INVITING writing

Sara Miller McCune founded SAGE Publishing in 1965 to support the dissemination of usable knowledge and educate a global community. SAGE publishes more than 1000 journals and over 800 new books each year, spanning a wide range of subject areas. Our growing selection of library products includes archives, data, case studies and video. SAGE remains majority owned by our founder and after her lifetime will become owned by a charitable trust that secures the company's continued independence.

Los Angeles | London | New Delhi | Singapore | Washington DC | Melbourne

INVITING *writing*

Teaching & learning writing across the primary curriculum

ADAM BUSHNELL & DAVID WAUGH

SAGE | LearningMatters

Learning Matters
An imprint of SAGE Publications Ltd
1 Oliver's Yard
55 City Road
London EC1Y 1SP

SAGE Publications Inc.
2455 Teller Road
Thousand Oaks, California 91320

SAGE Publications India Pvt Ltd
B 1/I 1 Mohan Cooperative Industrial Area
Mathura Road
New Delhi 110 044

SAGE Asia-Pacific Pte Ltd
3 Church Street
#10–04 Samsung Hub
Singapore 049483

Editor: Amy Thornton
Production editor: Chris Marke
Marketing manager: Dilhara Attygalle
Cover design: Wendy Scott
Typeset by: C&M Digitals (P) Ltd, Chennai, India
Printed and bound by
CPI Group (UK) Ltd, Croydon, CR0 4YY

Published in 2017 by Learning Matters Ltd.
© 2017 Adam Bushnell and David Waugh

Library of Congress Control Number: 2016960204

British Library Cataloguing in Publication Data

A catalogue record for this book is available from the British Library

ISBN: 978-1-4739-9161-3
ISBN: 978-1-4739-9162-0 (pbk)

At SAGE we take sustainability seriously. Most of our products are printed in the UK using FSC papers and boards. When we print overseas we ensure sustainable papers are used as measured by the PREPS grading system. We undertake an annual audit to monitor our sustainability.

Contents

Contents

Acknowledgements

We are grateful to all the teachers and trainee teachers and the organisations who shared case studies and gave us permission to use them.

About the editors

Adam Bushnell is a full-time author who delivers creative writing workshops in the UK and internationally in both state and private education to all ages.

His books have been selected by the School Library Association for the *Boys into Books* recommended reading list. Previously a teacher, Adam now also delivers CPD to teachers and others working in education on how to inspire writing in the classroom.

David Waugh is subject leader for Primary English at Durham University. He has published extensively in primary English. David is a former deputy head teacher, was Head of the Education Department at the University of Hull, and was Regional Adviser for ITT for the National Strategies from 2008 to 2010. He has written and co-written or edited more than forty books on primary education. As well as his educational writing, David also writes children's stories and regularly teaches in schools.

About the contributors

Rob Smith is the creator and curator of the award-winning website: The Literacy Shed www.literacyshed.com. After a 12-year career as a primary teacher, Rob now delivers writing workshops to students and professional development for teachers across the UK and around the world. Rob was a contributing author for *Beyond Early Writing* and is now writing his own English ideas website as well as creating a range of apps for teachers, the first of which 'DADWAVERS' has recently been released across Apple and Android platforms.

Sarah McAllister began her career in the food industry where she worked as a Senior New Product Development Technologist. Her work involved creating and launching new products for supermarkets including Tesco, ASDA and M&S. Sarah then worked for the Durham Education Business Partnership, informing young people about, and preparing them for, the world of work. She now delivers workshops in schools aimed at inspiring people of all ages to prepare healthy and nutritious fast food at home.

Pearl Saddington is the Centre Manager of the new Old Low Light Heritage Centre in North Shields. Pearl has considerable experience in museum and heritage education. Her ground-breaking educational Youth Outreach Project working with disengaged young people in South Tyneside won Bede's World Museum the prestigious North East Culture Club Award. Pearl works to create dynamic, audience-driven exhibitions and educational programmes.

Lynn Thompson is a Teaching Fellow in the School of Education at Durham University. She teaches maths to undergraduate and postgraduate primary teaching students and is co-author of *Understanding and Enriching Problem Solving in Primary Mathematics*. In addition to her earlier role as a teacher, Lynn was also a Primary Strategy Consultant for Mathematics.

Lynn Newton is Professor of Education in the School of Education at Durham University, where she is also Director of the Initial Teacher Training Division. Originally trained as a primary and middle school teacher and science specialist, she worked in schools and for a local authority as an advisory teacher for science and technology before moving into university. She has extensive experience of researching and writing on science issues for primary teachers, having written some 20+ books, over 100 research papers and curriculum software and schemes. Her latest book is *Creativity for a New Curriculum: 5–11* (Routledge, 2012).

Angela Gill is a Teaching Fellow at Durham University. She is part of the Primary English team, working with undergraduate and postgraduate students. For more than 20 years Angela taught in primary schools in Durham and Somerset, during which time she was subject lead for English and phonics. She has written a number of books and articles, including several about teaching phonics.

Rachel Simpson is subject leader for Primary Science at Durham University. Before working in Higher Education, she was a teacher, subject leader and assistant head teacher in primary schools in England, and also worked in an international school in Vietnam to develop an information literacy programme. Rachel moved into Higher Education as an Associate Principal Lecturer in Primary Education at Leeds Trinity University, before joining the School of Education in Durham in 2015.

Douglas P. Newton teaches science and D&T education, and productive thought in Durham University's School of Education. Of his many articles and books, his very successful *Teaching for Understanding* is now in its second edition (Routledge, 2012), and his current interest in how moods and emotions shape thinking led to the highly praised *Thinking with Feeling* (Routledge, 2014).

Rosie Ridgway is a teaching fellow in the School of Education at Durham University. Rosie was a teacher in mainstream and special schools in both primary and secondary phases. She now teaches Special Educational Needs and Disabilities (SEND) inclusive practices and primary computing to undergraduate, postgraduate students and trainee teachers. Her research interests are in education practices which support the learning and achievement of all pupils, developing innovative methodologies and using technologies to support a more inclusive pupil voice.

Tina Page is a lecturer in Education at the University of Hull. Tina teaches postgraduate students on the PGCE programme and is Lead Tutor for two partner institutions in School Centred Initial Teacher Training (SCITT). Tina's background in language teaching has led to a keen interest in comparative education with particular reference to policies, pedagogy and practice in France and Germany.

Nathalie Paris is a part-time primary languages teacher; she also specialises in French children's books and visits schools with her mobile library where she shares stories in French, Spanish and German with children of all ages. She was a full-time primary and secondary MFL teacher for 19 years before setting up Natta-lingo in 2014. In addition, Nathalie supports and trains primary languages teachers through the Association for Language Learning.

Andrew Joyce-Gibbons is subject leader for Primary History at Durham University. His primary research interest is the use of technology to support collaborative learning in History. Andrew left full-time teaching in 2013 to concentrate on his research career.

Emma Anyan is a music teacher who specialises in choral work. As well as her work in school, Emma is a member of 'Quintessential Voices', a five-part harmony group that performs at weddings and other functions. She has performed with Newcastle Chorale Society and was the conductor for the Darlington Youth Choir for five years. Emma has taken part in several Comenius projects with schools and has taken pupils to various European countries.

Mark Anyan combines his role as General Manager of the National Youth Choirs of Great Britain alongside a freelance career as a singer and conductor. He is currently Musical Director of Newcastle Choral Society and involved in the choral programme at Sage Gateshead. Mark spent 10 years as a singing teacher and animateur for Cheshire Music Service, and Durham Music Service, and is in demand as a workshop leader, adjudicator and singer throughout the North of England.

The Bowes Museum was created in the late nineteenth century by John and Joséphine Bowes and houses an internationally renowned collection of European fine and decorative arts spanning five centuries. The permanent collections are complemented by an eclectic mix of traditional and contemporary exhibitions. The Museum aims to foster a deeper understanding of art and culture for people of all ages and backgrounds through engagement with the fine and decorative arts. The Museum has a dedicated learning team which delivers an award-winning programme of school workshops and family activities.

The Durham Cathedral Education Team is an award-winning deliverer of learning outside the classroom. They cover all aspects of the curriculum in their offer to schools and welcome around 15,000 children and young people per year into their Norman cathedral situated within a UNESCO World Heritage Site. All the team are qualified teachers and come from a diverse range of subject specialisms.

Claire Patterson is an experienced classroom teacher, currently teaching in Year 6, and is also the lead for English within her school. As well as teaching full time, Claire is a fully qualified trainer for the organisation Educate and Celebrate, and delivers CPD on how to create LGBT-inclusive schools. She also plans English lessons with an SMSC focus for the organisation, which can be found on their website.

Jonathan Doherty lectured in PE at LeedsMet Carnegie for 13 years before joining the National Strategies as Regional Adviser. He was Co-director of an educational consultancy business and a School Improvement Adviser. Following senior leadership at Manchester Met and Leeds Trinity, he is heavily involved in ITE and CPD work with teachers.

David Bolden is a Lecturer in Mathematics Education and has worked at Durham University for the past 10 years. He is currently Programme Director of the PGCE Primary Education programme and also teaches on the BA Primary Education and MSc Mathematics Education programmes. His research interests include, and he has written and co-written on, creativity in mathematics, understanding in mathematics and teacher epistemologies, particularly in relation to primary mathematics. He is also co-author of the recently published book *Understanding and Enriching Problem Solving in Primary Mathematics*.

Introduction

Adam Bushnell and David Waugh

This book focuses on writing across the primary curriculum. Throughout the book, contributors show how writing can be an integral part of their subjects, offering opportunities for consolidation of ideas and creative responses to learning.

Every subject in the primary curriculum is covered, including religious education, social, moral, spiritual and cultural education and modern languages. We also devote a chapter to writing non-fiction.

The contributors have been drawn from schools, universities and organisations that are strongly involved in education and educational consultants. All have in common a passion for sharing good practice and a keen desire to develop children's ability to express themselves in writing.

Each chapter provides research focuses, critical questions, activities and reflections to encourage you to consider your own practice in the light of what you have read. There are also case studies to demonstrate how teachers and trainee teachers have used developed writing in the classroom. The chapters also include recommended further reading to enable you to develop stronger insights into how teachers can help children move beyond early writing.

In Chapter 1, David Waugh maintains that there is a misconception among some children that good writing has to be lengthy. He argues that it is important that we show that high-quality writing can be concise and convey powerful messages briefly, and provides several examples of writing that can engage children, which focuses on quality and concision.

Chapter 2 examines non-fiction writing across the curriculum in order to provide an overview of possibilities before individual subjects are explored. Adam Bushnell, Rob Smith and Sarah McAllister assert that non-fiction is a genre of writing that is extremely varied and offers lots of opportunities for multiple types of writing.

Lynn Thompson and David Bolden make a powerful case for the place of writing in mathematics in Chapter 3. Children need to develop fluency so they can *describe* their mathematical understanding; they need to develop this understanding so they can *explain* their mathematics; and they need to deepen their understanding in order to *communicate* and reason mathematically and to solve problems. The authors maintain that children should write in a variety of ways, using words as labels, short sentences to add clarity to their work, paragraphs and longer pieces of prose to communicate their understanding – to describe, compare, predict, interpret, explain and justify. The chapter includes thought-provoking examples of activities which bring writing into mathematics.

We make no apology for including two chapters on writing in science: science is a broad subject, which is subdivided into subjects at secondary school. In Chapter 4, Lynn Newton argues that one of the priorities in science education has to be to provide opportunities for the learners to communicate, record and interpret information. Children should be able to report findings from investigations, including written explanations of results, explanations involving causal relationships and conclusions. The chapter includes a fascinating forensic science activity, *Who Robbed Teddy?*

In Chapter 5, Rachel Simpson draws upon her own experience of visiting the Galápagos Islands and the work she subsequently did in school to show that creative writing about biology can inform, engage, demonstrate knowledge and develop understanding. She maintains that these are important skills for children to both recognise and practise, as they start to think like scientists and organise their knowledge through their writing.

Douglas P. Newton maintains in Chapter 6 that writing in design and technology offers specific opportunities for writing to support purposeful thought and, hence, develop competence in practical problem solving. In addition, it offers opportunities for descriptive and informative writing. His examples of activities and case studies are imaginative and have great potential for engaging young minds.

In Chapter 7, Rosie Ridgway discusses the opportunities that computing as a 'new' subject in the curriculum offers for developing writing. The chapter explores how computing supports learners to develop strategic approaches, organise activities, develop creative projects, evaluate and improve writing and communicate with authentic audiences. She offers vivid examples of writing through computing using a range of approaches. For example, demonstrating how with careful planning, social media (like blogging) can offer learners a global audience for their written work.

In Chapter 8, Andrew Joyce-Gibbons argues that we need to enable the articulation of balanced and evidence-based explanations of the past, explanations that use the language of possibility, of chronology and of compromise. Andrew provides interesting examples of historical writing and expresses clear views on what constitutes successful teaching and learning in his subject.

Adam Bushnell, Heather Jarvis and Emma and Mark Anyan look, in Chapter 9, at music as a stimulus for writing, providing examples across the primary age range. They also explore the possibilities that song lyrics provide for children to develop poetic writing. They argue that finding meanings within lyrics is also good for developing comprehension techniques. Difficult subject areas can be studied by looking at rap songs like Lowkey and Logic's *Relatives*.

Of all the subjects in the curriculum, PE may seem the least likely to provide opportunities for children's writing yet, in Chapter 10, Jonathan Doherty shows that being active and interacting with others and to solve problems through movement provide rich opportunities for classroom writing. Jonathan begins by offering 23 possibilities for getting children writing through physical education.

Angela Gill's Chapter 11 shows that writing in geography can produce outcomes such as a new mapping symbol for a local landmark, or a report debating and justifying opinions about opening a new mine near a settlement. Angela argues that we use geography and writing as part of our everyday lives: drawing a map to guide someone to a place or, perhaps, checking and sharing the weather app on our devices. Such writing activities enable children to collect, analyse, interpret and communicate.

Adam Bushnell and the Education Team at the Bowes Museum show how the written word can be stimulated by the beautiful and the grotesque through art. Chapter 12 includes examples of ways in which literature, portraits and ancient art works can be used so that art and writing can be studied side by side.

In Chapter 13, Tina Page maintains that writing in a foreign language can be supported with a cross-curricular approach: all primary curriculum subjects can be reference points. For example, English can be used to consolidate understanding a foreign language story or poem; geography can supply a foreign language focus on an ecological theme; and religious education can support a foreign language in intercultural awareness.

In Chapter 14, Adam Bushnell and Staff of Durham Cathedral Education Team provide practical examples of how Religious Education can produce not only effective learning, but also enhanced thinking skills and ultimately high-quality writing. The chapter looks at the potential for writing in the study of different religions and at common themes in world religions.

In the final chapter, Claire Patterson in association with Educate&Celebrate explore the teaching of British values, which is now part of the curriculum, and look at how children can be encouraged to become passionate about issues that are happening in the world they live in, including those surrounding LGBT+ (Lesbian, Gay, Bisexual, Transgender) equality. They provide examples which show how teachers utilise this to enable children to create exceptional, relevant pieces of writing which can then be shared with the world via blogs and social media.

We hope that you will enjoy reading the contributions of our various authors and will gain the same stimulation and enthusiasm for writing that we did as the chapters arrived.

Adam Bushnell
David Waugh
March 2017

Writing in English

David Waugh

Teachers' Standards

Standard 3 - Demonstrate good subject and curriculum knowledge

- have a secure knowledge of the relevant subject(s) and curriculum areas, foster and maintain pupils' interest in the subject, and address misunderstandings
- demonstrate a critical understanding of developments in the subject and curriculum areas, and promote the value of scholarship
- demonstrate an understanding of and take responsibility for promoting high standards of literacy, articulacy and the correct use of standard English, whatever the teacher's specialist subject

Standard 4 - Plan and teach well-structured lessons

- impart knowledge and develop understanding through effective use of lesson time
- promote a love of learning and children's intellectual curiosity

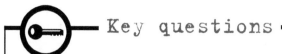 **Key questions**

- How can we make writing an inviting and exciting activity in English lessons?
- How can we balance the need for accurate transcription with the development of compositional skills?
- What is the role of collaborative writing and teacher writing?
- How can we give children a repertoire for writing by using texts as a starting point?

Introduction

The Department for Education (DfE, 2012) produced a report which synthesised research on children's writing. Using research reviews of international evidence (Graham et al., 2012; Gillespie and Graham, 2010; Andrews et al., 2009; Santangelo and Olinghouse, 2009), it claimed that one of the key pedagogical approaches which had been shown to improve children's writing was teaching pupils the writing process. The report provides examples of how this might look in the classroom.

- *Teach pupils strategies/tools for the various components of the writing process such as: planning; drafting; sharing; evaluating; revising and editing; summarising; sentence combining*

- *Gradually shift responsibility from the teacher to the pupil so that they become independent writers*

- *Guide pupils to choose and use suitable writing strategies*

- *Encourage pupils to be flexible when using the different writing components*

- *Engage them in pre-writing activities where they can assess what they already know, research an unfamiliar topic, or arrange their ideas visually*

(DfE, 2012, p12)

There is clearly an important role for teachers in modelling writing, but what aspects of writing might be involved? In this chapter, we will look at both the compositional aspects of writing in English and the transcriptional elements.

Composition and transcription

The marking system for SATs often leads to teachers encouraging children to insert fronted adverbials, semi-colons, adjectives and adverbs and similar features into their writing so that they can achieve higher marks. While it is laudable that children should be encouraged to make use of a range of literary devices, this approach can sometimes lead to rather stilted and formulaic prose which may tick boxes for gaining marks in a test, but would not be enjoyable to read. What is most important is that writers have a range of devices at their disposal, but know how to use them judiciously to make their text interesting and engaging for readers. Ivanič (2004) describes different approaches or discourses below.

 **Research focus**

Discourses of writing and learning to write

Ivanič (2004) looked at different approaches to teaching and learning writing and identified a *skills discourse* and a *creativity discourse*. In the former, the emphasis is upon accuracy, while in the latter the focus is upon content and engagement of an audience.

A skills discourse of Writing

Underlying a great deal of policy and practice in literacy education is a fundamental belief that writing consists of applying knowledge of a set of linguistic patterns and rules for sound–symbol relationships and sentence construction. At its most extreme, this is a belief that writing is a unitary, context-free activity, in which the same patterns and rules apply to all writing, independent of text type.

In this view, what counts as good writing is determined by the correctness of the, letter, word, sentence, and text formation ...

...These beliefs lead to 'skills' approaches to the teaching of writing, which focus on the autonomous linguistic 'skills' of correct handwriting, spelling, punctuation and sentence structure. A great deal of the teaching in this approach is explicit: children are taught spelling patterns and rules for grammatically correct and correctly punctuated written sentences. They undertake exercises which draw their attention to linguistic patterns and distinctions in written language, and their writing is assessed according to how accurately these patterns have been reproduced (p227).

A creativity discourse of Writing

The discourse of writing as the product of the author's creativity also focuses on the written text, but is concerned with its content and style rather than its linguistic form. In this discourse 'meaning' is central, with the writer engaged in meaning-making, and so it is concerned with mental processes as well as with characteristics of the text. Writing is treated as a valuable activity in its own right: the creative act of an author, with no social function other than that of interesting or entertaining a reader. This belief about the nature of writing generates value judgements about what counts as 'good' writing in terms of content and style, rather than, or in addition to, in terms of accuracy (p229).

Ivanič maintains that *Experienced, eclectic teachers of writing recognise the advantage of inspiring learners to write about topics which interest them and the opportunities this provides for implicit learning, alongside explicit teaching about linguistic rules and patterns (p230).*

It is, then, possible for children to develop their understanding of the transcriptional aspects of writing at the same time as they develop their compositional skills. In fact, Myhill et al. maintain:

> that teaching grammar as a discrete, separate topic, where the grammar is the focus of study, is not likely to help writing development because it does not make connections between grammar and writing, or between grammar and meaning …

> a writing curriculum which draws attention to the grammar of writing in an embedded and purposeful way at relevant points in the learning is a more positive way forward. In this way, young writers are introduced to what we have called 'a repertoire of infinite possibilities', explicitly showing them how different ways of shaping sentences or texts, and how different choices of words can generate different possibilities for meaning-making.

> (2011, p3)

Myhill (2012) asserts that grammar teaching is most effective when it is taught in the context of reading and writing, either in the context of the linguistic demands of a particular genre, or the writing needs of a particular child. In the case study below you can see how a teacher begins a writing activity in a very simple way, which all children can engage with, before developing writing which involves phrases, clauses, sentences and paragraphs.

 Case study

Six-word life stories

Sadiq had enjoyed a game played at a friend's house which involved people trying to tell their life stories in just six words. Afterwards, he searched the Internet for examples and discovered several websites which provided sample six-word stories, including the BBC's *Today*.

Sadiq's Year 5 class included several children who were reluctant writers, many of whom had good ideas when discussing themes orally. He decided to devote a lesson to six-word stories and shared some examples he had found online. He then asked children to think about famous people and fictional characters and to work in pairs to tell their life stories or to write something about their personalities or achievements, using only six words. Sadiq emphasised that the order in which the words were placed could have a powerful impact on the reader and urged children to reflect on their writing and discuss alternative vocabulary when appropriate. There were some interesting outcomes including:

Goals, fame, transfer, wealth, England captain

Sadiq then asked children to work individually, to think about themselves and tell the story of their lives in six words. He provided examples of what he and his wife had written the night before:

Worked hard, became a teacher. Happiness!

(Continued)

(Continued)

Children enjoyed writing their stories and sharing them with each other. Sadiq told them that they did not have to share their stories if they didn't wish to, as some wrote quite poignant things about the loss of relatives, pets, etc.

Sadiq explained that the six-word stories were sufficient in themselves and did not have to be developed, but that he would like the children to go on to create six-line stories and later six-paragraph stories, using verbs, adjectives, nouns and adverbs to embellish them.

Start simple: how do you get reluctant writers writing?

The case study illustrates that good writing can be concise, and also shows that short pieces can be developed when appropriate. There is a misconception among some children that good writing has to be lengthy. It is important that we show that high-quality writing can be concise and convey powerful messages briefly.

Many people, including some teachers, admit that they do not enjoy poetry. There is even a word, *metrophobia*, for hatred of poetry. It may be that they were put off poetry by being introduced to it through lengthy ballads and epics, and by unfamiliar and complex language styles, which they would never have wished to use in their own writing. However, there are many poetic forms with highly structured writing which may have restricted numbers of syllables or lines, but which enable writers to achieve good results using few words. Haikus, cinquains and tankas are popular in schools and have the advantage that they do not have to rhyme and so enable authors to say what they mean, rather than having to adapt to the need for a rhyme. Limericks and triolets do have to rhyme, but have simple rhyming schemes. These poetic forms provide an introduction to reading and writing poetry which may lead to a more positive attitude to more challenging and lengthy works.

Short, structured poetry

Haiku

A Japanese form of poetry with 3 lines, 17 syllables in the sequence: 5, 7, 5:

> *Doncaster Rovers*
> *Good days make up for the bad*
> *My team 'til I die*

Tanka

A Japanese poem based on a Haiku but with two additional lines to give a more complete picture of the event or mood. One person can write a haiku and then give it to another poet to add two lines to create a poem of 31 syllables with the sequence: 5, 7, 5, 7, 7. This would then be returned to the original poet:

> *Doncaster Rovers*
> *Good days make up for the bad*
> *My team 'til I die*
> *I wasn't born in Leicester*
> *But sometimes wish I had been.*

Cinquain

A poetic form invented by the American, Adelaide Crapsey, containing 22 syllables on 5 lines in the sequence: 2, 4, 6, 8, 2

> *Adder*
> *Sliding slowly*
> *Slipping through the long grass*
> *If I knew you were so close by*
> *I'd run!*

Triolets ('triplet')

A French verse form with the structure:

- 8 lines. Two rhymes.

- 5 of the 8 lines are repeated or refrain lines.

- First line repeats at the 4th and 7th lines.

- Second line repeats at the 8th line.

Louise McCarthy sits in front of me	A
She's the kind of girl I'd like to be	B
She has long hair	a - Rhymes with 6th line
Louise McCarthy sits in front of me	A - Identical to 1st line
I'd really like to ask her home for tea.	a - Rhymes with 1st line
I wouldn't dare.	b - Rhymes with 3rd line.
Louise McCarthy sits in front of me	A - Identical to 1st line
She's the kind of girl I'd like to be.	B - Identical to 2nd line

Limericks

Limericks have five lines and are usually humorous. The first, second and fifth lines rhyme and have the same rhythm. The third and fourth lines have five to seven syllables, the same rhythm and rhyme with each other. Some well-known nursery rhymes have a limerick form, for example:

Hickory, dickory, dock,

The mouse ran up the clock.

The clock struck one,

The mouse ran down,

Hickory, dickory, dock.

Rhyme can be introduced as children feel confident in using it. Rhyming dictionaries can be useful, as can websites like Rhyme Zone, which also provide near rhymes, but children need to be cautious about using the dictionaries' suggestions unless they are confident they understand the word they choose and know that it is appropriate. Used alongside ordinary dictionaries, rhyming dictionaries and websites can promote vocabulary investigations and help children broaden their lexicons while developing their reference skills.

All of the poetic forms above are complete writing entities in themselves and do not need to be expanded. However, these forms can be used as starting points for writing more extensively and per-haps even as a prelude to writing a story. Some authors introduce chapters in novels using *epigraphs*, quoting lyrics or extracts from poems to arouse the reader's interest. J.K. Rowling, writing as Robert Galbraith, does this to great effect in her Cormoran Strike detective thrillers, although these books are certainly not suitable for young readers.

Developing prose writing

If children can gain confidence from producing short, meaningful writing which enables them to succeed and receive praise from teachers and classmates, they are much more likely to approach more extended pieces with enthusiasm. However, they still need models so that they can see how such writing can be constructed and the kind of features which are appropriate. One way of doing this is to engage them in shared reading where they hear their teacher read as they follow text and then join in with the reading, often pausing to discuss the text and the language used. This can be followed by the teacher modelling similar writing, thinking aloud about different ways of expressing ideas as well as spelling and punctuating. Gradually, children can contribute their own ideas which can be incorporated. They might work in pairs to develop the next sentence before sharing their ideas with the class.

Roth and Guinee (2011) describe *interactive writing*, which involves teacher and pupils working together *to construct a meaningful text while discussing the details of the writing process* (p333). As in the developed stage of shared writing, the teacher invites children's contributions and draws upon their ideas to develop a piece of writing and acts as a scribe to model spelling, punctuation, sentence con-struction, etc. Interactive writing follows Vygotsky's (1978) zone of proximal development in that learners can achieve more when guided by an experienced teacher. Roth and Guinee maintain that *The instruction does not follow a specified sequence but evolves from the teacher's understanding of the stu-dents' strengths and needs* (p335).

In the case study below, Daniel, a Year 5 teacher, introduces a story opening as an example and plans to use it in a variety of ways to help children develop their own writing.

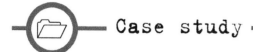

Case study

A story opening

Daniel planned a series of lessons for a three-week period. He began by putting up a display of first pages and covers of well-known children's stories, displaying the covers separately from the text and asking children to try to match covers to openings. He then invited the class to bring along their own favourite story openings and sought volunteers to read these to groups. There was a discussion about the features of good openings, which revolved around the following questions.

* What are the features of opening sentences which make you want to read on?
* What are the features of opening paragraphs which make you want to read on?
* What do you want to know after reading the first page of a story?

Daniel then introduced the children to a story opening from an as yet unpublished book written by his friend. He told them that his friend wanted to continue the story and would welcome their ideas, but he also wanted to know how he could improve the opening. Before reading the story opening, Daniel gave each child a card with a word which would appear somewhere in the text. He asked children to discuss with neighbours what the words were and what they meant, and then asked if anyone was unsure about how to say a word or its meaning. They could use dictionaries, if they wished. Cards with the following words were provided.

money	banknote	suitcase
bundle	sweat	padlock
stairs	footsteps	step uncle
cupboard	bed	millions
tickle	hasp	digit roller
door	playing field	receding

Daniel told the class that, after he had read the opening to them, he would ask them to discuss their words as they appeared in the story and then write a sentence or two which described the significance of the word in the story.

THE CASH STASH

CHAPTER ONE

CASH

I'd never seen so much money before. I bet hardly anyone in the country had ever seen that much money, unless they worked in a bank or had just robbed one. The suitcase was full almost to bursting. The neat bundles of banknotes were crammed in tightly and had visibly risen when I'd opened the case, as if stretching after being squashed into a small seat on a car journey.

(Continued)

(Continued)

I hesitated before touching the money, but then courage came quickly and I snatched up one of the bundles and flicked its edge so that the notes made a sort of zipping sound as I ran my finger along their edges. The top note was a twenty. I flicked through again to see if all of the notes in the bundle were twenties too – they were. Then I flicked through again even more slowly and tried to count approximately how many notes there were. Around fifty, I reckoned – a thousand pounds in a bundle and the suitcase was stuffed with bundles. There were forty-eight on the top row – £48,000! I delved into the case and found that there seemed to be six bundles in each pile. My head began to spin as I tried to do the maths. Forty-eight thousand times six: six eights made forty-eight and six forties made 240, so that was 288 thousand. £288,000! More than a quarter of a millions pounds! And there were three more suitcases. Could these, too, be equally well-filled with banknotes? If they were, that would make more than a million pounds.

I felt a drip of sweat trickle from my armpit. This was incredible. No wonder there was a coded padlock on the cupboard door. No wonder the case had a padlock too. How could anyone be so careless as to forget to lock the locks? Before I had time to give this another thought, I froze in terror. Someone was coming up the stairs. I could hear the familiar heavy tread of my step uncle's footsteps and their sound was getting louder.

I closed the suitcase and clicked its padlock together. As quietly as I could, I crawled out of the cupboard and back into my bedroom. Quickly, I tried to lock the padlock on the door, but it was stuck. Someone had tried to lock it but hadn't put the hasp into its hole. The padlock was locked, but not properly. There was no time to experiment with the four digit-rollers to try to unlock it, so I put it back onto the door as soon as I had shut it. Then I crawled under the bed and tried to hold my breath. Something was jabbing into my back and I worried that my legs might be sticking out, but when the door to my bedroom opened and footsteps moved across the room, there was no word from my step uncle to indicate that he knew I was there.

All I heard was one word: "Idiot!". Then I heard the sound of the padlock being removed and the door to the cupboard opening. The rustlings which followed had to be the sound of a suitcase opening. Within a minute it was all over. I heard the suitcase snap shut, the door close and the digit rollers turn before the padlock on the door was locked too. After that my step uncle left my bedroom and I heard the sound of his footsteps receding as he descended the stairs. I crept out from under the bed and wondered what to do next. Uncle Mark thought I was at the village playing field with my mates. I didn't want him to find that I was actually at home and that I'd been in the cupboard which he'd told me was kept locked for safety reasons.

(from Waugh, D., 2016, *Cash Stash*)

When Daniel had read the story opening, he took the children to the school hall and asked them to move around the room meeting different people and then discussing the words on their cards and their significance to the story. He wanted them to talk with children who did not sit at their tables and to gather as much information about as many words as possible. Back in the classroom, he found the class better able to discuss the text than usual and eager to contribute ideas about the story, its strengths and weaknesses, and how it might be developed.

Children could then choose to work individually or in pairs to write a letter to the author with their views and suggestions, and to include at least one paragraph to follow the opening. Daniel promised to show these to his friend and ask him to reply.

The case study illustrates how sharing and discussing a text can be a preparation for writing. A range of other activities might follow, often beginning with oral work, examples of which can be seen below to match this story opening or any other.

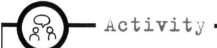

Activity

Look at the possible activities described below and consider the following.

- How could you adapt them to meet the needs of your class?
- Which other activities might you include for your own class?

Possible activities to follow story opening

Picture sheets for writing around

Provide A4 sheets of paper and ask children, in pairs, to make a quick sketch of a character or a scene from the story in the centre of the sheets. Ask them to pass these on to others, who can make notes around the pictures about the characters or events. Encourage brevity, with single words and phrases being used. After the sheets have been passed around to a few people, have children give them back to the original artists who can use the notes to create a short description.

Hot-seating

Ask for volunteers to assume the role of a character from the story and answer questions in role. Get the rest of the class to discuss and write questions for the character.

Dramatise an event from the story

In *Cash Stash* this might be the discovery of the suitcase or hiding under the bed. Get children to work together to plan a short dramatic sequence, perhaps asking characters to speak their thoughts aloud. They might produce a storyboard with notes and dialogue.

Collecting synonyms

Use the word cards and the story and invite children to find synonyms. From the story, they might look at:

courage   *approximately*   *reckoned*   *crept*   *delved*

You could also use the word cards as a starting point for this activity.

Write a blurb for the story

Display a range of book covers and ask children to look at books to get a feel for what is expected in a publisher's blurb. Ask them to write their own blurbs and to ask others how effective they would be in persuading them to buy the book.

Write the next two sentences/paragraph and make predictions

At different points in sharing a story with children, stop and ask them to discuss what might happen next. They could write down their predictions and then write the next few lines and share these with their group and the class.

Write the story so far in six words

An interesting follow-up to six-word story activities could involve children retelling this new story opening in six words. Ask them to decide what the key events are and to work in pairs or small groups to choose six key words.

Four-letter words

Ask children to describe a chapter in four words or four sets of four words, or even four sets of four-letter words. As with the six-word stories, this encourages careful reflection on content, as well as engagement with vocabulary and spelling (see also Chapter 12, Writing in Art).

Collect adjectives and adverbs

Although teachers often emphasise the importance of using adjectives and adverbs, real books tend to use these descriptive devices sparingly, making them more powerful and keeping the story flowing. Ask children to find examples of adjectives and adverbs in the story and to consider alternatives. Ask them to consider whether some aspects of the story might have benefited from more description. In *Cash Stash*, they might focus on the following:

| Adjectives: | neat | full | well-filled | small | heavy | |
| Adverbs: | tightly | visibly | slowly | quickly | quietly | properly |

Look for similes and metaphors

The first part of *Cash Stash* includes just one simile:

as if stretching after being squashed into a small seat on a car journey

Ask children if there could be opportunities for other similes or metaphors and if these could improve the writing and help paint a more vivid picture for the reader.

Write openings together and in pairs

Ask children to devise openings for their own stories, once they have looked at a range of published stories. They could then pass these on to other pairs or groups and ask them to continue the story by writing the next paragraph.

Developing writing

Note how the writing which can emanate from exploring story openings can be varied in style and presentation. There are lots of opportunities for developing an awareness of authorial devices, incidentally, as well as through direct teaching. The National Curriculum and SATs make considerable demands upon children and teachers, so that when writing takes place the focus is not always on composition. What about fronted adverbials, subordinate clauses, similes and metaphors? Do we need a liberal sprinkling of adverbs and adjectives? All of these can be deployed to make writing more varied and interesting, but children will use them more naturally and effectively if they see models of writing and have the opportunity to discuss style and its effect on an audience. A good resource to complement this is Wilcox's *Descriptosaurus,* which is a DfE-recommended text. It offers sample nouns, verbs and adjectives, as well as example sentences, to offer children extra support for their writing.

 Research focus

Teachers as writers

Cremin and Baker (2014, pp5-6) looked at two aspects of teachers' writing in the classroom: demonstration writing and writing alongside children, and argued as follows.

In demonstrating spontaneously, teachers can begin to share the blank spots, uncertainties and emergent nature of drafting thinking on the flip chart or interactive whiteboard. Some have found that by thinking aloud their concerns, voicing their choices and defending their decisions, they are able to demonstrate the genuine struggle of writing and that this was of value to the children (Cremin and Myhill, 2012). However, some studies suggest that teachers are concerned about demonstrating writing in the public forum of the classroom (Cremin, 2006; Turvey, 2007). As a consequence, they may pre-write the haiku or tanka for example in the privacy of their own homes, 'pretending' to demonstrate the act of composition in school. Others may simply avoid demonstration writing.

When writing alongside children, literally sitting alongside them, teachers may for example take part in journal writing, enabling children to draw on the 'texts of their lives' (Fecho, 2011) as a resource to retell, reinterpret, or remake their stories.

(Continued)

(Continued)

Others may undertake the same set writing challenges publishing their own work alongside the younger writers. Practitioners have found that working 'inside the process' in this way, helps them appreciate the challenge of the tasks they set and enhances their empathy for child writers (Cremin, 2010). It can also enable teachers to seize informal opportunities to discuss emerging issues and difficulties, writer to writer. Many have found that children settle more quickly when they write alongside them and that through engaging in informal conversations from the position of a fellow writer, they were able to offer informed support and advice (Cremin, 2010).

Children's comments have included: 'It's only fair that they write with us because we're all writing and the teachers aren't just standing around talking', 'I like it when she writes with us – she does the same thing as us, so she's one of us', 'It makes it easier - she doesn't interrupt', and 'Sometimes she finds it hard, sometimes writing is' (Goouch et al. 2009). These suggest that their teachers' positions as writers were influencing the younger writers' perspectives too.

Conclusion

In this book, writing is explored in every curriculum subject. A common theme is that children need to understand that there are different ways of writing which are appropriate for different situations. This chapter has focused on English, which is typically the subject in which there is the greatest focus on accuracy in writing and developing an understanding of different genres. As primary teachers, we need to extend this into all areas of the curriculum, so that expectations are consistently high and children understand what is expected. The keys to achieving this are:

- teacher modelling and shared writing;

- wide experience of texts;

- active involvement in writing, with oral work often preceding writing;

- the provision of interesting and often brief and manageable tasks designed to enable children to express their ideas and experiment with language usage.

▬ Further reading ▬

For examples of six-word stories see:

BBC *Today*. Available from: www.bbc.co.uk/radio4/today/reports/misc/sixwordlife_20080205.shtml

Fershleiser, R. (2008) *Not Quite What I Was Planning: Six-Word Memoirs by Writers Famous and Obscure.* New York: Harper Perennial.

For rhymes:

Rhyme Zone: rhymezone.com

Rhymer: rhymer.com

For ideas for short, imaginative poetry activities, three books by Sandy Brownjohn are packed with ideas.

Brownjohn, S. (1980) *Does it Have to Rhyme?* London: Hodder & Stoughton.

Brownjohn, S. (1982) *What Rhymes With Secret?: Teaching Children to Write Poetry*. London: Hodder & Stoughton.

Brownjohn, S. (1994) *To Rhyme or Not to Rhyme*. London: Hodder Stoughton.

━━ References ━━━━━━━━━━━━

Andrews, R., Torgerson, C., Low, G. and McGuinn, N. (2009) Teaching argument writing to 7–14 year olds: an international review of the evidence of successful practice. *Cambridge Journal of Education*, 39(3): 291–310.

Cremin, T. and Baker, S. (2014) *Teachers as Writers; a PETAA occasional research paper*. Sydney; PETAA, pp1–9.

DfE (2012) *What is the Research Evidence on Writing?* Education Standards Research Team, Department for Education. London: DfE.

Gillespie, A. and Graham, S. (2010) Evidence-based practices for teaching writing. Johns Hopkins University School of Education: New Horizons for learning. Available from: http://education.jhu.edu/ newhorizons/Better/articles/Winter2011.html

Graham, S., Bollinger, A., Booth Olson, C., D'Aoust, C., MacArthur, C., McCutchen, D. and Olinghouse, N. (2012). *Teaching Elementary School Students to be Effective Writers: A Practice Guide* (NCEE 2012- 4058). Washington, DC: National Center for Education Evaluation and Regional Assistance, Institute of Education Sciences, U.S. Department of Education. Available from: http://ies.ed.gov/ncee/wwc/publi cations_reviews.aspx#pubsearch.

Ivanič, R (2004) Discourses of writing and learning to write, *Language and Education*, 18(3): 220–45, DOI: 10.1080/09500780408666877

Myhill, D. (2012) The role for grammar in the curriculum, in *Meeting High Expectations: Looking for the Heart of English*. Available from: https://heartofenglishblog.files.wordpress.com/2013/09/high-expec tations.pdf

Myhill, D., Lines, H. and Watson A. (2011) *Making meaning with grammar: a repertoire of possibilities*. Available from: www.education.exeter.ac.uk

Roth, K. and Guinee, K. (2011) Ten minutes a day: The impact of Interactive Writing instruction on first graders' independent writing. *Journal of Early Childhood Literacy*, 11(3): 331–61.

Santangelo, T. and Olinghouse, N. (2009) Effective writing instruction for students who have writing difficulties. *Focus on Exceptional Children*, 42(4).

Vygotsky, L.S. (1978) *Mind in Society: The Development of Higher Psychological Processes*. Cambridge, MA: Harvard University Press.

Wilcox, A. (2013) *Descriptosaurus*. Abingdon: Routledge.

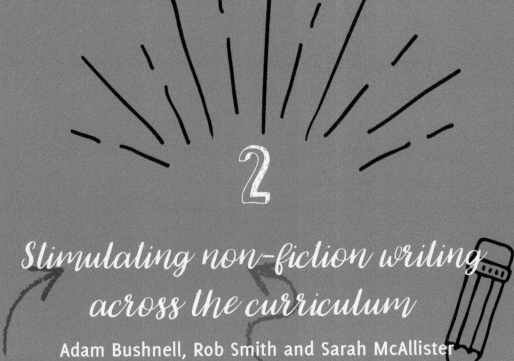

2

Stimulating non-fiction writing across the curriculum

Adam Bushnell, Rob Smith and Sarah McAllister
with staff of the Old Low Light Museum

Teachers' Standards

Standard 3 - Demonstrate good subject and curriculum knowledge

- have a secure knowledge of the relevant subject(s) and curriculum areas, foster and maintain pupils' interest in the subject, and address misunderstandings
- demonstrate a critical understanding of developments in the subject and curriculum areas, and promote the value of scholarship
- demonstrate an understanding of and take responsibility for promoting high standards of literacy, articulacy and the correct use of standard English, whatever the teacher's specialist subject

Standard 4 - Plan and teach well-structured lessons

- impart knowledge and develop understanding through effective use of lesson time
- promote a love of learning and children's intellectual curiosity

- What opportunities are there for writing using non-fiction as a stimulus?
- How can we ensure high-quality writing is produced using non-fiction?
- Which resources are best to aid writing in non-fiction lessons?

Introduction

Texts are commonly called 'fiction' or 'non-fiction'. But what is non-fiction? Is it fact-based books? Instructions? Encyclopaedic websites? Posters that advertise products?

Lots of fictional books contain stories based on real life events or include historical real life characters. The emergence of such books and movies, like *Abraham Lincoln – Vampire Hunter* for example, has blurred the lines even further. That particular book contains a well-researched, chronological biography of Lincoln's life, interspersed with the American president spending his evenings hunting the undead. The result of films like this is that lots of children in primary schools are often confused by what is real and what is not. They need to know that not all websites that appear to be factual are true. They also need to know that adverts on television or billboard posters may not necessarily contain facts, they are often opinion, yet are all classified as non-fiction.

Newspaper articles are officially classified as non-fiction too, yet the *Newcastle Journal* published the headline *Youngsters Catapulted Back Into The Roman Era* and the *Sun* published *Freddie Star Ate My Hamster*. These headlines are no doubt metaphor and hyperbole. The hamster eating has even since been disproved. It did not happen. Yet, still, these headlines are classified as being non-fiction.

Children, particularly boys, are interested and inspired by fact-based texts. The National Literacy Trust (2012, p13) quotes Phil Jarret in its report, *Boys' Reading Commission*, saying that boys *tend to read … non-fiction, autobiographies, newspapers and so on*. It also states that boys are often *turned off* by a lack of texts that interest them. That is why, in this chapter, we will focus on non-fiction texts, websites and activities that will inspire and engage both boys and girls to produce high-quality writing.

Crime scene investigators

Imagine arriving at the classroom door one Monday morning only for it to be sealed with police tape. Would you want to go in? Some of us would and perhaps some of us wouldn't, but we would all want to find out what had happened. Hopefully, this will never happen for real but it could be utilised by us as teachers to engage the children, to have them eager to investigate and explore what has happened inside their own learning environment. It is at this point of peak engagement when we should reveal key facts to children. When they are ready to learn they are most receptive to what is being taught. Of course, you couldn't use this 'hook' or one like it every Monday morning, but it is a useful launch to any writing topic or theme.

But what is inside the classroom behind the police tape? There could be a number of investigations for the children to explore and hypothesise over – such as a robbery, vandalism or even a murder.

In 2018, it will be a World Cup year, over 50 years since the World Cup was won by England and 50 years since the World Cup trophy was stolen from an exhibition in Westminster, the story of which can be found on the BBC's 'On This Day' website.

Children could be asked to write their own police report around these events or around the scenario created in the classroom.

Inside the classroom there could be found an evidence packet labelled 'POLICE: Top Secret'. The door could be closed, and with the teacher using a conspiratorial voice, the 'evidence' that has been found could be shared with the class. For the World Cup theft, the pack may include a photograph of a dog, an image of the Jules Rimet trophy, a page from a policeman's notebook, a ransom note and a photograph of a bundle of money. The children could discuss and develop a hypothesis as to what these clues could mean. They may come up with a number of hypotheses, each of which can be discussed and ranked according to their merit. At this point, more clues could be revealed, perhaps that the dog is called Pickles and that the trophy is called the Jules Rimet trophy. The children may even have the opportunity to research the real story themselves on the Internet or a pre-made fact file or worksheet.

Examples of police reports may need to be examined and discussed, looking at key features such as the orientation of the crime scene, reported speech and summaries.

This learning process could occur without the drama at the classroom door on that Monday morning but it does get the children involved and excited about their learning from the outset.

A variety of hooks can be used by teachers to inspire writing both digital and traditional written form. The point of the hook is to engage the pupils enough that they *want* to write about the topic that you have chosen to cover.

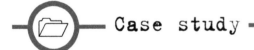 Case study

Year 3 class looking at newspaper articles

Harry had his class on the carpet and showed them a variety of newspaper covers. They looked at the common themes from all of them and listed these on the board. The list included the name of the newspaper, the date, headlines, subheadings, photographs, the name of the journalist and articles of news.

Harry then asked the class to name a verbal list of superheroes that they knew in talk partners. The list, mainly given by boys, was impressively large. The children were shown a poster with the headline 'Daredevil Collars Fisk' and the subheading 'Mystery figure brings end to daring escape' and 'Who is this kingpin of crime?'. They then read the article which outlines the fictional story of how the superhero Daredevil captures the escaped super villain Kingpin.

Harry then asked the class to choose a superhero and a supervillain of their own creation or one that they already knew about. He made a list of five heroes and five villains on the board. He encouraged the children to make up their own characters using animals. Heroes such as *Fish Boy, Giraffe Girl* and *Captain Meerkat* were invented, as were villains such as *Scorpion Woman, Leech Man* and *Doctor Nit*.

The children drew and labelled their two characters and returned to the carpet.

Harry then explained that they were going to write a fictional newspaper article using all of the elements of a non-fiction newspaper. They reviewed the common themes from real newspapers and were asked to start with the name, date, headline and subheading. Once these were written, children then went over the key features of the Daredevil article. This mainly featured two elements: what the villain had done and how the hero apprehended the villain.

Ideas were shared with talk partners and the children then returned to their seats to write the articles. These were finally shared on the carpet, again in talk partners.

The case study may seem a very boy-orientated example of fiction inspiring non-fiction style writing; however, the girls were utterly engaged when making up their own superheroes. It would seem that this genre of superheroes has mass appeal to both boys and girls.

 ## Activity

Writing a newspaper article

News can be written about anything from sports commentary to scientific discovery to heart-warming courageous acts.

- Superheroes were the inspiration for the case study above. What area of interest does your class have? What could they write a newspaper report on?

- Could you create a scenario to immerse your class in like the crime scene earlier? What props could you use? What images would support the writing?

- What framework or structure would you give the class? How could you encourage independent writing?

 ## Research focus

Boys and girls

In 2012 the DfE found that: *Overall, the evidence shows that there is a gender gap in pupils' performance in writing with girls outperforming boys throughout Key Stages* (p3). It goes on to state: *Evidence suggests that boys perform less well than girls in writing* (p3). Also, Clark (2012) says, *There is consistent evidence that girls enjoy writing more than boys* (p5).

(Continued)

(Continued)

If this is the case, if girls simply enjoy the process of writing more than boys, then should we offer writing opportunities that have more appeal to boys than girls in order to close this gender gap of performance?

The DfE goes on in the same report to state that the reasons for the boys performing less well than the girls are *factors related to the way lessons are conducted such as too much emphasis on story writing, not giving boys ownership of their writing, a discrepancy between boys' reading preferences and writing topics, using 'ounting down' time strategies and a dislike by boys of drafting and figurative language* (p19).

This would suggest that we need more non-fiction writing in the classroom in order to appeal to the boys. But we should be offering both boys *and* girls areas of interest in their writing. We should find what interests and inspires *everybody* in our classrooms and offer writing opportunities for all. Non-fiction is such a broad topic that there is something for everybody.

Using videos as a hook into non-fiction writing

One of the difficulties for many teachers is getting children to a point where they want to write. Using sources that are familiar to them is important. For many children, the main source of literacy in the home is from a screen, whether it is a television, laptop, tablet or mobile phone. Lots of children watch more YouTube films than they do live television. The National Literacy Trust (2014) statistics make for sad reading: 10 per cent of children do not own their own book before they leave primary school. The majority of children say that they prefer watching film and animations to reading, and almost 35 per cent of boys confess that they only read when they have to. It is for these reasons that using a text to stimulate writing, or for research, is not always the most efficient way of ensuring that children are motivated to write. It is with this in mind that teachers begin to plan stimulating lesson hooks, from physical objects or field trips to practical demonstrations. Even with these demonstrations, there can still be some difficulties in getting the children to write, as outlined below. Using visual literacy can help with this, as can be seen in the following case study.

 **Case study**

A mixed Year 4 and 5 class learning to write instructions

A Recently Qualified Teacher, Annette, was standing in front of a class of children in Years 4 and 5 teaching them about writing instructions. She asked the class to give her instructions on how to make a cup of tea. When she asked how she should make a cup of tea, some children felt that they knew how to do this and others didn't.

She followed their instructions, which included turning the kettle on. However, the children had not given the instruction that it needed to be filled with water. She was also told to add milk, but the class did not say how much. Another instruction given was to add sugar, but she was not told to stir it.

The results of these only partial instructions made for humorous viewing for the class, but the point was firmly made; instructions need to be chronological, thorough and accurate. The children were asked to write their own instructions for making a cup of tea. This was then shared and compared with each other.

Finally, the teacher showed the class the Wallace and Gromit TV advert for PG Tips. In it, the animation shows a very inventive way of making a cup of tea. The children were then told that they would be creating their own diagrams of tea-making machines which would be labelled with technical vocabulary using the animation for ideas.

Animations for instructional writing

As well as practical demonstrating from the teacher as in the case study above, another way of engaging children is to use a still or moving image. On YouTube there is a series of short Wallace and Gromit animations called *Cracking Contraptions*, each is around two minutes long and features the plasticine heroes with one of their madcap inventions which invariably go wrong. There is *Easy Iron Machine* which was invented by Wallace. Using these animations, children require no prior knowledge of how the machine might work. The animation is a visual demonstration that children could turn into the written word. Even with something as simple as making a cup of tea, children will need some prior knowledge – they will need to know that you boil the kettle, add a tea bag, stir, add milk and sugar, if required. However, with the 'Cracking Contraption' it doesn't matter as much in which order the children choose to complete their instructions. For example, with the 'Easy Iron Machine' it does not affect the outcome if one child thinks that you start to pedal first and then push the lever or another child may decide that you push the lever first and then start to pedal.

On the Literacy Shed website animations such as 'The Shirt Machine', 'Powerless' and 'Pigeon Impossible' can also help with inventing and describing new machines for a variety of purposes. These can be turned into instructions or used to extend descriptive writing, such as starting sentences with imperative verbs, using adverbs such as carefully, slowly, gently and adding in sequencing vocabulary, before going on to demonstrate correct structure and layout. Using animations like these means that children have no fear of getting things wrong as with making the tea; there is no right way to control their own invented machine as it is a creation from their own imagination.

Note-making using the moving image

Note-making is an integral part of lots of genres of writing, including non-fiction writing. Often, experiences of note-making for primary-aged children involve copying chunks from a textbook or 'copying and pasting' from the Internet. Unless the child is accomplished at note-taking, the absorbing of information is often minimal. There are a number of film sources that could be used to develop knowledge in order to inspire non-fiction writing. The BBC Learning Zone has lots of links that are suitable for this, such as the television series *Horrible Histories,* which teaches non-fiction content in an engaging and accessible way.

The use of film is inclusive as the information is presented both visually and audibly, which means that children who may have good comprehension skills but poor decoding skills find the content more accessible. For example, if children were writing a chronological report on a subject such as 'The History of Lego', they might find the information on a variety of sources on the Internet.

Children frequently go to Wikipedia as a source of information. This is the Wikipedia article on 'The History of Lego'.

> *The Lego Group began in the carpentry workshop of Ole Kirk Christiansen, in Billund, Denmark. In 1916, Christiansen purchased a woodworking shop in Billund which had been in business since 1895. [1]:8 The shop mostly helped construct houses and furniture, and had a small staff of apprentices. The workshop burned down in 1924 when a fire ignited some wood shavings.[2]:37 Ole Kirk constructed a larger workshop, and worked towards expanding his business even further. When the Great Depression hit, Ole Kirk had fewer customers and had to focus on smaller projects. He began producing miniature versions of his products as design aids. It was these miniature models of stepladders and ironing boards that inspired him to begin producing toys.[2]:39*

> *In 1932, Ole Kirk's shop started making wooden toys such as piggy banks, pull toys, cars and trucks and houses. The business was not profitable because of the Great Depression. Farmers in the area sometimes traded food in exchange for his toys; Ole Kirk continued producing practical furniture in addition to toys to stay in business. In the mid-1930s, the yo-yo toy fad gave him a brief period of increased activity until it suddenly collapsed. To reduce waste, Ole Kirk used the leftover yo-yo parts as wheels for toy trucks. [1]:15 His son Godtfred began working for him, taking an active role in the company.[1]:15*

Despite Wikipedia being a frequent source of information for children, this text is quite difficult for an 8- or 9-year-old to unpick in order to retrieve the relevant content for their own writing. When the text it too difficult, children often end up copying large chunks in the hope of capturing something relevant. When a film is used, children do not have the original text written down for them in order to copy; they hear the text being narrated and they have to put this into their own words or diagrams in order to reuse the information later. *The History of Lego* film can be found on The Literacy Shed website at: www.literacyshed.com/the-history-shed.html. In the first minute of this film, children are able to see where Lego was invented as well as when and by whom. They also get an insight into how the creator of Lego was feeling as he had to make his workers redundant. Teachers can also use this clip to show language features. In the first 30 seconds of the film the narrator asks three rhetorical questions, the first being 'Have you ever wondered where it all started and why it is named Lego?' When children are first introduced to note-making from films there will have to be lots of pausing and discussion of key points, but teachers will find that children are able to recall many facts. Technology in the classroom can also be utilised. If there are laptops or tablets which children can use independently, they can watch and rewatch sections of film in order to collect content.

The moving image in the film also aids comprehension. The following extract is from the narration of a BBC animated documentary about the life of Charles Dickens, which can also be found at: www.literacyshed.com/the-history-shed.html

> *Charles John Huffam Dickens was born on 7th February 1812 to John and Elizabeth Dickens. Charles was the second child of eight siblings in all, six of whom survived until adulthood.*

In this 25-second extract the children are presented with a number of facts: when he was born, what his middle names are, what his parents' names are and how many siblings he had. This is quite a lot of information for children to unpick; however, the moving images support what is being narrated. The viewer can see images of Dickens's parents and siblings; they can deduce that the children in the image are his brothers and sisters, if they were unsure of the meaning of the word 'siblings'. When the narrator says, 'six of whom survived until adulthood', the characters in the animation drop dead in a rather comical manner. Children often enjoy using visual stimuli such as animations when trying to remember events as they can use their visual as well as verbal memory to do this.

 Activity

Note-making and animation

Animations can be used to support note-making.

- Go to the website 'The Literacy Shed' and choose a topic that you would like your children to make notes on - perhaps on Vikings or the Great Fire of London. 'The Saga of Biorn' is listed for Vikings and 'Flight Over 17th Century London' is listed for the Great Fire of London.

- How could these animations support the topic? What will you ask the children to write? Where will you pause the animation? How would you support the note-making? How can you develop this into a piece of writing?

 Research focus

The benefits of visual literacy

The United Kingdom Literacy Association (2004) in its report on *Raising Boys Achievement in Writing* lists a great deal of benefits, particularly to many boys, on using visual elements of literacy. They say, *In terms of age differences, at Reception, children paid careful attention to reading visual images where later in Key Stage 1 they showed much more attention to reading their own writing, particularly checking punctuation. At Key Stage 2, there was evidence of pupils identifying characters' feelings and emotions from visual images but also closer reading of print text as more careful and attentive reading of visual text developed (p18).*

(Continued)

(Continued)

It is important that visual literacy is offered in our classrooms for both boys and girls as it can be a valuable resource, as stated in the same report, *One of the key factors for those involved in the project was the powerful impact that using the visual had not only on the pupils' writing but also on their reading* (p38).

Visual literacy is now readily available in our classrooms and is a resource that is essential for our children to develop all areas of literacy.

Food, glorious food

Food can be a useful stimulus for writing. Many children would agree that one of the most glorious of all foods is chocolate. Roald Dahl's *Charlie and the Chocolate Factory* remains one of the most popular books for children and adults ever written, and it is the tasty treat that is at the heart of the story. But the actual true story of where chocolate comes from is equally compelling.

The Spanish and Portuguese explorer knights, known as the Conquistadors, brought chocolate to Europe from South America, but it was not in the form that we enjoy today. The Aztecs would grind the cacao bean into a powder and mix it with water and chilli to make a bitter and spicy form of hot chocolate. The Conquistadors stole this and a great many other things from the Aztecs, but it was not a popular drink in Europe. It was only in Victorian times that chocolate was mixed with milk and sugar, making it into the more familiar form that we see today. Chocolate has evolved enormously since the Aztecs. In fact, the chocolate we see in shops today is reminiscent of Dahl's vision for chocolate in his book. There are dazzling varieties and combinations of flavours readily available. Children could design their own products and recipes for chocolate. They could describe methods for making different types in instructional writing. They could research and write about the history of chocolate. They could create posters to give opinions and persuade. The writing opportunities are many and varied.

 **Case study**

Year 2 class learning about Africa

Kasia, a food technologist and chef, was invited into a Year 2 class to prepare and cook several dishes from different parts of Africa, including her home country, South Africa. Individual children tasted new ingredients and the class described their opinion as to what it tasted like from the expression on the taster's face. Adjectives such as *bitter, sweet, chewy, smooth, tough* and *spicy* were offered.

Several dishes were prepared by chosen children and cooked by Kasia, and by the end of the interactive session each child in the class had participated in some way.

The class were then asked to vote for their favourite dish. Children were told that they would be preparing this dish to serve to their parents or carers the following week with the help of Kasia.

They were told that they would need to write letters of invitation for their chosen adult. This invitation would include persuasive language, detailed descriptions of the chosen dish, including adjectives to make it sound delicious.

Over the proceeding week the children wrote these invitations and edited for improvement. They also made posters to advertise the event, then rewrote the recipes made during the session with Kasia, including the method and instructions.

 Activity

Zombie apocalypse

Learning about other cultures, as in the case study above, can encourage children to try new and diverse foods. Another important lesson that we, as teachers, need to continually reinforce is to not waste the food that we buy and try. We have more food readily available in the United Kingdom than ever before but unfortunately, according to the 'Waste and Resources Action Programme' (2016), we throw away around 15 million tonnes of food away every year and almost 50 per cent of this comes from our homes. This makes for alarming reading. But what if we run out of food? What would we do? How would we survive? There are many films and books on the survival topic. Bear Grylls's *Mission Survival* books are a popular and informative series that children can learn a lot from. Another survival scenario that can be linked to food and survival is a zombie apocalypse

- Ask your class what they would do if the school came under attack from zombies. Where would they hide? How could they secure the school from the attack?

- Could you take them on a tour of the school to inspire some ideas? Could the children make notes or sketches in each location?

- Once all of the ideas are collated, then the next step is to ask about food and drink. Tell your class that the government are sending help, but they need to survive for two weeks on the food that they have in school. You may want to give your class a list of the rationed food including quantities. There may be a mixture of fresh, tinned or boxed food. Some might be dried or preserved in some way. Some might not.

- Tell your class that they are in charge of the rationing of the food once the school has been made secure and safe from attack. How can the food be rationed? What quantities will be given out? How will the food be prepared? Which food will be used first and why?

- The class could then write diary entries for each day explaining and justifying their choices made. They could not only describe what they did, but also how they did it and what they were feeling throughout the whole two-week experience.

- What other writing opportunities are there in this scenario?

- Could you adapt the scenario for younger children?

Obviously, describing a zombie apocalypse is not suitable for every year group or every school. But the activity above could be adapted for a natural disaster or for Second World War writing or an alien invasion. We, as teachers, need to know what is suitable for our own teaching environment. This is again fictional writing but written in the style of a non-fiction genre.

The power of food

With the introduction of the new curriculum, in 2014 children now learn about new food, cooking and nutrition throughout most age phases. From 'All About Me' in Early Years to 'Micro Organisms' in Year 6, children need to know the importance of healthy eating.

Inviting experts such as chefs into schools to explain, as seen in the case study earlier, is happening more and more. Children are being told why the government is spending millions on educating people of all ages as to why it is important to eat healthily. This is all very positive, and there are also writing opportunities that can be taken too.

Information leaflets can be written for younger children explaining the benefits of healthy eating. Posters could be created to explain about carbohydrates and fats on food packaging and what this means, or perhaps critical review writing of different drinks such as comparing fresh fruit juices to smoothies. The children could write letters that contain persuasive writing encouraging the inclusion of healthier ingredients to the manufacturers of ready meals.

Fair Trade projects that lead to a business and enterprise focus also provide opportunities for writing. Children can work collaboratively to design logos, and to order food to sell at break times to make a profit, but they need to be made aware that there is a risk that they may make a loss. This could then be written about, outlining the reasons as to how their business venture went and why it was successful or not.

Food is a subject that can make people feel passionate, but it is also one that can make people feel uncomfortable. There are children who develop issues with food at a very young age. Whatever your perspective on food, it is certainly a subject that can lead to vast and varied non-fiction writing.

 Case study

Year 6 class visiting the Old Low Light Heritage Centre

To give children a new perspective on the origins and rich history of their local area, they could interact with objects, artefacts and their own imaginations by visiting a historical site. A Year 6 class visited the Old Low Light Heritage Centre in North Shields in order to research local history for a non-chronological report that they would write back at school. The purpose of the visit was to gather as much information as possible.

After visiting the heritage gallery, children worked in small groups and were given their own artefact and Old Low Light volunteer. The children had to decide what the artefact was, how old it was, who might have owned their object, what it was made from and how old they thought it was. One arte-fact was a sextant that was interpreted by the group by imagining the adventures it had had during the Battle of Trafalgar and how many times it had sailed around the world. Another was a glass medicine bottle and children wondered if it had saved all the children who lived in the local area from dying of the plague.

By removing the glass case and putting the artefact in front of the students, all barriers to access were removed. The children were in the role of curators; they were involved in the story behind the artefact by giving it an imagined narrative and a voice.

They were told the real story behind each artefact and they made notes and sketches about these to be used back in school for their writing. The volunteer then asked the group whether the object they had been exploring should replace an existing artefact on display in the gallery that they had visited earlier. They had to give reasons for their decision. This was dis-cussed with the group and the volunteer. They made additional notes and shared these with the other groups.

 Activity

Objects

Think of your topics for teaching this year.

- What objects could be used from your home or a family member's home that might enhance the topic?

- Where can you source other objects from? Could you ask colleagues to fill a box in the staff room of objects linked to a particular topic?

- How will you use the object to its best effect? Will the children be able to handle the object? What is the story behind the object?

 Research focus

Using artefacts

In *The Writing Classroom*, Evans (2013) quotes researcher Frank Smith (1982): *In order to write effectively we must have something to write about, we need to plan the writing prior to starting and we need to talk with someone about the writing* (p16). He uses the term 'conference' to describe this discussion process. This is exactly why visits to places as in the case study are essential for the planning of writing as it enables children to have a 'conference' about what they will write about. The children are experiencing something that they can go back to the classroom and write about. It also offers opportunity to discuss what they are going to write about with other adults who are specialists in their subject area.

Conclusion

Non-fiction is a genre of writing that is extremely varied with lots of opportunities for multiple types of writing to be achieved. It is an area of writing that particularly appeals to boys, but also has a mass appeal to both genders when children's areas of interest are pursued. In this chapter we have looked at examples from police reports to superheroes, from inventions to Lego, from food to world culture, from zombies to Fair Trade to object handling. There are countless other topics and themes that could have been explored. It is our role as teachers to make our lessons as rich and varied as we can in order to seek the best possible outcomes in writing. Teaching is an on-going pursuit: a learning journey that we are all on, both child and teacher, to find what inspires us all to become better writers.

━━━ Recommended websites ━━━

BBC Learning Zone, Horrible Histories – www.bbc.co.uk/cbbc/shows/horrible-histories

Flight Over 17th-Century London – www.literacyshed.com/the-history-shed.html

History of Lego on the Literacy Shed – www.literacyshed.com/the-history-shed.html

History of Lego on Wikipedia – https://en.wikipedia.org/wiki/Lego#History

Life of Charles Dickens – www.literacyshed.com/the-history-shed.html

Pigeon Impossible – www.literacyshed.com/the-fun-shed.html

Powerless – www.literacyshed.com/the-inspiration-shed.html

Saga of Biorn – www.literacyshed.com/the-myths-and-legends-shed.html

The Shirt Machine – www.literacyshed.com/the-inventors-shed.html

Wallace and Gromit PG Tips advert – www.youtube.com/watch?v=gfG2ZujlIZU

World Cup Theft 1966 – http://news.bbc.co.uk/onthisday/hi/dates/stories/march/20/newsid_2861000/2861545.stm

━━━ References ━━━

Clark, C. (2012) *Young People's Writing in 2011*: Findings from the National Literacy Trust's annual literacy survey. London: National Literacy Trust

Dahl, Roald (2016) *Charlie and the Chocolate Factory.* London: Puffin.

DfE (2012) *What is the Research Evidence on Writing?* London: Department for Education.

Evans, J. (2013) *The Writing Classroom.* Abingdon: Routledge.

Grahame-Smith, Seth (2011) *Abraham Lincoln Vampire Hunter.* London: Little, Brown Book Group.

Grylls, Bear (2008) *Mission Survival Series*. London: Red Fox.

National Literacy Trust (2012) *Boys' Reading Commission*. London: National Literacy Trust.

National Literacy Trust (2014) *Children and Young People's Reading in 2014*. London: National Literacy Trust.

United Kingdom Literacy Association (2004) *Raising Boys' Achievement in Writing*. Hertfordshire: United Kingdom Literacy Association.

Waste and Resources Action Programme (2016) Handy facts and figures on food surplus and waste in the UK. Banbury: Waste and Resources Action Programme. Available from: www.wrap.org.uk/content/uk-handy-waste-facts-and-figures-retail-sector?_ga=1.179900068.126911944.1470123508

3

Writing in mathematics

Lynn Thompson and David Bolden

Teachers' Standards

Standard 3 - Demonstrate good subject and curriculum knowledge

- have a secure knowledge of the relevant subject(s) and curriculum areas, foster and maintain pupils' interest in the subject, and address misunderstandings
- demonstrate a critical understanding of developments in the subject and curriculum areas, and promote the value of scholarship
- demonstrate an understanding of and take responsibility for promoting high standards of literacy, articulacy and the correct use of standard English, whatever the teacher's specialist subject

Standard 4 - Plan and teach well-structured lessons

- impart knowledge and develop understanding through effective use of lesson time
- promote a love of learning and children's intellectual curiosity

Key questions

- Can writing help to develop understanding of mathematical concepts?
- How do children learn to communicate their mathematical understanding?
- How can we engage children in writing about mathematics so that they can articulate ideas and concepts, as well as developing their understanding of written problems?

Start writing, no matter what. The water does not flow until the faucet is turned on.

Louis L'Amour

Introduction

Literacy is essential to functioning as part of society and necessary for most forms of employment; it is a creative, exciting subject that pupils enjoy individually and collectively. Do you agree with these statements?

Now substitute mathematics for literacy. Do you still agree? Literacy and mathematics are often seen as lying at opposite ends of the curricular spectrum, with literacy at the creative edge and mathematics at the formal, methodical edge (see Bolden et al., 2010). For this reason, mathematics and literacy are rarely taught in a cross-curricular manner in the classroom and learning from one subject is not often consolidated or enhanced in the other. Yet, mathematics and literacy may have more in common than you think and there are opportunities to create exciting lessons that combine both, leading to extended learning for pupils. Communication through writing connects all subjects, including mathematics.

The Mathematics Programme of Study (DfE, 2013a) specifically mentions that pupils should, from Year 1, be able to read and spell appropriate mathematical vocabulary, but the writing of technical words is not the only opportunity for writing in mathematics. The three aims of the new curriculum are fluency, reasoning and problem solving, and writing is key to mastering each of these curricular aims. Children need to develop fluency so they can *describe* their mathematical understanding; they need to develop this understanding so they can *explain* their mathematics; and they need to deepen their understanding in order to *communicate* and reason mathematically and to solve problems.

Regular opportunities to write in mathematics lessons should be planned in advance and children should expect to write using sentences and paragraphs, just as they do in other subjects. They should write in a variety of ways, using words as labels, short sentences to add clarity to their work, paragraphs and longer pieces of prose to communicate their understanding – to describe, compare, predict, interpret, explain and justify.

Prompts to promote writing in mathematics

Prompt	Purpose
What does two-dimensional mean?	Describing
How could you find out if 162 was a multiple of 9? Are there other ways to find out?	Comparing
How many star jumps could you do in one minute?	Predicting
What does this graph tell you about ...?	Interpreting
How could you use your knowledge of triangles to help you work out the sum of the interior angles in a hexagon?	Explaining
If you did this again, would you use a different method? Why/why not?	Justifying

Look at David Waugh's section on 'Developing prose writing' (Chapter 1) and consider how this might support you to introduce or extend children's use of writing in mathematics. Allowing children to *gain confidence from producing short, meaningful writing* to inspire and elicit purposeful, quality mathematical prose is excellent advice to ensure all learners can engage in the activity. Following David's suggestions will also support you as a teacher as you embark on your own pedagogical journey towards mathematical writing. He offers ideas for a progressive route from thinking, reading and speaking to writing, which is as applicable to mathematics as it is to any other subject. The modelled, shared and interactive writing he discusses will be addressed in a mathematical context later in this chapter.

When children begin to write paragraphs and prose to communicate their mathematics there are educational benefits in both subject areas. Editing and redrafting mathematical writing refines reasoning, deepens understanding and helps to *enhance the effectiveness of what they write as well as increasing their competence* (DfE, 2013b, p23).

 Research focus

Language in learning

For many years, researchers have discussed the position of language in learning and educational development. Vygotsky (1986) believed that use of language helped children to develop higher-order thinking skills, and his views underpin many current, accepted research theories. In the primary classroom, the idea of developing language use through shared experiences is common practice to promote learning, with most pupils and teachers engaging in regular shared and scaffolded writing activities across curriculum subjects. This practice is based on and informed by a plethora of research, which indicates that writing supports high levels of learning in all subjects. The *National Writing Project* and Nagin (2006) state that because of this, writing *matters in any classroom where inquiry, knowledge, and expression are valued and recognized by students and teachers* (p104).

Research also shows, however, that despite a wealth of research into the benefits of writing as language use in mathematics, writing in and about mathematics is still a departure from the pedagogical norm (Kuzle, 2013, p41), *thus creating a gap between research and the realities of practice* (p46).

As teaching is a research-based profession, what are the perceived benefits of writing in mathematics that as educators we seem reluctant to take up and why is that?

Miller (1991) states that the purpose of writing outside the literacy lesson is to improve the quality of writing and, as Martin (2015) observes, this has largely been the focus of research into writing across the curriculum. Academic enquiry into the benefits of writing in mathematics is much more recent. The purpose of writing in mathematics is to allow pupils an opportunity to focus closely on the subject matter, to reflect upon, analyse and deepen their understanding, refine their reasoning and improve their ability to communicate.

Burns (2004) agrees that writing supports children's mathematical learning in this way, providing pupils with an opportunity to consolidate their thinking and, in addition, that mathematical prose allows teachers to explore children's understanding in depth and therefore to make more accurate assessments when teaching for mastery: ... *when students write, their papers provide a window into their understanding, their misconceptions and their feelings about the content they're learning* (p30).

There is much academic debate in relation to the benefits of writing in mathematics. Porter and Masingila (2001) reflect upon the extensive research conducted and suggest that benefits to mathematical understanding may not be due to the actual activity of writing, but to the processes children go through in order to write - thinking about their maths and refining those thoughts to communicate to others. Wilcox and Monroe (2011) state that many teachers struggle to link writing and mathematics, as they may feel that a writing activity detracts from the mathematical content, though they conclude that the activity continues to be one of educational worth.

Wilcox and Monroe (2011) argue that writing in mathematics promotes learning in both areas; that drafting and editing work improves the quality of writing while also extending mathematical thinking. They offer six suggestions to integrate writing and mathematics.

- Writing without revision (*Learning logs*)
- Think-Write-Share (*in response to questions*)
- Note taking/note making
- Writing with revision (*shared and edited writing*)
- Class book (*shared writing*)
- Alphabet books (*shared writing - maths dictionaries*)

Wilcox and Monroe put these ideas forward as starting points for teachers introducing writing into mathematics lessons and they encourage teachers to augment them with additional strategies as they become more aware of the range of writing opportunities. Case studies in the article reveal that teachers valued writing as an engaging strategy to promote understanding in mathematics. Reflecting upon the benefits to both writing and mathematical learning, Wilcox and Monroe conclude that *such opportunities are not superfluous or simply nice to do if there is enough time. They are too important to ignore* (p529). Burns (2004) goes further, affirming that *I can no longer imagine teaching maths without making writing an integral aspect of students' learning* (p30).

Opportunities for writing in mathematics

 Case study

Outdoor learning

Each year Durham University students on the PGCE Primary Education and those in the 2nd year of the BA Primary Education programme take part in an outdoor maths trail with local KS2 pupils. This is a structured maths trail with a booklet of questions designed to promote mathematical discussion among pupils and challenge within problem-solving. Students are encouraged to support and challenge the pupils and to help them communicate their understanding in a variety of written styles. In some questions, the writing is modelled to support independent writing of sentences further into the trail booklet, as in the following examples.

Q1. Estimate the girth of the tree.

A. We estimate that the girth of the tree measures .... cm/m/km. (Cross out the two you don't need)

Explain how you worked it out.

....

....

....

....

....

....

Q1a. What mathematical word could be used to describe the 'girth'?

....

There are planned opportunities in this activity for single-word answers, full sentences and longer pieces of prose, and pupils are encouraged to discuss their responses as a group and also to share ideas for how to communicate their understanding in writing. This allows for children at different stages of competence in writing to contribute at their own, level to the final response, and also for children to extend their learning in both mathematics and literacy through shared writing and learning from their peers.

Upon return to school, there are further opportunities for research and extended writing related to the maths trail.

Hayley brought her Year 6 class to one of the PGCE maths trails at the Botanic Garden. A large portion of the children in her class were EAL learners from both the beginning to advanced stages of learning English. Initially, some of the children were reluctant participants, perhaps because they had been told they were going on a trip to do maths and problem solving all afternoon. It was soon apparent, however, that the children were enjoying the activity; they were enjoying doing maths, were absorbed in mathematical reasoning with their peers, and were able to justify their choices and

When you get back to school you could use the Internet to find out more information about the Botanic Garden.

Puck's charm

Is there a piece of waste-land in your school grounds you could transform into a garden? Can you produce a design? How much will it cost? How long will it take?

There is a headstone in the Garden dedicated to a soldier who died in World War I. Can you find out more about him?

Did you notice the sculpture about Puck of Pook's Hill? Find out more about him and his charm. Would you travel with him? Where would you go and what would you do?

The Visitor centre was opened in 1988 by Dame Margot Fonteyn. What is she famous for?

Design a leaflet to promote the Botanic Garden.

Where did you see this?

Figure 3.1 Botanic Garden Maths Trail booklet: back cover

shared ideas to communicate their understanding in the booklet. Hayley was surprised at the level of engagement and also the standard of both the maths and the written work her pupils produced on the day. After completing the trail, one pupil whom Hayley described as a 'reluctant learner' announced that it had been the best day of his life. He was eager to discuss his problem-solving strategies and to ensure that everyone in the vicinity was aware of his contribution to the written explanations.

Hayley kept in touch after the trip and shared some of the success her class achieved in follow-up research and extended writing. They produced leaflets to advertise the Botanic Garden, including within them some maths problems of their own and they also took on the suggestion to find out more about Puck of Pook's Hill. As part of their research, the children listened to excerpts of Kipling's short stories and wrote their own fictional works based on Puck and his magical powers. Hayley shared her belief that the outdoor maths trail had extended her pupils' learning in both writing and in mathematics, stating that she would never have thought it possible that a day of maths would lead to children's fictional writing based on classic literature.

Another local school following a maths trail activity with 2nd year undergraduates used the university booklet as a model for Year 6 pupils to create their own trail within the school grounds. This was particularly powerful, as children used a shared writing approach to construct their own mathematical problems, editing and redrafting to clarify meaning and also considering whether the problems they created would be better served by word, sentence or paragraph responses.

In the next section you will find further ideas for fieldwork activities.

Classroom ideas for outdoor learning

The best teachers are always looking to improve their practice and for ways to engage learners in learning – that is why you are reading this book. The benefits of writing to enthuse pupils and consolidate understanding across the curriculum are evident in practice and supported by academic research, but these could be augmented by taking your new ideas beyond the classroom. Dillon et al. (2006) argue that ... *fieldwork, properly conceived, adequately planned, well taught and effectively followed up, offers learners opportunities to develop their knowledge and skills in ways that add value to their everyday experiences in the classroom* (p107).

1. Visitor centres often offer maths trail activities for schools to undertake as part of their field trip. Ask when you book your school trip and incorporate the trail into your day.

2. Create your own booklet to facilitate a structured maths trail in a local park or in the school grounds. This will take time to prepare but can be used with future cohorts, so is well worth the time spent. Ensure that you consider opportunities for writing alongside opportunities for children to develop and practice their mathematical skills. NRICH offer advice on constructing your own maths trail available from: http://nrich.maths.org/2579

3. Provide opportunities for unstructured maths trails. These might be during school trips or when exploring the school and its grounds. Unstructured trails develop as you explore and therefore take little time to prepare beforehand. They still offer the opportunity for children to deepen their mathematical understanding and to write at length, based on practical experiences and stimuli.

4. The venue you choose for your maths trail can provide links to other subject areas, helping children to develop understanding across disciplines, supported by communication through writing. For example, a maths trail in a park can help children to examine their surroundings much more closely and can link to work in geography. Similarly, a maths trail in a church or cathedral can support learning in RE. Look at Chapter 14, 'Writing and RE', in which a 'Year 4 Class visit Durham Cathedral to learn about the Northern Saints' (case study and research focus) and consider how you could combine learning in mathematics, RE and writing.

Maths through stories

Tucker et al. (2010) maintained:

> Often children develop anxiety about math because they must learn it, but they do not understand it. Teachers and researchers have found that using storybooks about math concepts can help because they present the abstract concept through a story in which children can relate and explain the concept in terms the child understands (p154).

Which books support mathematical learning?

- Maths dictionaries that define vocabulary.

- Story books that teach or practise a mathematical skill.

- Regular children's fiction.

All of these can be used to promote learning in maths and have a place in the maths classroom. A quick glance at the bookshelves in a primary classroom, however, will inevitably reveal examples of regular children's fiction, sometimes display examples of maths dictionaries, but rarely books about maths or stories that teach a skill or concept. This is a missed opportunity, as maths story books are an engaging way to teach and consolidate skills, and learning can go beyond that which is immediately apparent.

Father Christmas Needs a Wee by Nicholas Allen is a counting book that goes from 1 to 10 and back again. As he visits each of the ten houses, Father Christmas drinks and eats the treats left out for him. Very soon, he desperately needs a wee and forgets to leave the presents. He has to dash back to each house to deliver the presents in order to get home in time ... but there is a problem ...

This book can be used to consolidate counting forwards and backwards to ten in Early Years, but there are also opportunities to explore number bonds and addition, subtraction in Key Stage 1 and to problem solve in Key Stage 2. There are also great opportunities to write mathematically here. Children in Nursery and EYFS can make marks to describe the numbers and tell the story. In Key Stage 1, calculation stories can be written to reflect the storyline, as in the following example.

Father Christmas had one treat at number one, two treats at number two and three treats at number three. Father Christmas had 6 treats altogether $1 + 2 + 3 = 6$.

In Key Stage 2, the book can be used as a model for children to write problems related to the story or to write their own book that teaches a skill. These activities both provide opportunities for children to think about maths, to refine their understanding and to improve their ability to communicate with others.

Case study

Writing a story about maths

A Year 6 class read *Father Christmas Needs a Wee* and *Four Twits, A Dragon and a Princess - A Story about Learning the Four Times Tables* by Professor Paradox. In groups of four, the children discussed the stories, sharing their views before writing a review of each. Their shared writing reviews were drafted and edited, then shared with other groups for peer review. During this activity, they refined their opinions on the style of writing and the efficacy of the story as a mathematical learning tool.

Each group then worked together to choose a mathematical topic that they could use as the basis of their own maths story book. Topics covered included shape, measure and number. Each group

(Continued)

(Continued)

worked together to plan their story and to create scenes, characters and dialogue. At the end of each lesson, each group shared their progress with another group and received feedback to help improve their writing. Groups wrote in different styles – one group choosing to write in poetic prose in the style of *Father Christmas Needs a Wee* to illustrate properties of shape. Another group took the idea of the princess and castles from *Four Twits, A Dragon and a Princess* and used that to write about number bonds. In this story an evil magician (called Al Gebra) casts a spell to eradicate numbers from the whole land, causing chaos for the townspeople. Fortunately, they are saved when the king convinces the wizard to remove the spell by letting him live in the castle.

When their ideas were complete the children drafted storyboards, then used an online resource to create their book (www.storyboardthat.com/storyboard-creator).

Figure 3.2 Excerpt from Oh No, Where Are All the Numbers? *created in StoryboardThat*

The school above holds weekly peer coaching sessions where children move to different classes and support others in areas in which they are having difficulty. The Year 6 children read their stories with other children and used them as a stimulus to share their understanding of the mathematical concept within.

Case study

Problems related to stories

PGCE students went into a local school to carry out an activity related to creative problem solving through literature. Students read to EYFS and Key Stage 1 pupils from a selection of stories including *Six Dinner Sid*, *The Gruffalo*, *The Gruffalo's Child* and *Handa's Surprise*.

After sharing the book, students presented groups of children with a selection of practical mathematical problems they had developed, based on the story, and complemented these with effective questioning to challenge learning and to elicit full responses. The children were encouraged by the students to discuss their ideas with a partner and to communicate their responses in writing, whether it was through mark-making, writing a word or constructing a sentence.

For Key Stage 2 children, problems were based on myths, legends and fables including *The Lambton Worm*, *The Crafty Fox* and aliens spotted in Durham city centre. Again, the stories were shared before pupils, in small groups and supported by a student, solved related mathematical problems. Language use, including technical vocabulary, was developed through discussion and pupils were encouraged to communicate their reasoning and understanding in writing on whiteboards. After children solved the problems, students used the children's written responses to focus follow-up activities on areas for development they had identified through this communication.

Classroom ideas for maths through books

1. Provide opportunities for children to develop a mathematical dictionary. This can be an independent activity for each child or a shared writing activity where children contribute their definitions for a class dictionary. *Dictionaries of this type, which are developed by the children in response to their own learning needs, result in deeper understanding and better retention of technical terminology* (Barmby et al., 2014, p44).

2. Review the story books available in the classroom or school library. If necessary, consider augmenting these with books that could be used as a stimulus to promote writing in mathematics.

3. Read stories about maths to your pupils and support them to create their own story that helps to practise or consolidate a mathematical topic.

4. Liaise with your local secondary school to enable their students to develop mathematical problems related to stories, myths, legends and/or fables for you to use. The secondary teachers can use these to assess their students' conceptual understanding and writing skills. You can use them as an opportunity to combine writing and mathematics in your classroom.

Maths board games

Learning maths through games allows pupils to interact with mathematics in a non-threatening way similar to when learning maths through stories. Gough (1999, p12) identifies a 'game' as having two or more players, who take turns and compete to win. The players are able to influence the outcome of the game through the choices they make. Games are different from activities because of this 'choice'. Snakes and Ladders is not categorised as a game because there is no interaction between players and no chance to influence the outcome, as winning relies purely on luck.

Research focus

Learning through games

Gyöngyösi Wiersum (2012, p25) identifies research that proposes the benefits of learning maths through games include among other things, increased levels of motivation, a positive attitude and increased learning. Increased learning, she asserts, is in comparison to levels of learning in more formal activities and occurs because there is a high level of interaction between players, resulting in good opportunities to test intuitive ideas and problem-solving strategies.

It can be expensive to buy ready-made board games, so if you would like to save some money consider making your own. If you would like to save some money *and* increase learning through writing in mathematics, ask your pupils to invent their own games This is an engaging activity where children have to develop a deep understanding of the mathematical concept behind the game in order to design the board and devise the game, rules.

Writing opportunities can include making preparatory notes, perhaps in relation to the mathematical content of other known games, identifying key mathematical vocabulary and writing rules and instructions which may be edited to improve the quality of the writing and the clarity of the mathematical content. When games are completed, they can be played by other children in the class, who then have an opportunity to rate the game and give feedback to the developers in written form.

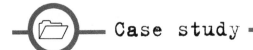

Case study

Board games

A maths subject leader had attended a course on learning maths through games and felt that children in her school would benefit greatly from practising basic skills in this way. She developed a handful of basic board games, which covered topics such as odd and even, place value and calculation strategies. She shared these with her Year 4 pupils, who found all but one of them very engaging. Through discussion, she discovered that this was because the children found the rules to this one game rather confusing. She used this as an opportunity to integrate writing into learning mathematics and asked the children to work in small groups to review the game and offer feedback on how to improve it. Early responses showed that the children could offer sensible suggestions to clarify the rules, but they were quite unclear as to how to describe the maths learning in the game.

The teacher spent time with the children writing a shared class review of one of the other board games and modelled how to describe the mathematical content and how to decide if the game met its stated mathematical objective. Children used this piece of shared writing to inform their previous reviews which resulted in higher quality written work and a deeper understanding of the mathematical content.

The children's deeper understanding informed their choices when designing their own games which were peer reviewed within a further shared writing activity and which are still used by other classes in the school.

Classroom ideas for maths through board games

1. Ask children in groups to play and review popular board games in an effort to discern opportunities for mathematical learning. These could include chess, Monopoly, Battleships, Connect Four, Guess Who? or indeed any games or board games that lurk at the back of your classroom cupboard. This can be a powerful mathematical exercise as children become aware of maths skills they are using in everyday activities and begin to see the meaning and application of their learning. There are opportunities here for independent note-making and shared writing as children combine ideas, perhaps culminating in a written report. To ensure that the best learning takes place within this activity, it should be modelled first by the teacher producing a piece of shared or interactive writing that children can use to structure their own thoughts and ideas.

2. Ask children to invent their own mathematical game using resources like dominoes, cubes, playing cards and dice. They should begin by thinking about the mathematical skill to be practised and then combine ideas as they construct their game. Groups will need to produce a set of rules, a 'how to play' brief and a sentence or two to outline the mathematical content. Completed games can be peer reviewed and adverts could be designed to promote their games or letters written to the head teacher to persuade them to invest in more of the resources they have used.

Problem solving and writing to communicate understanding

If children are to become proficient problem solvers they also need to be able to reason, to consider their own thinking, justify their choices and communicate these mathematically (Barmby et al., 2014, p57). Think about this in relation to your own class: using this definition, how many of your pupils can you now describe as proficient problem solvers? In recent years, Key Stage 2 maths SAT questions that asked for a written explanation or justification were more often than not graded informally at level 5. This meant that as teachers we felt we had some justification for our level 3s and 4s making no attempt to communicate in writing or producing something that just did not quite make sense.

As a class teacher, how often have you said or heard something along the lines of 'if I could mark what's inside your head you'd get it right, but you have to improve your written explanations and make them clearer to get the marks'? Pupils who hear this from their teacher may come to believe that reasoning and communicating are not linked to their understanding, but are an exercise to gain a mark in a test. Problem solving, reasoning and communicating were seriously threatened under the previous curriculum and testing format of becoming the domain of the elite mathematicians, the 'rapid graspers', those we fondly remember as 'the more able children'. Teaching for mastery within the new curriculum at the very least demands that we expect ALL children to be problem solvers who are metacognitively aware, able to reason, justify and to communicate in writing.

So, how do children learn to effectively communicate their mathematical understanding in writing? The ability to do so is actually the next step after they have learned to think about their thinking, have learned to reason and have learned to justify. So, the questions we should perhaps be considering are how do they learn these skills and how do we teach them?

In many classrooms we do not explicitly teach or train children how to think about their thinking, but we ask children:

- can you explain what you are doing?

- why have you done this?

- how would you explain this to someone else?

We then expect that, by asking these questions frequently, children will come to realise what we expect as an answer (Barmby et al., 2014, p58).

Waring (2008) suggests a progressive teaching model to use in the classroom that supports and leads children to communicate effectively in mathematical writing.

Stage 1: Convince yourself (mental justification).

Stage 2: Convince a friend (oral justification).

Stage 3: Convince a pen friend (informal written justification).

Stage 4: Convince your teacher (formal written justification).

If this or a similar model is introduced where skills are taught and refined and feedback is given, children develop their skills progressively from considering their own thoughts through to independent written communication of understanding. With a very strong link to teaching for mastery, this progress to quality writing in maths enables ALL children to communicate their understanding.

Classroom ideas for effective written communication in maths

1. Consider your approach to teaching reasoning skills and compare this with those of your colleagues. Would a model that allows you to teach these skills leading to effective written communication benefit your pupils' learning? If so, agree how the model might be implemented throughout school – by what age would you expect children to have achieved a particular stage of understanding?

2. If appropriate, allocate extra time to teach children the skills of writing effectively in maths until their ability is in line with your expectations.

3. When appropriate, consider using sophisticated problems like those from the NRICH website to promote thinking and writing skills: http://nrich.maths.org/frontpage. Stringy Quads, for example, asks children to consider how they might convince someone else that their shape has only one line of symmetry: http://nrich.maths.org/2913. There are also tasks based on the book If the World Were a Village by David J. Smith and Shelagh Armstrong, which ask for children's opinions on the most effective representation of data: http://nrich.maths.org/7725. For any of the problems, even if they do not specifically suggest writing, you could consider:

- writing key words;
- justifying choices and methods in sentences;
- explaining in writing how the problem was solved;
- writing to convince someone else the answer is correct;
- and so on ...

Different types of mathematical writing

Remember to start off small if you are introducing your pupils to writing in mathematics – a word to describe something, a title on a graph, or a sentence to clarify meaning is enough to begin with. This can be followed by longer prose when the time is right – when children have been taught the skills that will enable them to communicate their understanding.

Some academics (Beveridge, 1997; Lim and Pugalee, 2004) and practitioners advocate the use of a dedicated maths journal where pupils write about their daily learning and their feelings towards particular maths topics. Some may believe that mathematical writing should take place in the child's maths book alongside evidence of the maths work it relates to. This might take the form of a description of what the child has learned today alongside the highlighting of particular aspects they found hard or easy, underneath a photograph of them carrying out a practical or group activity. These are considerations for you as the class teacher – you know your pupils.

As Urquhart (2009) helpfully notes, incorporating writing activities into your maths lessons does not mean you need to start from scratch. Existing lessons can be tweaked to add opportunities for writing that will both improve pupil engagement and heighten cognitive demands.

Conclusion

Mathematical writing should be modelled by the teacher and children should feel that their efforts are meaningful and acknowledged. They should also understand the purpose of the mathematical writing and be able to see how it promotes and consolidates understanding.

As mentioned previously, some practitioners may be concerned that by focusing on the quality of writing they may be neglecting learning in mathematics. Porter and Masingila (2001) identify academic literature which argues the opposite; research which suggests that through the use of writing to learn mathematics pupils may actually become more engaged as they begin to see mathematics as meaningful, and that the process of writing helps them to understand the material. Miller (1991) states that:

> Students come to mathematics class having a variety of real-world experiences on which to continue the construction of their knowledge of mathematics. The construction of knowledge requires active engagement in thought-provoking activities. Because writing leads people to think, improved mastery of mathematics concepts and skills is possible if students are asked to write about their understanding. Because writing in mathematics involves many of the thought processes teachers would like to foster in their students, every mathematics teacher should seriously consider the use of writing as a part of the daily routine of the mathematics class.

(p517)

In addition to these perceived benefits to the pupil as a writer of mathematics, Porter and Masingila (2001) point out that research also identifies benefits to the teacher as a reader in relation to more accurate formative assessment, and also notes benefits to the student–teacher interaction.

In response to the friend who suggested that the biggest drawback to writing in maths lessons was that it slowed everything down and took up too much time, consider a quote from a very famous mathematician.

> 'Can you do addition?' the White Queen asked. 'What's one and one and one and one and one and one and one and one and one and one?' 'I don't know,' said Alice. 'I lost count.' 'She can't do addition,' the Red Queen interrupted.

Lewis Carroll, *Through the Looking Glass and What Alice Found There*, 1871

Sometimes maths is just easier when it is written down

━━━ Recommended websites ━━━

How to use maths trails

www.ncetm.org.uk/public/files/5274603/organise-maths-trails.pdf

Maths problems

https://nrich.maths.org/frontpage

Meaningful Maths Trails

http://nrich.maths.org/2579

Online storyboard creator

www.storyboardthat.com/storyboard-creator

Writing in Mathematics

http://mathwire.com/writing/writing1.html

References

Allen, N. (2009) *Father Christmas Needs a Wee* London: Hutchinson.

Barmby, P., Bolden, D. and Thompson, L. (2014) *Understanding and Enriching Problem Solving in Primary Mathematics*. Northwich: Critical Publishing.

Beveridge, I. (1997) Teaching your students to think reflectively: the case for reflective journals. *Teaching in Higher Education*, 2(1): 33–43.

Bolden, D.S., Harries, A.V. and Newton, D.P. (2010) Pre-service primary teachers' conceptions of creativity in mathematics. *Educational Studies in Mathematics*, 73(2): 143–57.

Burns, M. (2004) Writing in maths. *Educational Leadership*, 62 (2, October): 30–3.

DfE (2013a) *Mathematics Programmes of Study: Key Stages 1 and 2*. National Curriculum in England. Available from: www.gov.uk/government/uploads/system/uploads/attachment_data/file/335158/PRIMARY_national_curriculum_-_Mathematics_220714.pdf (accessed June 2016).

DfE (2013b) *English Programmes of Study: Key Stages 1 and 2*. National curriculum in England. Available from: www.gov.uk/government/uploads/system/uploads/attachment_data/file/335186/PRIMARY_national_curriculum_-_English_220714.pdf (accessed June 2016).

Dillon, J., Rickinson, M., Teamey, K., Morris, M., Choi, M.Y., Sanders, D. and Benefield, P. (2006) The value of outdoor learning: evidence from research in the UK and elsewhere. *School Science Review*, 87(320): 107–11.

Gough, J. (1999) Playing mathematical games: when is a game not a game? *Australian Primary Mathematics Classroom*, 4(2): 12–17.

Gyöngyösi Wiersum, E. (2012) Teaching and learning mathematics through games and activities. *Acta Electrotechnica et Informatica*, 12(3): 23–26.

Kuzle, A. (2013) Promoting writing in mathematics: prospective teachers' experiences and perspectives on the process of writing when doing mathematics as problem solving. *Centre for Educational Policy Studies*, 3(4): 41–59.

Lim, L. and Pugalee, D.K. (2004) Using journal writing to explore: they communicate to learn mathematics and they learn to communicate mathematically. *Ontario Action Researcher*, 7(2): 1–15.

Martin, C. L. (2015) Writing as a tool to demonstrate mathematical understanding. *School Science and Mathematics*,115(1): 302–313.

Miller, D. L. (1991) Writing to learn mathematics. *The Mathematics Teacher*, 84(7): 516–521.

National Writing Project and Nagin, C. (2006) Because writing matters: improving writing in our schools (2nd edition). San Francisco, CA: Jossey-Bass.

Porter, M., and Masingila, J. (2001) Examining the effects of writing on conceptual and procedural knowledge in calculus. *Educational Studies in Mathematics*, 42(2): 165–77.

Professor Paradox (2012) *Four Twits, a Dragon and a Princess – A Story about Learning the Four Times Table (The Numberland Tales – Help with Times Tables and Multiplication for Children Book 4)*. Kindle Edition, Paradox Theatre. Available at: www.amazon.co.uk/Four-Twits-Dragon-Princess-Multiplication-ebook/dp/B008LK89AE

Tucker, C., Boggan, M., and Harper, S. (2010) Using children's literature to teach measurement. *Reading Improvement,* 47(3): 154–61.

Urquhart, V. (2009) Using writing in mathematics to deepen student learning. Denver, CO: Mid-continent Research for Educational and Learning. Available at: http://files.eric.ed.gov/fulltext/ED544239.pdf (accessed July 2016)

Vygotsky, L. S. (1986) *Thought and Language* (translated and edited by Alex Kozulin). Cambridge, MA: MIT Press.

Waring, S. (2008) *Can You Prove It?: Developing Concepts of Proof in Primary and Secondary Schools.* Leicester: Mathematical Association.

Wilcox, B. and Monroe, E.E. (2011) Integrating writing and mathematics. The Reading Teacher, 64(7): 521–29.

4
Writing in science
Lynn Newton

Teachers' Standards

Standard 3 - Demonstrate good subject and curriculum knowledge

- have a secure knowledge of the relevant subject(s) and curriculum areas, foster and maintain pupils' interest in the subject, and address misunderstandings
- demonstrate a critical understanding of developments in the subject and curriculum areas, and promote the value of scholarship
- demonstrate an understanding of and take responsibility for promoting high standards of literacy, articulacy and the correct use of standard English, whatever the teacher's specialist subject

Standard 4 - Plan and teach well-structured lessons

- impart knowledge and develop understanding through effective use of lesson time
- promote a love of learning and children's intellectual curiosity

---

Key questions

- What are the expectations on primary children to record their ideas in writing in primary science?
- How do we incorporate opportunities for recording in a variety of ways to use and enhance writing skills in science?
- What approaches can we use to encourage writing in science?

Introduction: science in the lives of primary children

Science is (and always has been) one of the three core areas of the statutory school National Curriculum, having the same status as English and mathematics. As such, all children in primary schools must be taught science – it is a key part of the primary school curriculum today for Key Stages 1 and 2. Children's science ideas build on their prior experiences of the world around them acquired during informal experiences gained out of school, and during their earlier school experiences in the Foundation Stage (3–5 years). Their primary school experiences also prepare the ground for their later work in science in secondary school. Consequently, primary teachers need to think about how to support primary children's thinking and working in science through the primary science curriculum experiences they offer and the approaches they use.

Young children of primary school age enjoy science. They like doing the activities and, when encouraged to do so, ask lots of science-focused questions and discuss their experiences. With a knowledgeable and enthusiastic teacher, the foundations are laid for a positive attitude to science in their later education. Yet research shows that even some experienced primary teachers still feel uncertain about how to teach some aspects of science effectively. To do so, teachers need to feel secure in the 4Ps of science. This involves thinking about:

- science as a *process*, a way of thinking and working (the skills and processes);

- science as a *product*, a body of knowledge (the key concepts and ideas);

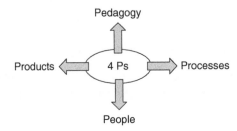

Figure 4.1 The 4Ps of science

- science and *people,* as a human enterprise that affects us all (its relevance); and

- science *pedagogy* appropriate to primary-aged teaching and learning.

 Research focus

Engaging science

How are the 4Ps achieved? The concept of *engaging science* provides a basis for good practice. What constitutes engaging science has been studied by Darby (2005). Based on observations of science lessons, she identifies two dimensions of teaching that have a major impact on children's engagement with a science lesson: an *instructional dimension* and a *relational dimension.*

The Instructional Dimension relates to how the teacher:

- provides for engaging children's *interest*; and
- supports children's development of *understandings.*

The Relational Dimension is about the teacher's:

- *enthusiasm* for the topic and the children's success in learning;
- ability to create an encouraging, non-threatening, mentally comfortable *atmosphere*; and
- provision of support at the *individual* level.

The former emphasises the teacher's planning, while the latter emphasises the nature of opportunities for interaction and the nurturing learning environment.

In 1986, in a policy statement for science (DES, 1986), HMI outlined ten principles of good practice in science teaching and, given Darby's dimensions, these principles are still relevant a quarter of a century later. They require science provision that has: *breadth, balance, continuity, progression* and *relevance.* It should also provide *equal opportunities,* and be *differentiated.* There should be *variety in approaches used* and opportunity for *cross-curricular activity* and it should be appropriately *assessed.*

The National Curriculum's expectations

The current National Curriculum (NC) framework became operational in schools in September 2014. The aims of the NC are to provide all pupils with:

> *an introduction to the essential knowledge that they need to be educated citizens. It introduces pupils to the best that has been thought and said; and helps engender an appreciation of human creativity and achievement.*

> (DfE, 2013b, section 3.1, p6)

Thinking about the 4Ps mentioned earlier, science in the National Curriculum is both a *process* (a way of thinking and working – Science 1) and a *product* (the concepts and ideas that underpin working scientifically – Science 2, 3 and 4). It also incorporates opportunities to show the *people* in science, through exemplification of the contributions of people to the scientific endeavour past and present, and making the relevance to our lives today explicit. In science, the Programmes of Study reflect the aims of the NC, to ensure all pupils:

- develop scientific knowledge and conceptual understanding through the specific disciplines of biology, chemistry and physics;

- develop understanding of the nature, processes and methods of science through practical activity; and

- are equipped with the scientific knowledge required to understand its uses and implications today and for the future.

While the NC requirements for Key Stage 1 (KS1) and Key Stage 2 (KS2) identify what to cover (summarised in Table 4.1), the NC does not specify how to deliver it. Teachers have freedom to use approaches and experiences from across the full school curriculum. Thinking particularly about recording and communicating in science, the NC requires that the younger primary children in KS1 record their findings using standard units, drawings, diagrams, photographs and simple prepared formats such as tables and charts, tally charts and displays.

In lower KS2 they should be encouraged to record findings using simple scientific language, drawings, labelled diagrams, bar charts and tables, and report their findings from their investigations, including written explanations of results and conclusions, displays or presentations.

In the final phase of their primary schooling, upper KS2, they must record data and results of increasing complexity using scientific diagrams and labels, classification keys, tables, bar and line graphs, and models. They should also be able to report findings from investigations, including written explanations of results, explanations involving causal relationships, and draw conclusions. Finally, they are expected to present reports of findings in written form, displays and presentations.

So, one of the priorities in science education has to be to provide opportunities for the learners to communicate, record and interpret such information. By the time they leave primary school, children need to be able to express themselves clearly, both in speech and in writing, to use scientific vocabulary appropriately, and to use a variety of methods to present ideas and information. Therefore, carefully planned and controlled methods of recording can satisfy this need, introduced gradually from an early age.

It can be seen from this that, for science, the use of language arts skills (reading, writing, speaking and listening) is crucial to communicating in science. The remainder of this chapter will look at children recording in science.

Children recording in science

One of the priorities for science in the DES policy statement mentioned above was to provide pupils at all stages in their education in science with appropriate opportunities to: *communicate (verbally, mathematically and graphically) and interpret written and other material* (DES, 1986, p2).

Table 4.1 National Curriculum – Science Key Stages 1 and 2

Working Scientifically (Science 1)	Year	Concepts and Ideas (Science 2, 3 and 4)
Key Stage 1: – observing closely using simple equipment; – performing simple tests; – identifying and classifying; – recording findings using standard units, drawings, diagrams, photographs, simple prepared formats such as tables and charts, tally charts and displays.	1	Plants Animals including humans Light
	2	All living things Plants Animals including humans Habitats Everyday materials Uses of everyday materials Forces and motion
Lower Key Stage 2: – setting up simple comparative and fair tests using a range of equipment, including data loggers; – beginning to make accurate measurements using standard units; – recording findings using simple scientific language, drawings, labelled diagrams, bar charts and tables; – reporting findings from investigations, including written explanations of results and conclusions, displays or presentations; – using results to draw simple conclusions and suggest improvements and predictions for setting up further tests.	3	Plants Animals including humans Everyday materials Rocks Sound Forces and magnets
	4	Classification of living things Animals including humans Habitats Evolution and inheritance States of matter Light Earth and Space Electricity
Upper Key Stage 2: – planning investigations, including, recognising and controlling variables where appropriate; – taking measurements using a range of scientific equipment with increasing accuracy and precision; – recording data and results of increasing complexity using scientific diagrams and labels, classification keys, tables, bar and line graphs, and models; – reporting findings from investigations, including written explanations of results, explanation involving causal relationships and conclusions; – presenting reports of findings in written form, displays and presentations; – continuing to develop the ability to use test results to make predictions to set up further comparative and fair tests.	5	All living things Animals including humans Properties of everyday materials and reversible changes Forces Static electricity and magnetism
	6	All living things Evolution and inheritance Changes that form new materials Light Forces Electricity

This goal is as relevant today as it was 30 years ago and, while few teachers would argue against such a priority, many might make a distinction between communicating and recording. Good communication skills – reading, writing, speaking and listening – are fundamental to success in most areas of life and are useful, if not essential, in most contexts in which primary children and their teachers work. It would seem appropriate, therefore, that such skills are fostered and used in a planned and measured way across the whole curriculum, including science.

But communication is both a mental and a physical activity. It is valuable in the context of science because both children and teachers can learn from the communicative act (Newton, 2000). From a teacher's viewpoint, he or she:

- provides a role model for effective communication;
- introduces new scientific vocabulary at appropriate points in the learning experience;
- creates opportunities to explore scientific ideas and thinking more fully;
- notices and notes gaps in a learner's skills, knowledge and understanding; and
- scaffolds the learning that is taking place.

The children, on the other hand, are helped to:

- make sense of their experiences, clarifying thinking and constructing new understandings;
- sort ideas into a logical order, sequencing procedures and events, and prioritising what is important;
- synthesise ideas to produce mental structures or frameworks or models to represent the overall experiences;
- experience new vocabulary and develop and use scientific terminology appropriately in different contexts;
- apply various language skills in different contexts for different purposes and audiences; and
- stand back to examine and review experiences from different perspectives and reflect upon them.

Science has its own specialist language and vocabulary. This, in turn, raises some challenges. For example, *material* to a child usually means the fabric that makes up the curtains or the bed covers, whereas in science it is the state of matter. When and how to introduce particular words and terms is left to the judgement of individual teachers, although the NC framework does help to point the way. Science also has its own particular method – way of working – that has embedded in it an approach to recording science experiences. Many teachers will recall their own experiences of recording in science at secondary school which involved a formulaic *Apparatus, Diagram, Method, Results, Conclusion*. How do we prepare primary children for this? Teachers need to view communication activities within science as part of the overall science learning experiences being afforded to the children. While it is important from the NC viewpoint that children are engaged in the collection of evidence in science, how they record and communicate those experiences can provide good learning opportunities for them as well. Teachers need to build such opportunities into their planning in science.

Some might argue that it is doing the practical activities in science that is important, and that having to record and communicate findings and ideas inhibits this. So, why should children record during their science lessons? There are good reasons for doing so from the teacher's point of view, such as credibility, accountability and record keeping. However, even more important are the benefits to the learners in terms of aiding the development of their scientific skills, knowledge and understanding and the promotion of positive attitudes towards science.

Recording ideas in some way may, of course, be a *necessity* – some form of recording may be an integral and essential part of the activity. For example, the children may be required in some way to record the pulse rates of members of their group during different types of physical activity and then, later, construct a graph and draw conclusions from the data. Even when it is not a necessity, by recording ideas and findings in different ways during their science activities under the teacher's direction, children gradually *practise* and become skilled at different methods of recording. Later, they can select independently the recording method most appropriate to the science activity when carrying out investigations and problem-solving tasks. If children are recording their ideas and findings in science, they should be thinking more deeply about them and internalising their ideas and constructing new understandings. Thus the recording process acts a *reinforcement* for learning and concept acquisition. The recording process may also act as a *stimulus* for further questions, enquiry and investigations, stimulating further science work either through the replication of activities or the use of findings to raise new questions from themselves or others.

Of course, children do not need to record everything they do in science. Recording can, on occasions, be unnecessary, inappropriate or a waste of time. Recording is pointless if it is not fulfilling a worthwhile educational role. It can become nothing more than a time-consuming chore, especially when the same recording method is used over and over again. When this happens frustration can build in the children, with boredom leading to negative attitudes forming. But this does not have to be the case. If children are asked to record their findings, thoughts, plans, experiences, then it is crucial that the type of recording is matched to the type of science activity going on, as well as to the needs and prior experiences of recording of the learners. To be able to do this, teachers need to have available a variety of recording methods and introduce this variety in a planned way across the science programme, providing opportunities for children to use the methods, initially under the teacher's control, to practise and refine their ability to use each method and then, eventually, to select and justify which one they think is the most appropriate.

Activities for children to encourage recording in science

There are numerous ways that children can be encouraged to record in science. They vary with the age and ability of the children, but if they are introduced to the range available at appropriate points in their science work and given opportunities to practise them in different contexts, they can become competent and independent in recording, adding to their communication repertoire. These can be loosely grouped as written, graphic and other recording methods.

Written records

Free writing about science activities

The first stage in the writing process will be to encourage the children to describe in their own words what they did in their science lesson and, perhaps, generate some kind of explanation for what they found out. Oral questioning by the teacher (see Table 4.2) will help to guide and structure this process.

In the case of the youngest children or those who are less competent at writing, sometimes asking the children to produce a drawing first can be a good starting point. Then the teacher or a classroom assistant could ask questions about the drawing and, after listening to the child's response, help write down his or her answer by annotating the drawing. A key word list could also be useful at this point.

As children's writing skills develop, they can begin to do this for themselves, either annotating their own drawings or writing a prose account of their science activity with the support of a key word list. Initially, such accounts are likely to be descriptive and events from the science process may be listed out of sequence (children often write as the thoughts pop into their heads). Again, oral discussion during the plenary or, if possible, one to one, can guide and focus attention on what is important and develop understandings in science: *What did you already know? What did you do? What happened? Can you think of a reason why that might have happened? If you did it again, what would you do?*

Structured writing about science activities

Once children's reading and writing skills are developed, a shift from oral to written questioning is possible. Structured worksheets and frameworks for writing become useful to:

* focus children's attention on what is relevant;

* encourage them to answer questions;

* make predictions;

* enter descriptive observations;

* present results in numerical data form;

* put forward ideas and give reasons for what they have found; and

* draw some conclusions.

Initially, a simple writing framework might be helpful.

1. First write about what you were trying to find out.

2. Next write about what you did.

3. Then write about what happened or what you saw.

4. Finally, write about what this tells you.

If exercise books are not being used for recording, worksheets may be stored in files or glued into folders, making the addition of related work or supplementary materials possible. They can also be scanned into e-portfolios for assessment purposes.

In the early stages, as well as writing frames and word lists, some teachers use Cloze procedure (literally, 'filling in the gaps') to extend ideas and support the writing process. An account of the science activity is provided with key words or phrases or definitions or explanations omitted. The children have to draw on their prior knowledge and new experiences to fill in the gaps, providing the missing words or phrases. Again, to scaffold learners in the early stages, a list of possible words, phrases, definitions or explanations can be provided separately, in random order and with some 'red herrings' to encourage thinking.

 Research focus

Writing frames

Medwell et al. (2014, p132) discussed the use of writing frames which include key words or phrases related to the text form children are asked to write in, arguing that they provide a structure within which children can *concentrate on communicating what they want to say, rather than getting lost in the form.* Medwell et al. argue that such writing frames scaffold writing in several ways.

- *It does not present writers with a blank page. There is comfort in the fact that there is already some writing on this page. This alone can be enough to encourage less confident writers to write at greater length.*

- *The frame provides a series of prompts to children's writing. Using the frame is rather like having a dialogue with the page and the prompts serve to model the register of that particular piece of writing.*

- *The frame deliberately includes connectives beyond the simple 'and then'. Extended use of frames can result in children spontaneously using these more elaborate connectives in other writing.*

- *The frame is designed around the typical structure of a particular genre. It gives children access to this structure and implicitly teaches them a way of writing this type of text.*

Writing about science activities and investigations

Eventually, children will be writing their prose account independently and be ready to move on to a more scientific structure for their account. The writing frame points them in this direction, but using a 'science template' can be useful. Their accounts look more like a scientific report and this paves the way for their secondary school experiences. A standard pattern could be as follows.

Primary school framework	Alignment to secondary school pattern
What we wanted to find out	Aim
What we used	Apparatus
Picture of what we did	Diagram
Description of what we did	Method
What we found	Results
What we think about what we found	Conclusion

Writing using such a structured approach provides a detailed record of the scientific procedures in the order in which they were carried out, and allows the children to develop and use particular skills related to scientific method convention. Initially, they can be given the template to complete, but later a card with the labels should be sufficient and then, eventually, even this could be withdrawn.

There is a danger, of course, that such a structured way of writing can degenerate into thoughtless descriptive responses. The important elements in developing scientific understanding are pulling forward relevant prior knowledge and understandings, interpreting findings, predicting, explaining and applying ideas in new contexts. A structure like that described above does not necessarily allow expression of such important aspects of working scientifically. This emphasises the importance of seeing recording in science as one (albeit very important) aspect of communicating in science, and opportunities for other free forms of writing, as well as teacher and pupil questioning and group discussion in science lessons, is crucial to support this writing process. In science, questioning for a purpose is important. Table 4.2 provides a framework for focused questioning, showing the kinds of questions that can be asked at the different stages of a lesson or sequence of lessons.

Graphic records

Graphic records are those constructed in pictorial form and they range in complexity from a full representation of the concrete object to abstract and stylised representation of concepts and ideas. There is an extensive range of graphic methods available. Although this chapter focuses on writing in science, graphic representation can be the starting point for writing in other subjects, in that the graphics can be annotated and written about.

Pictures

Most children enjoy drawing pictures and even before their writing skills develop this is a natural form of expression. Encouraging younger children to make pictures to show what they have been doing in science is an appropriate way to record their experiences. No constraints on the medium being used are necessary, giving the children the opportunity for free expression of their experiences and helping build their confidence and enthusiasm. Using prepared labels to put words on their diagrams, then encouraging the children to copy the words on to their pictures, can be a useful starting point. By talking with a child about his or her picture, an account can be prepared and written underneath by a classroom assistant and then possibly copied by the child. Some computer packages may also allow writing support for this.

Table 4.2 *Questioning framework for primary science*

QUESTION PURPOSE	QUESTION TYPE (choose specifically for task)	RESPONSE (could be either verbal or written)
• Setting the scene • Making the relevance explicit	How many of you ...? Have you ever ...? What happens when ...? Who knows anything about ...? Did anyone see ...?	
• Encouraging recall of relevant prior knowledge ready for use	What is a ...? What did we do ...? Can you remember when ...? What did ... do when ...? What is ... doing ...? How did you ...? What happened when ...?	
• Setting expectations • Guiding thinking and action • Focusing on what is needed	What do you think we could do to ...? What is it we need to find out? What we need to find out is ... so we need to ...? How do you think we might ...? Does it matter if ...?	
• Encouraging connections in ideas • Using ideas in new situations • Making predictions from findings • Explaining ideas to others	How was this like ...? Why is ...? Why does ...? Why do you think ... happened? What might happen if ...? Can you ...? What if ...?	

Diagrams

The conventional graphical representation for science is the two-dimensional, labelled, line diagram. As the children become more competent in writing, they can be introduced to the idea of diagrams (2D line drawings) to represent ideas. Initially, asking the children to draw their science activity as a side-view line drawing is the starting point. They are likely to try to depict what they see in three dimensions and will need support (by examples) of drawing in two. Teachers need to encourage them to add labels to their diagrams. These can be labels that, for example, name the parts of a plant or the stages in the water cycle or the apparatus used in an investigation. As they become more confident, they can begin to draw things from unusual angles (above or below, for example) and in cross-section. The latter is difficult for primary age children and many will not get to this point.

An extension of developing diagrams is to encourage children to draw before-and-after diagrams, showing the beginning and conclusion of an investigation, and to write an explanation to go with them. This is particularly useful for physical science, where events often involve change in some way.

Children are familiar with cartoon strips in comics. Producing a sequence of diagrams extends the before-and-after approach into a longer format for more complex investigation. Writing speech bubbles into the comic strips or annotating each slide extends writing skills in a natural way, and is an ideal springboard into encouraging children to produce PowerPoint slides on a computer for presentations.

Charts, tables and graphs

These are often essential components of a scientific investigation. Charts and tables (a particular type of chart) allow children to record their findings in an organised and concise way, particularly when there is a large number of observations or sets of results to collect. Tables and charts enable trends and patterns to be identified and observational data to be converted to graphs for this purpose.

Graphs are a valuable way to summarise findings and show patterns and trends over time. They require writing skills for both the labelling of the graphs themselves (the x and y axis, the header) and also for producing an analytical report on what is noticed in the graphic patterns. With younger children, early graph work can use coloured wools or tapes as bars to represent, for example, growth over time. Pictures and words can also be glued to form block columns, representing groups, choices or observations. All require labelling. With older children, the picture graphs become block graphs and the wool and tape become bar or line graphs. Computer technology can be introduced at some point, with alternatives such as pie charts being introduced, useful for comparisons and proportions. A number of software packages exist for children to use. Labels and written interpretations are still essential, regardless of type.

Other ways to encourage writing in science

There are other, less conventional, opportunities for recording in science that lend themselves to writing. Drama can often be used to explore scientific ideas (for example, acting out a year in the life of the solar system or telling a story from the history of science). Storyboarding the action and writing scripts can encourage the children to use writing skills. The use of video and digital cameras during activities and fieldwork (for example, a visit to a garden centre) also enables children to write about their film or pictures, explaining the context and the observations or findings. Model making (for example, making a cardboard house and fitting 'lights' using their experience of serial or parallel circuits, switches and buzzers) also requires planning and recording ideas. Finally, collective class displays in the classroom, a corridor or the school hall, enable children to share their experiences, not only with others in their class but also with the whole school, and also encourages children to value those experiences. Such displays should be produced by the children themselves, include their scientific writings (as full a range as possible) and be interactive to encourage others to read, ask and answer questions and possibly replicate some of the activities.

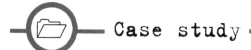 **Case study**

Who Robbed Teddy?

An example of an approach that combines a range of writing opportunities is the *Who Robbed Teddy?* forensic science activity. This was initially designed as a task for trainee primary teachers, but has been used in schools by teachers with older primary pupils.

The activity emerges from work on materials and their properties (Science 3) and brings together opportunities for investigative activity to explore some of the concepts. In essence, the children, having already explored concepts to do with types of materials, changes in materials and simple chromatography, use skills and processes to observe situations and generate ideas and explanations.

The children are given a page from a newspaper, *The Gossiper,* that reports on an incident that occurred involving a burglary and robbery at Teddy's house. (This can be found at the end of this chapter.) Children are given some clues in the newspaper report and also have the crime scene set up in their classroom (photographs are also helpful to work on at tables). The children on each table have to work as a forensic team to explore the clues they have been given and can see at the scene. They can use equipment to do tests on the clues: perhaps a cheque that might have been forged (chromatography), a hot drink on the table made just before the incident occurred (the time frame), or some fibres found on Teddy's clothing (materials). Having carried out their tests, the children have to reach a conclusion – who robbed Toytown Teddy? Was it his so-called friend, Big Ted, or was it his girlfriend, Krystal? And what was the motive?

Having completed their investigation, the children must then prepare a scientific report for the police and also a more general newspaper report for tomorrow's *Gossiper*.

Conclusion

Children do not compartmentalise their learning experiences. We do that as teachers when we break the curriculum into labelled chunks of English or mathematics or science. Nor do children automatically transfer learning in one area of experience to another, like learning about graphs in mathematics but using them in other subjects like science. The same applies to aspects of language. Pointing the way in terms of the development of writing skills through opportunities to write for a purpose in other subjects (recording and communicating experiences in science) is an opportunity not to be wasted.

━━ Recommended websites ━━

Websites are a useful starting point for pictures, photographs and tests to stimulate discussion and writing. Some useful ones for science are:

Association for Science Education – www.ase.org.uk

BBC Science Clips – www.bbc.co.uk/schools/scienceclips/

Dinosaurs – www.hmag.gla.ac.uk/dinosoc/

Eureka Museum – www.eureka.org.uk

Exploratory Museum – www.exploratorium.edu

Flying Pig! Mechanisms – www.flying-pig.co.uk

Franklin Institute Science Museum – www.sciencegems.com

Free Photograph Gallery – www.freefoto.com

Health Education – www.kidshealth.org/kid/

Interactive Whiteboard Science – topmarks.co.uk/interactive

International Centre – www.centreforlife.co.uk

Maps and aerial photographs – www.multimap.com

Museum of the History of Science – www.mhs.ox.ac.uk

Museum of Science and Industry – www.msin.ac.uk

Natural History Museum – www.nhm.ac.uk

Primary Games – www.primarygames.co.uk

Primary Investigations – www.science.org.acu/pi/

Primary Resources – www.primaryresources.co.uk

━━ Further reading ━━

Hand, B., Lawrence, C. and Yore, L.D. (2001) A writing in science framework designed to enhance science literacy. *International Journal of Science Education,* 21(10): 1021–35.

An easy-to-read introduction to an approach to encourage children to write in science and support their scientific literacy.

Newton, L.D. (2000) What do we mean by key skills in primary science? In: *Meeting the Standards in Primary Science.* London: RoutledgeFalmer, pp145–70.

The importance of the use of communication and literacy skills in primary science is discussed and elaborated upon.

Newton, L.D. (ed.) (2012) Creativity in science and design and technology. In: *Creativity for a New Curriculum: 5–11*. London: Routledge/David Wilson, pp48–61.

This book provides ideas to stimulate writing in science that encourage the children's creative thinking skills in a science and D&T context. Starting from discussions and investigations, writing opportunities emerge.

▬▬ References ▬▬

Darby, L. (2005) Science students' perceptions of engaging pedagogy. *Research in Science Education*, 35: 425–445 (DOI: 10.1007/s11165-005-4488-4)

DES (1986) *Science 5–6: A Statement of Policy*. HMSO: London.

DfE (2013a) *Teachers' Standards: Guidance for School Leaders, School Staff and Governing Bodies* (July 2011 with introduction updated June 2013).

DfE (2013b) *National Curriculum: Science*. Available from: www.gov.uk/dfe/nationalcurriculum (Reference: DFE-00178-2013)

Medwell, J., Wray, D., Minns, H., Coates, E. and Griffiths, V. (2014) *Primary English: Theory and Practice* (7th edition). London: Sage.

Newton, L.D. (2000) *Meeting the Standards in Primary Science*. London: RoutledgeFalmer.

The Gossiper
All the Latest Libel

Teddy Robbed!

Toytown Teddy found brutally robbed. P.C. Badger says, 'We've no idea who did it'. Police CSI teams called in.

A recent photo of Toytown Teddy

Teddy, 25, a rich diamond mine owner of Toytown Farm, Redling-hall, was brutally robbed last night. The police say that when they arrived at 7 p.m., in response to the burglar alarm, Teddy was laid out on the floor with a whisky glass with half-melted ice cubes in it on the table beside him. 'It were 'orrible,' said PC Badger, 'e was hit' and it'll be us who 'as to find the robber!'

According to our source at the farm, Teddy's girlfriend, Krystal, aged 23, grey fur and fancy coat, says Teddy was alive and well and sitting with his glass of whisky when she left at 6 p.m.

Our roving reporter, Soya Sam, visited Krystal at her home in Bridgeton. Krystal told him, 'Teddy had just taken some diamonds to the jeweller's shop and had this diamond ring made for me. I called at the shop and picked it up before all this brutal bashing. When I showed the ring to Teddy he didn't seem too pleased with it but I think it's lovely – just look at the size of that diamond! I am very upset.'

Soya Sam learned from Krystal that the shop was *Teddy Boy the Jeweller's: Purveyor of Fine Baubles for the Oh, So Rich!* in the High Street. The owner, Big Ted, 26, blue fur and yellow tie, said, 'Yes, I buy diamonds from Toytown Teddy and make them into rings and things to sell. I haven't been to his farm or seen Ted since he brought me some diamonds to make into a ring a month ago. How is he?' CSI science experts from Stockton are to be called in to solve the dreadful crime.

Toytown Farm and famous diamond mine.

Our source at Toytown Farm

Photographs:

Figure 4.1 Teddy

Figure 4.2 Big Ted and krystal

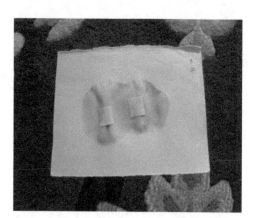

Figure. 4.3 Chromatography on cheque

Figure 4.4 Fibres

Figure 4.5 Sand from shoes

Figure 4.6 Children's work

5

writing in biological science

Rachel Simpson

Standard 3 - Demonstrate good subject and curriculum knowledge

- have a secure knowledge of the relevant subject(s) and curriculum areas, foster and maintain pupils' interest in the subject, and address misunderstandings
- demonstrate a critical understanding of developments in the subject and curriculum areas, and promote the value of scholarship
- demonstrate an understanding of and take responsibility for promoting high standards of literacy, articulacy and the correct use of standard English, whatever the teacher's specialist subject

Standard 4 - Plan and teach well-structured lessons

- impart knowledge and develop understanding through effective use of lesson time
- promote a love of learning and children's intellectual curiosity

Key questions

How can creative writing activities enable children to:

- demonstrate their subject knowledge of animals and plants?
- explain their understanding of biological concepts?
- apply their knowledge and understanding of important ideas about the natural world to real life issues?
- reflect upon the importance and purpose of science in their lives and their futures?

Introduction

Purposeful writing tasks in science can enable children to become effective writers and successful scientists. When children write creatively, their internalised knowledge of scientific concepts can be expressed using their own language. Bereiter (1990, 1994) discusses using writing as a tool for learning: ideas about science can advance further if the writing task is reflective, enabling children to clarify their knowledge and develop their learning. Understandings – and sometimes misunderstandings – emerge and can be consolidated or challenged. Writing about science can also be referred to a long time after memories of the first-hand experiences have faded: writing can help scientific outcomes to be remembered with accuracy. For you as the teacher, creative writing can be a wonderful opportunity to assess a child's developing understanding of scientific concepts and be used as a starting point to ask further questions.

The children you teach may already be using an instructional writing style in their science lessons to record scientific investigations. This chapter will introduce the idea of children writing creatively to represent their scientific observations and explain their ideas, using imagery, metaphors, analogies and emotive language. Thoughtful and reflective writing tasks can be both creative and scientific, engaging an audience as well as the writers. At times, Charles Darwin did this in his observations of the natural world. Imagery and metaphors can be found in his most famous work *On the Origin of Species* (Darwin, 1859). Darwin's audience included non-scientists, who would have been able to relate to his analogies, such as that of a tree's growth used to explain the theory of evolution.

Darwin had a fascination with the natural world – as it would seem do most children. They are eager and interested observers and questioners of the environments, ecosystems, animals and plants around them, and this curiosity can be captured permanently in their creative writing. The National Curriculum devotes over half of the science programmes of study to biology (DfE, 2013) in Key Stages 1 and 2. Children of all ages will explore the morphology (size, shape and structure) and physiology (the life-supporting structures) of animals and plants. Some year groups will also focus on habitats, interdependence and the new addition of evolution. Although it is important that children develop an in-depth understanding of all aspects of science, this increased focus on biology in primary schools, coupled with children's enthusiasm as young explorers of the natural world, justifies its focus in this chapter.

What are the benefits of writing creatively about biology?

Children need both a secure knowledge and understanding of science and appropriate literacy skills to be active citizens in future scientific communities (Lakin, 2006). The problem with this is that communication tasks in science lessons may not be engaging; indeed, Lakin uses the term 'notoriously dull', suggesting that teachers need to use rich and lively literacy techniques. Writing creatively about science can be engaging and motivating, giving children time to develop as thoughtful learners and opportunities to realise the importance of science to their lives. Carefully planned creative writing activities can enable children to:

1. build and consolidate scientific knowledge;

2. make personal sense of science and develop understanding;

3. apply scientific knowledge and understanding to a real life issue.

These three benefits will be discussed in this chapter, but first it is important to add a note of caution. Creative writing or 'narrative' is not considered to be scientific writing by the science community, as explained by Wellington and Osborne (2001), narrative accounts are ... *notable for their total absence of the graphs, diagrams, illustrations, mathematics and pictures that are prominent in normal science text* (p75).

However, the authors explain that although some scientists question the value of narrative writing, it can be a motivational tool, providing enjoyable opportunities for children to express scientific knowledge and understanding, alongside producing an engaging final product for an audience of non-scientists. It is therefore important for children to recognise and use different types of scientific writing and understand the benefits and limitations of these when reporting, describing and explaining ideas. Whichever writing style is used to explain scientific ideas, the teaching emphasis needs to be on developing accurate scientific understanding (Wellington and Osborne, 2001).

Theme 1: Using creative writing to build and consolidate scientific knowledge

Writing about science can help children to organise, consolidate, expand and adjust their knowledge of science. Children develop their scientific knowledge by internalising and then expressing scientific ideas using their own language. This differs from simply being knowledge-tellers; instead, children are knowledge-builders (Yore et al., 2002). Webb (2010) describes writing as being a *minds-on* experience, which can lead to children raising further questions and pursuing new lines of scientific enquiry. Thoughtful writing tasks also give children time to select accurate vocabulary choices to create descriptions and explanations of scientific concepts that they have observed or researched.

Research focus

Science writing

Flynn (2015) described an example of a creative writing project that demonstrated children's science knowledge. This project encouraged children to write science-themed haiku poems for publication. Children were challenged to explain scientific concepts concisely yet accurately within the strict haiku syllable structure (5 syllables in the first line, 7 in the second, and 5 in the third and final line).

The importance of collaborative editing through peer review was emphasised throughout the project, as this was used to redraft and improve the poems. Children aimed for accurate meaning through careful word choices, as well as writing to entertain the audience.

The children enjoyed using poetry techniques to explain scientific phenomena, and the use of humour was evident in many poems - something that would not be appropriate in formal science assessments. For some children it increased their confidence in and enjoyment of science, and they were enthused by the creative nature of the task, as seen in 'Friction'.

Friction

I walked down the street
And slipped on a banana
Reduced resistance

(Flynn, 2015, p78)

 Case study

Writing poetry to build and consolidate scientific subject knowledge

Focus: Key Stage 1

NATIONAL CURRICULUM LINKS (DfE, 2013)	
ENGLISH	**SCIENCE**
Key Stage 1: Composition	**Y1: Animals, Including Humans**
To develop positive attitudes towards and stamina for writing by writing poetry.	To identify and name a variety of common animals. To describe and compare the structure of a variety of common animals.

(Continued)

NATIONAL CURRICULUM LINKS (DfE, 2013)	
ENGLISH	**SCIENCE**
To write down ideas and/or key words, including key vocabulary. *Children might draw on and use new vocabulary from their wider experiences.*	**Y2: Living Things and Their Habitats** To identify that most living things live in habitats to which they are suited and describe how different habitats provide for the basic needs of different kinds of animals and plants, and how they depend on each other. To describe how animals obtain their food from plants and other animals, using the idea of a food chain, and identify and name different sources of food.

A Year 2 class studied a variety of living things in and around the school pond. The teacher, Nizam, helped the children to identify animals found there, and encouraged them to carefully observe how the animal's body shape helped it to move. Nizam asked the children to explain their observations to each other, and ask and answer questions. These conversations were audio-recorded; writing did not take place at this stage to allow the children to concentrate on observing using their senses. This is an example of one conversation between two children and Nizam.

James: 'Look! The frog jumped!'

Nadia: 'No, he hopped!'

Nizam: 'How did it do that?'

James: 'He pushed with his legs.'

Nadia: 'Not all of his legs! I don't think he pushed with all his legs.'

Nizam: 'Didn't it? Which legs did it use?'

James: 'His back.'

Nadia: 'No, his front!'

Nizam: 'The frog is hiding now. How can we check which legs he used to push?'

Back in the classroom, further research was carried out. Secondary sources of books and videos were used to learn about the frog's carnivorous diet and the children linked this to the smaller animals they had observed.

Nizam planned for these science observations to be used to inspire poetry writing. To prepare for this, the children had already studied animal-themed poems. Nizam listened to the audio recording from the pond area and wrote down the children's vocabulary used to describe the animals. This formed a baseline assessment of the class's range of scientific vocabulary and was a useful starting point to discuss the meaning of familiar words. More scientific words were introduced ('camouflage' and 'amphibian') and there was a discussion about the differences between words such as 'jump' and 'leap'. Together the class created a poem that described the frog's features, movement and diet.

Our Frog

Mud-coloured, camouflaged,
Watching, waiting.
Jumping!
With strong hind legs,
Bug-eater,
Amphibian.

Nizam then provided differentiated activities. Some children studied the class poem and chose new words to replace words that had been underlined by the teacher, such as 'jumping'. For support, they used the word bank created in the class discussion. Other children wrote their own verses about another observed animal. They were encouraged to be scientifically accurate with their choices of words. In a peer review task, Nizam encouraged the children to look for and discuss scientifically precise word choices in each other's work and the children then improved their word choices.

A final challenge for the children was to examine some poems about frogs and discuss the scientific accuracy. This was a very popular activity, with great criticism of poems about frogs eating soap.

In the case study, poetry was chosen as a genre so the children could express their scientific knowledge of an animal using carefully chosen vocabulary, but also tell a story of the animal's actions. The children's writing was inspired by their first-hand observations in the pond area. Individual interpretations of their observations emerged, and the scientific accuracy of these was later reconsidered in the light of secondary research and discussions with peers and the teacher. A deeper level of understanding started to develop when the children critically examined other animal poems, from the viewpoints of scientists.

Classroom ideas for using creative writing

- Think about the local environments around your school. If you don't have a wildlife area, these can be the school field, tiny nooks and crannies between paving slabs or tufts of grass around the edge of the playground. Plan an activity for children to make first-hand observations of the animals and plants found there. Audio-record the conversations and encourage questions. Use these recordings for writing activities such as poetry back in the classroom.

- Select a range of poetry books that include animal poems, suitable for the age group. From these poems, choose ones that you think would teach children about the features of animals and reasons for these features, for example: body shape, colour, feeding adaptations.

- Consider poems such as 'Caterpillar' by Christina Rossetti. Outline how you would use these in your teaching, thinking about the poetical features but also the scientific accuracy.

Suggested resource to support the activity

Lewis, P. (ed.) (2012) *National Geographic Book of Animal Poetry: 200 Poems with Photographs That Squeak, Soar, and Roar!* England: National Geographic Society.

Theme 2: Using creative writing to make personal sense of science and develop understanding

Writing about science allows children to share their ideas in a scientific writing community. This can be a revelatory moment as children start to realise that scientists see the scientific world from personal perspectives. By comparing their written interpretations of scientific concepts, children will begin to grasp that their interpretations of the same scientific event may be different (Mason, 2001). Through peer and teacher-led discussion, they will see how scientific ideas can be adjusted and a shared understanding can (sometimes) be reached.

Using metaphors can help children as young scientists to make meaning of unfamiliar scientific phenomena and express their conceptual understanding (Ogborn et al., 1996). Indeed, metaphors are commonly used in scientific language, for example, a 'magnetic field' or a 'computer virus'. During *The Voyage of the Beagle*, Charles Darwin described marine iguanas as *hideous … imps of darkness* (Darwin, 1835) after observing these reptiles basking in great piles on the black lava rocks of the Galápagos Islands. This metaphor not only gives an indication of their appearance (black with 'imp'-like faces), but also Darwin's feelings about the creatures.

Children can include metaphors in creative writing, engaging both the writer and the audience, as we will see in the next two case studies. Before considering these, it is important to examine the value of using metaphors to engage children in scientific learning, as explained in the following research focus.

 **Research focus**

Using metaphors

Bloom's studies (1992) concluded that using metaphors was an integral part of a child's learning experience.

> *For each child who generates his or her own metaphor, a connection or understanding is established that is not only personally meaningful but also extends that understanding beyond the basic concept.*

(p406)

One example Bloom gave is that of a child, Emily, who described the 'nose' (tip) of an earthworm to be like the whiskers of a cat. She used her knowledge of a familiar animal (the cat) to develop her understanding of the sensitivity mechanism in an unfamiliar animal (the earthworm).

More recently, Jakobson and Wickman (2007) researched children's use of spontaneous metaphors in science in elementary schools in Sweden. Interestingly, the authors identified the children's metaphors as indications of their attitudes towards the science experience (as we saw with Darwin and the marine iguanas). For example, salt crystals were described by some children as 'pearls', indicating a positive association, whereas wet soil was described as 'mush', and this was seen to be negative. Jakobson and Wickman concluded that children's metaphors could be used to *enliven and humanise the subject* (2007, p287), and, in agreement with Bloom, to develop conceptual understanding. However, their discussion also highlighted that children tended to use metaphors as *temporary stepping stones in making sense of scientific phenomena* (p284) rather than always developing understanding directly from the metaphor - as we saw with Emily. Therefore, teachers need to respond to children's metaphors carefully to ensure that scientific learning is developed.

 ── Case study ─────────────────────────

Writing a diary entry to express personal understanding of animal adaptation

Focus: Lower Key Stage 2

NATIONAL CURRICULUM LINKS: Lower Key Stage 2 (DfE, 2013)	
ENGLISH	**SCIENCE**
Writing - composition To plan writing by discussing and recording ideas. To draft writing by composing and rehearsing sentences orally and organising sentences around a theme. To evaluate and edit by assessing the effectiveness of their own and others' writing and suggesting improvements.	**General:** To be familiar with and use technical terminology accurately and precisely. To build up an extended specialist vocabulary. **Animals, including humans** To identify that animals need the right types and amounts of nutrition and that they cannot make their own food; they get nutrition from what they eat. To identify that some animals have skeletons and muscles for support, protection and movement. *From the Year 6 Programme of Study: To identify how animals and plants are adapted to suit their environment in different ways and that adaptation may lead to evolution.*

Introduction: Diary writing gives children the opportunity to write with empathy. For children to understand the purpose of an animal's morphological and physiological adaptations, it can be useful - as well as highly engaging - for them to imagine they are the animal. What does the animal need to do in order to survive in its environment and how has its body adapted to accommodate these needs?

The case: As part of a 'Living Things and their Habitats' study, children in Year 4 studied the marine iguana. The teacher, James, chose this reptile because he wanted to challenge the children's understanding of animal groups, by adding in the only marine lizard. He used a film

(Continued)

(Continued)

clip of the marine iguanas in action, pausing the film at key points and asking the children questions, such as: 'How did the marine iguana warm up its body before it dived into the sea?'. The questions were discussed in pairs and then an answer was collaboratively written, in note form. Targeted pairs explained their answers to the class and James checked for accurate scientific understanding, as well as highlighting good examples of concise note-taking. He also encouraged the use of metaphors, enabling children to explain their understanding from their viewpoints.

James then planned a creative writing activity, allowing children to individually internalise and explain their understanding of how the marine iguana's physiological features and behavioural adaptations enabled it to swim underwater and why this was so important for its survival (to obtain its food source of algae). To enthuse the children with this task, they were asked to draft diary entries from a marine iguana's point of view; these would be used to inform an audience of younger children about the creatures. The use of metaphor was encouraged to help the younger children to understand their explanations. For example, a child wrote: 'The sea was a freezer compared to the baking lava rock'.

The children used their initial notes to support their diary writing, enthusiastically explaining the importance of avoiding exhaustion by only staying underwater for ten minutes, and then violently releasing salt from their nostrils once back on land. Humour was used effectively, as children enjoyed creating the diary accounts to entertain younger children in the school. Formative peer review opportunities helped the children to edit and improve their work.

During the formative peer review task, the children were interested to see that their interpretations of the marine iguanas' physiology and behaviour sometimes differed. James helped them to identify that their vocabulary choices often accounted for the differences. For example, there was great debate about the way the marine iguana positioned and used its body when feeding on algae underwater and a shared understanding was only reached by rewatching the film. The editing stage that followed peer review was crucial, allowing children to improve both the quality of their creative writing and the accuracy of their scientific ideas.

 Activity

- Think about the science topics you teach. Could the children use a diary-writing genre to express their understanding of scientific ideas? You could consider ideas such as: 'A day in the life of a yeast cell', 'My life as a water molecule'.

- What resources will you use to help them to develop their scientific understanding?

- How will the work be assessed: teacher assessment, self-assessment or peer review?

Theme 3: Applying scientific knowledge and understanding to a real-life issue

Writing about science gives children the opportunity to develop opinions about real-life issues that involve science. When children need to use their writing to reason and justify their views about an issue, they can be encouraged to recognise the importance of supporting an argument with scientific evidence. Lakin (2006) maintained discussion and persuasion are important strategies to use with children, allowing them to communicate their understanding of science. In the world outside the classroom, scientific knowledge is not used in isolation to fuel debates and inform policies. It is therefore important for children to make connections between subjects such as geography, history and science, as children develop their ideas about important issues and prepare to become informed citizens.

Children can become engaged in writing by preparing speeches for debating contentious science-related issues, such as the effects of climate change or testing medicines on animals. If they can relate to the issue, then they may develop an emotional response to it (Eccles and Taylor, 2013), and this can be expressed using persuasive devices, including emotive language and rhetorical questions. Stringer (1998) explains that children can develop *independent thought, respect for evidence* and *rational argument* (p93) when considering environmental issues, and these are illustrated in the case study below. Identifying an audience who will be judging the quality of the speeches can encourage children to support their emotive arguments with scientific evidence. Children's speeches for a debate can be excellent assessment evidence: science needs to be clearly understood in order to be clearly expressed.

 Research focus

Understanding science

Hulleman and Harackiewicz (2009) conducted an empirical study in the USA to explore factors that motivated pupils in science lessons. They concluded that children became more interested in science and motivated to succeed if they understood the relevance of science to their lives. This randomised controlled trial introduced a science-related task to two groups. The treatment group's task included an aspect that was personally relevant to the pupils; however, this personal aspect was omitted from the control group's task. The pupils' work and their attitudes towards science were compared once the task had been completed. The researchers noted that for pupils with low expectations of their success in science, attainment and attitudes improved in the treatment group compared to the control group.

Although this research explored science in high schools, its conclusions translate into primary education. This is a crucial time when children are forming their attitudes towards subjects. Hulleman and Harackiewicz explain in their study that children can develop positive attitudes towards science by making connections between science and their lives. If they understand early on that they may be able to make a positive contribution to important real-life issues, such as environmental concerns, they could become more motivated to succeed in science.

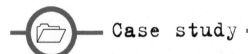 **Case study**

Applying scientific knowledge and understanding to write a speech for a debate about a real-life issue

Focus: Upper Key Stage Two

NATIONAL CURRICULUM LINKS: Upper Key Stage Two (DfE, 2013)	
ENGLISH	**SCIENCE**
Aims: Children's confidence, enjoyment and mastery of language should be extended through public speaking, performance and debate.	**Purpose of study:** Science has changed our lives and is vital to the world's future prosperity.
UKS2: writing - composition **Planning.** To identify the audience for and purpose of the writing, selecting the appropriate form and using other similar writing as models for their own; To note and developing initial ideas, drawing on reading and research where necessary.	**Aims:** To be equipped with scientific knowledge required to understand the uses and implications of science, today and for the future.
Drafting and writing: To select appropriate grammar and vocabulary, understanding how such choices can change and enhance meaning.	The social and economic implications of science are important but [should be] taught in the wider school curriculum.
Evaluating and editing: To assess the effectiveness of their own and others' writing. To propose changes to vocabulary, grammar and punctuation to enhance effects and clarify meaning. To perform their own compositions, using appropriate intonation, volume and movement so that meaning is clear.	

For this case study, like Darwin we travel to the Galápagos Islands. A Year 6 teacher, Ruth, was inspired by her recent trip, observing animals and plants such as giant tortoises, frigate birds with their magnificent red pouches, and towering candelabra cacti. She planned a cross-curricular Galápagos-themed topic to match the newly introduced science topic 'evolution' in the National Curriculum. Ruth was also aiming for the children to be *equipped with the scientific knowledge required to understand the uses and implications of science, today and for the future* (DfE, 2013, p144). From the moment the children stepped on to the 'aeroplane' destined for the Galápagos, set up in the school hall, they became immersed, developing their understanding of not only the ecosystems but also the people, the climate, the geography and the history of these Ecuadorian islands.

Towards the end of the topic, the children prepared to take part in a debate. To present their views of the impact of humans on this fragile environment, they addressed the question: 'Is tourism good or bad for the animals and plants of the Galápagos Islands?' Each child chose a role, such as a Galápagos conservationist or a Galápagos boat driver, and decided whether they would present a speech for or against the argument.

To prepare the children to write using the language of debate, Ruth modelled persuasive writing techniques including rhetorical questions, emotive language and connectives to demonstrate links between ideas. Careful use of metaphors was discussed to emphasise points and add interest to the arguments. The children drafted, edited and rewrote their speeches, with constructive peer support to check the scientific accuracy of claims. An audience of Year 5 children had voting cards and had to consider ideas such as:

> I believe that tourism is bringing in introduced species: quinine trees are swamping the islands. Although these can be used for medicines, they are altering food webs and some species will not survive for much longer.

and persuasively worded summaries:

> Do you want unique animals, like the giant tortoises, to die out? The futures of these endangered species are in your hands!

Children were invited to apply their scientific understanding by offering counter-arguments to the opposing side. Ruth used this as evidence for assessment purposes of a deeper level of understanding and application of scientific knowledge.

The children took their roles in the debate very seriously. They were passionate and, importantly, informed speakers. They attempted to think like scientists by finding weaknesses in each other's arguments.

Classroom ideas for debating real-life issues

- Think about your science topics – are these taught within a wider theme? Is there an opportunity to apply scientific knowledge and understanding to a speech for a debate?

- Have you visited a place that could inspire a cross-curricular topic or debate? Examples include: deforestation of the Amazon rainforest; the destruction of the coral found on the Great Barrier Reef; the endangered orangutans of Sumatra.

- Alternatively, consider an environmental issue in your school's locality, such as river pollution or increased traffic on roads. Are there 'for' and 'against' arguments?

Conclusion

Science needs to be accessed by a wide audience. Literature that explains scientific phenomena, and its importance to our lives, cannot be accessible only to science academics. Creative writing about biology can inform, engage, demonstrate knowledge and develop understanding. It is an important skill for children to both recognise and practise, as they start to think like scientists and organise their knowledge through their writing.

Scientists might not all agree that science can be accurately expressed through creative writing. However, have a look at this rhyming couplet, describing the Galápagos finches:

On every island finches fly,
Adapted beaks they all hold high.

The study of the Galápagos finches played a crucial part in developing Darwin's understanding of his theory of evolution. This couplet gives an indication of a child's level of knowledge of the finches' special variations in beak morphology. Reading this couplet may arouse curiosity in the reader to find out more about these 'adapted beaks', and the creative process of writing this couplet may inspire the writer, as language and science combine to produce a memorable outcome.

By reading this chapter you will have understood how creative writing activities enable children to demonstrate their subject knowledge and understanding of animals and plants. You will have read about ways for children to apply their knowledge and understanding of important ideas about the natural world to real-life issues, while reflecting upon the importance and purpose of science in their lives and their futures.

▬ References ▬

Bereiter, C. (1990) Aspects of an educational learning theory. *Review of Educational Research*, 60(4): 603–24.

Bereiter, C. (1994) Constructivism, socioculturalism, and Popper's World 3. *Educational Researcher*, 23(7): 21–3.

Bloom, J.W. (1992) The development of scientific knowledge in elementary school children: a context of meaning perspective. *Science Education*, 76(4): 339–413.

Darwin, C. (1835) *Charles Darwin's Beagle Diary.* English Heritage. Available from: http://darwin-online. org.uk/content/frameset?itemID=F1566&viewtype=text&pageseq=1

Darwin, C. (1859) *On the Origin of Species.* London: John Murray.

DfE (2013) *The National Curriculum in England Key Stages 1 and 2.* Framework Document. London: DfE. Available from: www.gov.uk/government/uploads/system/uploads/attachment_data/file/335133/PRIMARY_national_curriculum_220714.pdf

Eccles, D. and Taylor, S. (2013) Promoting understanding through dialogue. In: Harlen, W. (ed.) *ASE Guide to Primary Science Education.* Hertfordshire: ASE.

Flynn, S. (2015) Sciku: writing science in haiku. *School Science Review*, 97(359): 75–80.

Hulleman, C. and Harackiewicz, J. (2009) Promoting interest and performance in high school science classes. *Science, New Series*, 326(5958): 1410–12.

Jakobson, B. and Wickman, P.O. (2007) Transformation of language use: children's spontaneous metaphors in elementary school science. *Science and Education*, 16: 267–89.

Lakin, E. (2006) Science in the whole curriculum. In: Harlen, W. (ed.) (2006) *ASE Guide to Primary Science Education*. Hertfordshire: ASE.

Mason, L. (2001) Introducing talk and writing for a conceptual change: a classroom study. *Learning and Instruction,* 11: 305–29.

Ogborn, J., Kress, G., Martins, I. and McGillicuddy, K. (1996) *Explaining Science in the Classroom*. Buckingham: Open University Press.

Stringer, J. (1998) Environmental education. In: Sherrington, R. (ed.) (1998) *ASE Guide to Primary Science Education*. Hertfordshire: ASE.

Webb, P. (2010) Science education and literacy: imperatives for the developed and developing world. *Science,* 328(5977): 448–50.

Wellington, J. and Osborne, J. (2001) *Language and Literacy in Science Education*. Buckingham: Oxford University Press.

Yore, L.D., Hand, B.M. and Prain, V. (2002) Scientists as writers. *Science Education,* 86: 672–92.

6

Writing in design and technology

Douglas P. Newton

Standard 3 - Demonstrate good subject and curriculum knowledge

- have a secure knowledge of the relevant subject(s) and curriculum areas, foster and maintain pupils' interest in the subject, and address misunderstandings
- demonstrate a critical understanding of developments in the subject and curriculum areas, and promote the value of scholarship
- demonstrate an understanding of and take responsibility for promoting high standards of literacy, articulacy and the correct use of standard English, whatever the teacher's specialist subject

Standard 4 - Plan and teach well-structured lessons

- impart knowledge and develop understanding through effective use of lesson time
- promote a love of learning and children's intellectual curiosity

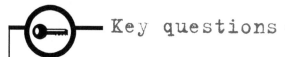

- How do we show children that writing can be a tool to support thought and learning?
- How do we practise that in design and technology (D&T) lessons to foster learning in D&T and develop competence in using writing as tool?
- How do we incorporate this tool in D&T lessons in engaging ways?

Introduction

Design and technology (D&T), a relative newcomer in the primary school curriculum, tends to be associated largely with the *making* of physical objects. What can it possibly contribute to competence in *writing*? In connection with writing across the curriculum, Young (1999, p1) wrote that *students use written language to develop and communicate knowledge in every discipline and across disciplines*. The key references here are to:

- developing knowledge; and

- communicating knowledge.

D&T is not simply having children make things. They have to do so *thoughtfully*. Writing is a valuable tool which can support that thought and develop knowledge. Moreover, it is not only for use in a child's time in school; it has the potential to be a valuable, long-term supporter of lifelong learning. While this writing is for themselves, writing can also be for others, as when communicating knowledge. Again, this is a valuable life skill, often undervalued outside the arts and humanities (Hart-Davidson, 2000). Of these, writing for communication (transactional writing) may be practised across the curriculum more than writing for thinking (self-dialogic writing). While the same is true of D&T, it offers a wide range of opportunities for writing to support purposeful thinking, such as retaining and recalling information, understanding, creative thinking, decision-making and evaluating (Newton, 2012, 2014, 2016). This chapter will give particular attention to using writing to support such thought. At the same time, transactional writing cannot be ignored as there are times when the two overlap. At this point, a few words about the nature of D&T may be appropriate.

What is design and technology?

D&T is the process of inventing or altering something to solve a practical problem. For example, mice are not welcome in the home and there are very effective mousetraps which kill them. Often, people find these traps repugnant. There is a need for a humane mousetrap which catches the mouse and allows it to be released elsewhere unharmed. Can you invent one? If you do, you'll probably find that you need, at least, to:

- explore the problem;

- recall what you know or collate what you find out about mice and traps;

- play with ideas and develop those that look promising;

- construct a plan of action for your best bet;

- make a version of it (all the while thinking carefully about those things you did not anticipate); and

- test it.

There is a lot of purposeful thinking going on here, including interpreting the problem, thinking creatively, understanding your invention clearly (particularly those special bits which make it work), constructing an ordered sequence of actions, taking decisions and evaluating the outcome. Solving the mousetrap problem is not a routine, mechanical matter, and it can be mentally demanding.

In the primary classroom, D&T can be seen as developing in children a belief in their ability to solve everyday practical problems for themselves, and fostering a disposition which inclines them to try. It commonly involves focused tasks to develop knowledge and know-how and, crucially, creative designing and making activities. It is a valuable life skill (Newton, 2005). Writing in D&T offers a tool to help children meet the mental demands of practical problem solving now and in adulthood, and is also a means of communicating their ideas effectively to others. This will now be illustrated.

Writing to support the interpretation and understanding of problems

Often, the hardest part of a problem is to understand it. With an understanding, the problem becomes personally meaningful, relatable to experience and amenable to dissection into manageable parts. Children, however, have limited experience and few appropriate words to discuss it. Where is the way in to the problem?

Take a popular topic in the primary school: *Houses and Homes*. At common D&T problem for young children stems from a Winnie the Pooh story, *A New House for Eeyore* (A.A. Milne, Egmont, 1999). Eeyore, the doleful donkey, is out in the field when it begins to snow. The snow becomes deeper and deeper, but Eeyore has nowhere to shelter and keep warm. He needs a place to live. Can we make one for him? Young children often need to have their thoughts focused and some words to think with. Vocabulary can be developed using the Thinking Flower (Figure 6.1). The teacher writes the problem in the centre and adds the children's responses to the 'petals' around it. This collection of relevant needs is now available to the child for use in their account of 'What I will make for Eeyore'. Each 'petal' may become the centre of a new flower and explored further. The Thinking Flower can be used at any age to collect ideas and supplement vocabulary.

A popular aspect of *Houses and Homes* for older children is *Houses through the Ages*, tied to work in history. In the UK, this enables a timeline to be constructed ranging from early round houses with thatched roofs to recent eco-friendly homes. A major factor in what a house is like is what materials

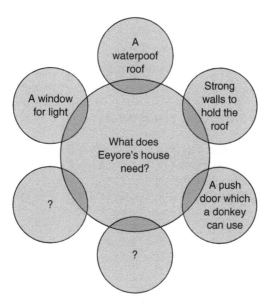

Figure 6.1 The Thinking Flower as a device used to explore a problem

are readily available, which can relate to work in science on the properties of materials. A problem for older children is that they are shipwrecked on a desert island and they need a house to sleep, eat and live in. What will it look like? The Thinking Flower is used at least twice, first to explore what a desert island might be like, and, second, to explore the potential of the available materials to make a comfortable, durable home. The whole can make an interesting story.

 **Case study**

Sanjeev and the Tiger

Children's stories often raise a predicament for the central characters and then resolve it. Stopping at the predicament and having the children construct their own solution to the problem makes good use of their engagement with the story. The traditional story *Sanjeev and the Tiger* was read to some Year 2 children.

Sanjeev lived in India where there are tigers. Every day, he had to walk through the forest to where he worked. One day, in the middle of the forest in a clearing, his heart beat fast with fright - there was a tiger looking at him. But he was safe because hunters had trapped the tiger in a cage.

'Please help me', begged the tiger. 'I'm hot and thirsty and feeling very sick. Please let me out'.

Sanjeev knew that tigers are very fierce and could gobble him up in a few mouthfuls. He also knew that there aren't many tigers left in the world, and he felt sorry for this one, trapped in a cage. Nervously, he approached the tiger.

(Continued)

(Continued)

> *'But if I let you out, you'll eat me', he said to the tiger.*
>
> *'I promise I won't eat you. Just let me out', pleaded the tiger.*
>
> *After much discussion and paw-on-heart promises by the tiger, Sanjeev opened the door of the cage and let it out. Of course, tigers being tigers, it licked its lips and made a dash for Sanjeev. Sanjeev ran to the nearest tree, climbed it, and looked down at the waiting tiger.*

Sanjeev was correct, there really aren't many tigers left in the world, so he had tried to do the right thing. But how could he set this tiger free without being eaten? The children were asked to solve the problem. The children used the Thinking Flower to explore it. The teacher showed them a picture of a crane and drew attention to its hook. She also showed them a real hook which was passed around and discussed and included as a petal in the flower. They then devised solutions. For instance, one group used a long piece of rope with the hook on the end, hanging over a tree branch. Sanjeev was to attach the hook to the cage and pull on the loose end of the rope from a safe distance. The children then completed the story and included their solutions so that Sanjeev could free the tiger in safety.

The story provided a clear, meaningful context for the writing, and the children developed their solutions as they wrote. Afterwards, the teacher continued the original story. A fox entered the clearing and expressed doubts about how the situation arose. After some heated expostulation by the tiger, it showed the fox how it had happened by returning to the cage, trapping himself in it, and, once again, pleading with Sanjeev to help him. And so it all began again.

 Activity

Show Key Stage 1 children a 'Jack and Jill'-style well with a simple crank handle for winding up a 'bucket' (such as a screw top from a bottle). Read a spider story (like *Charlotte's Web*, by E.B. White) and ask the children if they can make a spider which comes down from its web over their heads. Have them explore it small groups with a Thinking Flower, one for how to make the spider, and one for the device to raise and lower it.

 Activity

In Key Stage 2, it's someone's birthday. If we had a birthday party, what would we do? Help the children to use several Thinking Flowers to explore food and games. The children then prepare a menu and a programme of games. With older children in this Key Stage, try telling them about the enormous amount of paperwork you have. (Have your desk piled high to show it.) Tell them that as more piles up, you can't remember everything you have to do. Have them work in small groups to construct their own Thinking Flower and use it to help to write a letter to you describing a solution.

Research focus

Variety – the spice of life

Knipper and Duggan (2006) have found very short writing activities to be useful tools for fostering, organising and clarifying thought. For example:

- 'Quick Writes' help children recall what they know, making it available for use. They are given a card and quickly list what they know about the next topic. Later, they list what they now know and compare it with their first attempt. Seeing progress in this way can be motivating.
- 'Word Maps' can be used rather like the Thinking Flower. Printed ready for use, they can have an empty circle at the centre for the topic, surrounded by questions, such as: 'What does it look like?', 'What does it do?' and 'Think of three examples'. The children list their responses in their own words after each question.
- 'ABC lists' can be used at the end of the topic to consolidate and extend vocabulary. The letters A to Z are listed in a column on the left of a sheet of lined paper. The challenge is to write a relevant word about the topic next to as many letters as possible.

Activities like these add variety to the kinds of writing we commonly expect of children.

Writing to support imagination and creative thinking

Invention implies that the children will create something that is somehow new, at least new to them. That is, something they make will come from their own creative thinking and imagination, a kind of playful thinking in a 'What if … ?' world. Being creative to solve a practical problem is not a task that can be done to order. It needs time, space and a relaxed mind (Newton, 2014). Arthur Koestler, the writer, saw creativity as the bringing together of two or more ideas that we have not previously connected. Children, being of limited experience, also benefit from handling the available materials. To begin with, this creative thinking can be relatively free and wide-ranging, bringing together ideas that may not be entirely practical. This can be fun. The process of writing, often in conjunction with pictures, helps children focus on the task and allows time for ideas to be brought together.

If, however, the invention is to be turned into a practical solution, it will have to measure up to reality and the laws of nature at some point. The second part of creative thinking in D&T is to apply some critical thinking to weed out the impractical or make it practical. Children will have to consider the availability of materials and components, the details of structures and mechanisms, and their making skills. To emphasise that thought must, eventually, go beyond flights of fancy. It can help to think of practical problem solving as creative thinking followed by critical thinking. (If critical thinking is applied too soon, it can dampen or stall imaginative thought.) Writing helps critical thinking as it focuses the child's mind on particular parts of their solution. The need to elaborate and consider some of the detail helps to turn the idea into something feasible.

Note that the two kinds of writing are different. The first, to support imagination, has a broad brush and may amount to annotated sketches with callouts (like speech bubbles) that say a few words about some part of the invention. The second, to support critical thinking, has a finer brush and is more organised and detailed. Its task is to produce an organised, coherent and fairly detailed account of the proposed solution. Going beyond a draft, it may also serve to communicate the idea to others (see also the section below, 'Writing to integrate thoughts into coherent wholes and communicate understandings').

Fairly routine examples of these kinds of thinking are seen when children are asked to invent 'a new playground' or when older children 'design a new school'. Tasks of this kind, drawing on personal experience, often need few prompts. Annotated drawings with elaborations offered in callouts let children develop ideas and change their minds. The follow-up activity of describing their ideas prior to making models is intended to clarify those 'special bits', mechanisms and structures that make the ideas work. The children, however, need to know what kind of writing is expected at each stage, something the teacher may have to model or scaffold for them.

Case study

A Car of the Future

It is easy to stifle children's imagination if we constrain them with thinking critically early in a task. It can also take the fun out of flights of fancy. Activities which allow free rein to imagination are useful. This one, used with Key Stage 2 children, encourages creativity and, at the same time, requires some writing to clarify the designs.

The car manufacturer, Toyota, invited children to design a Car of the Future. The responses of Key Stage 2 children can be remarkable (see, for instance, those among 'Images for Toyota Car of the Future competition' on Google), both for their variety (which is what we want if children are thinking for themselves) and for their imagination. Some designs include the comforts of home, with bubble baths and carpets; others include solar panels to supplement the fuel and extra wheels to make the car run smoothly.

The richness of the designs is not always evident from the pictures alone. Writing, in the form of labels and explanatory callouts, are useful in themselves, but can also increase thought about details.

Activity

In connection with teaching about scissor action, ask some Key Stage 1 children to invent a scary animal, draw it and annotate it. (Usually, this involves making large jaws from card, which work like a pair of scissors.) When this task has been completed, they should write an explanation of how the 'special bits' (usually the jaw action) will work.

Activity

Have Key Stage 2 children design a Car of the Future or a House of the Future, and annotate it with callouts. Sight of the *Wallace and Gromit* cartoons and inventions might set the tone. (Use the names as key words to identify several useful websites.) Older Key Stage 2 children can be introduced to drawings like those of W. Heath Robinson, an illustrator with a particular interest in things mechanical. His cartoons show amusing and remarkable mechanisms for simple every-day tasks which stand up to detailed scrutiny (see, for instance, www.bpib.com/illustrat/whrobin. htm). Have the children choose one, colour or number the parts, and, record a journey through them in writing, following the mechanism's movements in detail. They may enjoy constructing their own Heath Robinson drawings. Inventive flights of fancy can be fun at any age: *chindogu*, from Japan, is the invention of feasible but bizarre or outrageous artefacts, purely for amuse-ment. The Internet will find lots of examples to amuse older children and prompt them to do something similar themselves.

Research focus

Writing as 'talking with oneself'

Mason and Bosolo (2000) describe writing as 'talking with oneself'. They see it as helping children to:

- clarify tasks, thoughts and ideas, making them meaningful to the child;
- organise thoughts and ideas;
- reflect on learning experiences.

Working with 9-year-olds, they also found that writing in their own words led to better understanding and, usefully, the children were aware that it helped them. The children came to view writing as a useful tool for supporting thought.

Writing to support recall and structure actions

Products in D&T often require several materials and various tools to work them. This calls for *lists* of materials and tools which the child uses to prepare for the action of making. Omitting a need from the list is rarely of great consequence, but having children develop the habit of com-piling a list is useful, if only as a preliminary step in preparing an *ordered list* of actions. Making things generally requires a number of steps, taken in the right order. Recall the child who glues wheels on both ends of axles then takes them to the buggy only to find there is now no way of sliding the axles through the holes they made for them. An ordered list of actions would have helped. The child first draws up a list of anticipated actions as they come to mind. This list is then put in order. Such lists are aide-memoires. *Instructions*, however, are an ordered list which someone writes for another person to follow so they must be clear. Teaching children the purpose of instructions can come from writing instructions and examining instructions like those in recipe books. (See also The English National Curriculum which includes ways of teaching and presenting instructions.)

Young children will need to have listing modelled for them: 'These are what we will need', 'This is what we will do'. Given the activities of very young children and the limits of their ability to anticipate actions in the future, their lists are usually short. At times, materials and tools are only card, adhesive tape and scissors. Similarly, their ordered lists are often short: 'I will do ... first, then ... second', with further steps added after these have been completed. Older children, of course, can compile quite long lists of needs and steps. Compiling and following instructions is similar. All can practise by listing the components of everyday objects, like plastic sunglasses, ball-point pens, pencils with attached erasers, and well-bound books (they may notice the stitching, but miss the glue). (Try the 'How many different materials can you find in a ... ?' challenge.) Compiling an ordered list of instructions may be practised for many everyday activities, ranging from 'How do we tidy the classroom?' through 'How do I make a sandwich?' to the quite demanding 'How do I tie a shoelace?'

 **Case study**

Minibeasts

When some Year 2 children were learning about minibeasts in science, the teacher took the opportunity to have them make a ladybird as a focused practical task in D&T.

The Ladybird activity involved drawing the shapes, cutting them out, colouring the components, punching a hole and, finally, joining the parts at the head with a paper fastener so that the wings move. She also gave them a blank flow chart (Figure 6.2, much reduced), and described the first step. The children wrote this in the first blank place of their charts and then completed the first step. She then asked them what they thought they should do next, and this was entered and completed. This continued to the task's conclusion.

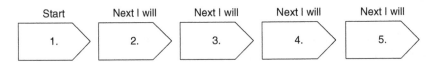

Figure 6.2 A blank flow chart for planning a sequence of actions

In subsequent tasks, the teacher expected the children to complete more of the flow chart themselves, prior to their making activity. As they engaged in each making activity, they ticked each step to show it had been completed and saw the usefulness of writing for themselves.

 Activity

Have Key Stage 1 children write a list of what is in the toy box. They then cut up the list and put in it order, from the largest toy to the smallest. They use the list to put the toys back in the box, beginning with the largest. Older children in this stage may construct a 'dictionary' of tools, materials and simple mechanism names, ordered alphabetically.

 Activity

In Key Stage 2, try giving the children a dismantled object in a tray, such as a press-top, ball-point pen. Their task is to write instructions for its assembly. Show older Key Stage 2 children some board games and their instructions. Have the children invent a board game, make it and write instructions for playing the game.

Practice in listing will, of course, largely come from the D&T tasks the children engage in.

 Research focus

Following instructions – a life skill

The ability to follow instructions is a well-researched subject because so much in everyday life depends on it, both in childhood and adulthood. The ability to follow instructions depends on a child's verbal working memory - the capacity to hold and organise verbal information. This usually improves over time, benefiting from experience of language use generally and instructions specifically. Nevertheless, some children lag behind the others. For instance, those with Attention Deficit and Hyperactivity Disorder (ADHD) have difficulty focusing and maintaining attention so their minds drift away from the instructions, even while writing them. Try having a child write and 'play back' to you a manageable number of steps in the flow chart (Figure 6.2) immediately before they are to use them. Also have them cross out completed steps so that the next one stands out clearly (Jaroslawska et al., 2016; Schutte and Hopkins, 1970).

Writing to support evaluative thought

An expectation in D&T is that children evaluate the quality of the products. This evaluative thought (a specific kind of critical thinking) answers questions, such as the following.

- Does it do what it is supposed to do? If not, why not? What does it do well? What could be improved? If you were to improve it, what would you do?

- Does it look/feel/sound good? If not, why not? If you were to make it again, what would you do differently?

- What about how you made it? Can you use the tools properly, or do you need more practice?

This reflective dialogue that children are expected to have with themselves takes time. Casual responses to these questions are likely to be shallow. Writing slows the process and can allow thinking to become more focused, reflective and balanced. Nevertheless, some children seem predisposed to be overly self-critical, and others over-generous with themselves, and their first drafts may need moderation. The process can be modelled by the teacher reflecting on and talking through his own thinking aloud, writing an evaluation of something he made himself.

The purpose of this kind of evaluation is to make a child aware of the strengths of their work and areas which may need more attention. It does, however, need to be handled sensitively and carefully – the aim is not to make the child lose confidence or a willingness to try, but to clarify how to improve.

The process of evaluation can be practised using everyday artefacts. For example, a collection of clothes hangers, old and new, shows a variety of materials and functions, some achieving their end better than others. The children are asked to put the hangers in order of age (with reasons) and consider which fits its purpose best (and why). Something similar can be done with tea-pots where even the most recent may not pour as well as an old pot. Contrasting an early and a recent artefact in this way, such as telephones, clothes irons or kettles, allows lists of pros and cons to be constructed. Writing is a valuable part of the exercise; it is not simply for collecting together ideas expressed orally, but focuses attention on specifics. Figure 6.3 shows one way children might list pros and cons, assuming they know how a see-saw works. The pros and cons are listed in the blank boxes. Children should not assume, however, that it is always the

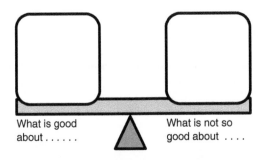

What is good about . . . . . .   What is not so good about . . . .

Figure 6.3 A pros and cons see-saw. The words are adjusted to suit the situation

numbers of pros and cons which determine the outcome. This diagram may be used to support writing which leads to a decision or a conclusion and generally includes one or more reasons, signalled by 'because'.

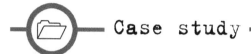 Case study

Modelling a holiday hotel

Following some work in geography, children in Year 6 had the problem of designing and modelling a holiday hotel. A task like this has many parts, many of which offered opportunities for (and even required) writing. The materials available were largely strip wood, sheet card and cardboard boxes. Using the computer, they also had to design and make letter-headed paper, blank bills, key fobs and signs for the hotel. An extended piece of writing came from the evaluation of the various solutions to this composite problem. This evaluation became the basis of an article for a newspaper from a 'hotel inspector', presenting an overview of the hotel's amenities.

The task exercises a variety of kinds of writing, some of which needed research (what does letter-headed paper and a blank bill look like?), others, for public attention, needed careful presentation (for example, signs) and a report (the hotel inspector's report). Some tasks of this nature allow children to practise a variety of skills, and integrate learning widely across the curriculum.

 Activity

Artefacts can be evaluated at any age but need careful selection to suit the age and interests of the children. Safety also needs to be considered. Try evaluating objects like different kinds of pencils, balls or other toys with Key Stage 1 children. The questions they are to answer could include: Which is best? Why do you think that? Which looks best? Why does it look better than the others?

 Activity

In Key Stage 2, older children may be given pairs of objects to compare and contrast, such as an old camera and a modern one, or an old iron and a modern one. Their questions could include: How are they the same? How are they different? Which is the older of the two? Why do you think that? Who would use them? When would they use them? Where would they use them? Are they safe to use? What about their appearance? Which looks/feels good? Which is better at what it does? Which do you think would be easier/cheaper to make? Why do you think that? (Note that children can be inclined to think that more recent versions of artefacts must be better. This may be challenged in the discussion which could follow the writing.)

When applied to the children's own solutions to problems, this kind of writing and discussion generally conclude a D&T task.

Research focus

Forming a balanced view

It can be difficult to be objective about something we have created ourselves so we should not be too disap-
pointed when children are somewhat partisan in their evaluations. Even adults can find constructing an unbi-
ased evaluation difficult (Leitão, 2003). Children do, however, identify relevant positives and negatives about
their work, although they may put too much weight on one side or the other. Nevertheless, this is useful if it
is taken forward to identify how strengths can be built on and weaknesses remedied.

Writing to integrate thoughts into coherent wholes and communicate understandings

We often think we understand something until we have to explain it. Trying to explain it reveals the
gaps and errors in our mental pictures of the world. Writing an explanation, however, can make thinking more deliberate so that deficiencies become evident. Moreover, as we write, we examine our mental
pictures more closely and adjust them to make good those deficiencies (Newton, 2012). This clearly supports the process of designing and takes imagination and creative thinking forward (see also above) so it
can be a use of writing to support thinking. But there are many occasions when writing of this kind is to
tell others about the solution, that is, to support *their* thinking, so it must be clear and meaningful – notes
are rarely enough. This may involve capturing what needs to be said with the help of a key word list and
story map, putting it in order (see also above), writing a draft and then making it as clear as possible.

There are various versions of this kind of writing in D&T which are worthwhile. The first and
obvious one is when children write a personal narrative about what they did to solve the particular problem. If the children keep a Project Book, they generally begin with a statement of the
problem, their thoughts about its solution and their detailed design of it. This may be followed by
a photograph of the finished object and its evaluation. A short personal narrative may conclude
the account. These accounts accumulate over time and can be attractive books to remind the children of what they did and the teacher of their progress. Purists might see no place for illustrations
in narrative writing as they remove the need for some verbal expression, but pictures are common
and legitimate aids to understanding in D&T. Children need to learn how to 'read' pictures, when
to use them and how to incorporate them in the text.

Case study

Making puppets

A class of Year 4 children saw a puppet show and, in D&T, set about making puppets for a show
of their own. The teacher showed pictures of different kinds of puppets with some real examples,
including glove puppets, articulated shadow puppets and simple string puppets. The children
looked for other pictures of puppets on the Internet and considered which they might be able

to do with the materials made available to them. Titles to sequence the activity were provided. As they worked through the task, they recorded their thoughts and ideas in their Project Book. After this episode of designing, the children made their puppets and evaluated them. A narrative account of the process was written in the Project Book, following pictures of the puppets. It concluded with a picture of the pros and cons scales and a written evaluation. Elsewhere, the children wrote a short story/play involving their puppet. Meanwhile, the teacher gave a large cardboard box the appearance of a television. The children acted out their play with the puppets from the back of this 'television' and the teacher video recorded the show.

This project extended over half a term and was used to integrate activities in D&T with those in English. In addition to writing in their D&T Project Books, which the children liked to browse through, the children wrote short plays for their puppets. As a whole, D&T was not just about making, and English was not just about writing, but together they formed an engaging learning experience.

Writing for understanding and communication in D&T can be quite varied. Here are some ideas to try.

 Activity

Point out to Key Stage 1 children that litter around the school has become a real problem. The school needs signs which remind people not to drop litter and to use the litter bins provided. Have the children design, make and display signs to achieve this.

 Activity

Let Key Stage 2 children examine some advertisements, and have them write one for a household artefact or, preferably, for something they have made themselves. This would involve extracting key points about the object to include in the advertisement. Older Key Stage 2 children can read stories about inventors. You might have the children turn one into a short cartoon strip (including speech bubbles, of course). Inventors apply for patents so that other people can't steal their inventions. A simple explanation of the practice will set the scene for older Key Stage 2 children to write a patent application for something they have made. The application (including illustrations) has to be accurate and clear.

 Research focus

Is writing for communication obsolete?

In this age of digital and electronic media, information comes from diagrams, pictures, videos and animations, with, perhaps, a few written words scattered around them. Is writing to communicate obsolete? James Carter (2014) argues cogently that it is not, and that it is essential for interpreting such information. One of his

(Continued)

(Continued)

examples is that of an exhibition in a museum. Museums have changed over the last decade or so and are much more hands-on and interactive than they once were. Nevertheless, they need instructions and explanations to make the activities meaningful.

You might try having the children set up an interactive display of 'old' artefacts in D&T and write instructions and explanations for visitors to their 'museum'. Carter points out that it is the power of the word which moulds what the visitors experience.

Some concluding thoughts and cautions

To sum up, writing in D&T offers specific opportunities for writing to support purposeful thought and, hence, develop competence in practical problem solving. In addition, it offers opportunities for descriptive and informative writing. Because D&T often draws on other areas of the curriculum for its content, consolidating, integrating and making learning more meaningful, these opportunities are usefully diverse. While the potential of D&T for fostering writing competence is considerable, there may be a danger of imbalance. Writing in D&T can support *both* competence in thought *and* competence in communication. This duality of function brings with it the problem of evaluation. Should the writing be assessed or corrected? This depends on its purpose. It would be easy to slip into the practice of correcting all writing as though it was narrative or explanatory prose meant to be read by others. There are, of course, times when this is appropriate, as in children's writing of a display sign or an advertisement. But, when the writing is purely for personal consumption and was an aid to thought, it could be judged more with that in mind (Davies and Moss, 2000). It may help if children are also made aware of the distinction between writing to help them think better and writing to tell others about what they invented. Finally, while reflective writing is an integral and valuable part of working and thinking in D&T, and a valuable competence to develop, it is important to remember that it is not the sole reason for teaching D&T.

References

Carter, J. (2014) Rejoice in the wordhoard. Available from: www.jamescarter.cc/wp-content/uploads/2014/09/Writing_interpretation_James_Carter.pdf

Davies, C. and Moss, J. (2000) *Issues in Teaching English*. London: Routledge.

Hart-Davidson, W. (2000) The core competencies of technical communication. *Technical Communication*, 48(2): 145–55.

Jaroslawska, A.J., Gathercole, S.E., Logie, M.R. and Holmes, J. (2016) Following instructions in a virtual school. *Memory & Cognition*, 44(4): 580–9.

Knipper, K.J. and Duggan, T.J. (2006) Writing to learn across the curriculum. *The Reading Teacher*, 59(5): 462–70.

Leitão, S. (2003) Evaluating and selecting counterarguments. *Written Communication*, 20(3): 269–306.

Mason, L. and Bosolo, P. (2000) Writing and conceptual change. *Instructional Science*, 28: 199–226.

Newton, D.P. (2005) *Teaching Design and Technology 3–11*. London: Paul Chapman.

Newton, D.P. (2012) *Teaching for Understanding*. Abingdon: Routledge.

Newton, D.P. (2014) *Thinking with Feeling*. London: Routledge.

Newton, D.P. (2016) *In Two Minds*. Ulm: The International Centre for Innovation in Education.

Schutte, R.C. and Hopkins, B.L. (1970) The effects of teacher attention on following instructions in a kindergarten class. *Journal of Applied Behavior Analysis*, 3(2): 177–222.

Young, A. (1999) *Teaching Writing across the Curriculum*, Upper Saddle River, NJ: Prentice Hall.

7

Writing in computing

Rosie Ridgway

Teachers' Standards

Standard 3 - Demonstrate good subject and curriculum knowledge

- have a secure knowledge of the relevant subject(s) and curriculum areas, foster and maintain pupils' interest in the subject, and address misunderstandings
- demonstrate a critical understanding of developments in the subject and curriculum areas, and promote the value of scholarship
- demonstrate an understanding of and take responsibility for promoting high standards of literacy, articulacy and the correct use of standard English, whatever the teacher's specialist subject

Standard 4 - Plan and teach well-structured lessons

- impart knowledge and develop understanding through effective use of lesson time
- promote a love of learning and children's intellectual curiosity

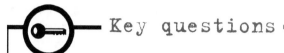

Key questions

- Does computing offer opportunities for writing?
- What aspects of computing are relevant for writing?
- How can we foster writing through computing in our classrooms?

Introduction

In UK primary schools computing is a relatively new phenomenon: the subject before this was Information and Communication Technologies (ICT). This change in focus requires an adjustment in approaches to understanding and working with information technologies in the classroom, where planning for learning shifts from an end-user based approach (where learners are taught how to use technologies for different purposes) to a producer one (where learners are encouraged to understand how and why technologies work, as well as how to apply technological solutions to problems). This chapter will consider whether the greater focus on computer science and problem solving in the curriculum narrows our opportunities for using computing and writing together, or whether the assumption that it does narrow opportunities is false.

What is computing?

The computing curriculum for primary schools was introduced in 2013, replacing the previous National Curriculum subject of ICT. There are three distinct strands to the computing curriculum: computer science, information technology and digital literacy. Its stated aims are that all pupils:

- *can understand and apply the fundamental principles and concepts of computer science, including abstraction, logic, algorithms and data representation*

- *can analyse problems in computational terms, and have repeated practical experience of writing computer programs in order to solve such problems*

- *can evaluate and apply information technology, including new or unfamiliar technologies, analytically to solve problems*

- *are responsible, competent, confident and creative users of information and communication technology*

(DfE, 2013, p1)

These aims can be met in a number of ways, and through a range of approaches, and the programme of study allows for some flexibility. Schools and teachers can plan to deliver this curriculum in a way which is suited to their particular context. It is worth noting that as the pace of change in information technologies continues to move rapidly, we need to keep flexibility in mind, and not become reliant on a particular piece of hardware, software or online materials to approach the subject in our teaching. For example, offering pupils an opportunity to learn using a range of platforms and interfaces, such as tablets, mobile phones and digital cameras as well as classroom laptops and interactive whiteboards, will allow them to use evaluative skills in selecting appropriate technologies, and also develop awareness of the range of skills required to use different technologies.

Of the above aims outlined in the curriculum, the first two relate to computer science, the third to information technology, and the fourth to digital literacy. The computer science strand offers some challenges in terms of opportunities for writing, whereas teachers are far more skilled and experienced in teaching information technology, and to some extent digital literacy, and so these areas present less of a challenge than the computer science strand. However, opportunities for writing in computing arise in many ways.

Developing skill in writing to develop projects in computing enables:

- developing logical thinking: organising thoughts (analytic and convergent skills);
- developing, structuring and managing projects: organising activity;
- developing creative and divergent skills: production;
- evaluating and assessing: reflecting and learning;
- writing for communication: meaningful work.

This chapter will address these approaches and use specific examples (focus activities) to explore how these skills can be developed and put into practice in our classrooms.

Writing to develop systematic and computational thinking

Systematic approaches and logical thinking are important skills for learners to develop and these can be developed in a number of ways by means of writing through computing. These skills are also needed for problem solving in school and in later life. Logic is often associated with mathematical and non-linguistic skills, yet there are strong connections between reasoning and logic. Logic should not be viewed in isolation from language. Vygotsky (1978) describes language as a tool for thought, and so it is. Systematic approaches can be fostered by writing and, in turn, writing skills can be fostered by adopting systematic approaches – something of a virtuous cycle.

In order to support learners less confident in their writing, or whose writing does not reflect their ability in other areas, there are several strategies which will improve performance. One strategy is to offer additional structure to order thoughts (for example, using a graphic organiser). This allows the learner to plan and then revisit their ideas, without having to remember the whole thing. Graphic organisers give concrete reference points (rather than abstract, memory-based ones – which rely on working memory and recall) reducing the cognitive load of the task. They also model one way for learners to structure and approach their writing in a strategic manner. By using a structuring tool, we encourage learners to be systematic and view their writing in a different way (although we should take care gradually to reduce this support as learners' skills develop, to allow them to make progress). An example is provided below.

Example of writing structure/graphic organiser

Writing structure example – persuasive writing: opinion

1. Introduction

    _____ is good/fun/great.

    My favourite _____ is _____.

    I think _____ is _____ for many reasons.

2. Reasons

    First/ First of all _____ is _____ because_____.

    Second/ Also/ In addition _____ is _____ because _____.

    Third/ Last/ Finally _____ is _____ because _____.

3. Conclusion

    That is why I think _____ is _____.

    As you can see, I like _____ very much.

This example offers structure for learners to plan out their writing, so that the sentence structure, grammar and punctuation, much of the word selection and the structure of the text as a whole are already on offer. This allows learners to think about the content of their writing (the actual opinion part) and the format, and concentrate on the core objectives of the task.

 **Research focus**

Writing structures

Instructional design is heavily influenced by constructivist theories of learning. One relevant strand of this is Cognitive Load Theory (Mayer, 2010), which suggests that by reducing task complexity and memorisation or recall requirements, learners have more available working memory capacity to focus on performing the task. *People learn better when extraneous material is excluded rather than included, when cues are added that highlight the organization of the essential material* (Mayer, 2010, p6). Offering scaffolding to tasks, such as writing structures, is one way to reduce task complexity in the way suggested by Mayer, and this can be taken into consideration in task design (Plass et al., 2010).

The National Curriculum Programme of Study (DfE, 2013 p2) states that Key Stage 1 pupils should be taught to *understand what algorithms are; how they are implemented as programs on digital devices; and that programs execute by following precise and unambiguous instructions; create and debug simple programs; use logical reasoning to predict the behaviour of simple programs.*

It also outlines that Key Stage 2 pupils should be taught to:

> *design, write and debug programs that accomplish specific goals, including controlling or simulating physical systems; solve problems by decomposing them into smaller parts; use sequence, selection and repetition in programs; work with variables and various forms of input and output; use logical reasoning to explain how some simple algorithms work and to detect and correct errors in algorithms and programs.*

(DfE, 2013, p2)

One of the key concepts in teaching computer programming is that computers follow a simple set of instructions (algorithms) to perform processes, and that these underpin the principle definition of a simple machine: Input–process–output. One commonly adopted approach for introducing this principle in Key Stage 1 is to ask learners to write and sequence a set of simple instructions. This might be how to build a sandcastle, or putting together the elements of a story in the correct order. Important in the development of the understanding of algorithms is a move from concrete to abstract principles, and there are many bridging strategies which can be used to support this shift in understanding. For example, process charts are a useful method for developing early programming skills as they help us to work out a precise, systematic approach for outlining a process. One reason they are particularly useful is that they make the abstract (code or programming language) more concrete by dividing the whole process into distinct blocks. Process charts can be introduced even to very young learners as simple quizzes and games such as *Guess Who?* and for organising the plot of a story or planning writing or other events.

 **Research focus**

Developing coding

Hutchison et al. (2015) used the Scratch app with learners to support literacy instruction. They claim that the language skills used in developing coding relate well to the language skills in the development of literacy. They also argue that the highly engaging visuals, well-structured materials and fun game-like quality of the tasks support motivation and engagement with learning. Scratch (MIT labs) and other online introductions to programming (commonly called *coding*) use a building-block structure to support this move to abstraction, where different sets of instructional code are presented in colourful chunks and learners can place the blocks in together to effect the outcome. For basic orientation into how a simple program should run, trial and improvement may suffice, but in order to develop more complex programs and to debug these, where necessary, learners will need to have a clear idea of the input process and outcome of their programs.

Key ideas

Sometimes, offering additional structure allows learners to focus on the learning task more easily. Teaching strategies which adopt a structured approach can develop writing and programming skills, and these same logical reasoning skills are benefited by practice in a range of domains and contexts; for example, writing a simple set of clear instructions in computing develops similar strategic and logical skills as story planning using a simple functional structure.

Writing to develop projects: analytic and convergent skills

The systematic and strategic approaches discussed in the first theme apply in a grander way to project development. Computing offers some exciting opportunities to develop projects which are reasonably long term (will last more than a few lessons). Here, functional strategic approaches which encompass planning, time management and organising the sequence of events can be shared and developed with learners (as appropriate according to the phase being taught). This is a useful way of encouraging purposeful writing with an authentic aim. For example, a six-week time block to put together a multimedia production such as a stop-motion animation: pupils need to research, draft the story, design sets and characters, then construct them, film the animation, record sound, edit and finish the product. To do so and ensure the project is successful, a clear, specific, and time and resource-bound strategy for managing the project is needed, and your learners (as the film makers) need to develop this (with teacher support). This may seem like a great deal of pressure and expectation to place upon young learners; however, because such work is highly engaging and motivating, they are likely to rise to this challenge and surprise you (and if you are really worried about it you can offer your own model plan for them to tweak and adapt).

 Case study

Retelling familiar tales

Angela's mixed Year 1 and 2 class had some reluctant writers. She decided to use a stop-motion animation project to help them engage with retelling familiar tales (with a twist). Angela prepared some background 'sets', printed out character images on to card (with extra arms, legs and faces with different expressions) and she also provided a range of different props which could feature in the story (such as a magic wand, a football, a pumpkin, a glass slipper, a teapot). The children each wrote a surprising version of the story with a beginning, a middle and an ending for the character. Then the class decided which elements of the story they preferred and then recorded it as an animation. In their version of the Cinderella story, the glass slippers were replaced with magic football boots. Every child had a chance to be involved in the filming of the animation and retelling the story with a twist.

Example: Animated projects

Stop-motion animation uses lots of still images in sequence to create the appearance of movement – like a technological flip book. Using a camera linked to a laptop or PC, still photographs are taken and put together at short intervals using free software (such as iMotion). The still photographs can be edited together with sound titles and end credits to create an animated film. Animations can create any situation or scenario from moments in history, pure fantasy, retelling familiar tales with a new twist or creating impossible events.

There are both risks and benefits, as follows.

Risks

Stop-motion animations are time-consuming and integrating such projects into class teaching requires forward-planning and realistic timeframes (a half-term/six-week block is reasonable for a short animated project). Another consideration is that the quality of the input directly affects the quality of the output, so, for example, taking care that fingers are out of sight before the photographs are taken saves time in editing the animation. Production problems can be avoided by adopting a practice of counting down before capturing the picture (some classes like to use a studio-style practice 'lights, camera, clear, action!' as a reminder).

Benefits

Animated projects can become the highlight of the school year for many pupils and offer a platform for purposeful writing with a meaningful outcome.

Tips and tricks

The more pictures put together per second of film, the more smooth and life-like the moving image will appear: animated television programmes put together about 24 frames per second (fps), but for a classroom animation project, about 12 fps will work quite effectively. Take care to control the environment when animating: be aware of light and shadows and don't change the focus of the recording device while taking photographs or the quality of the images will be compromised. If you use a bright light source such as a reading light while you are filming rather than relying on daylight or regular classroom lighting, the images will appear much more consistent when putting them together.

Key ideas

Organising a project such as a multimedia production requires planning, organisation, strategic management and great clarity about the aims and outcomes involved. The opportunities for writing during such projects offer learners authentic purposes and aims for their work, in addition to developing their strategic planning and problem-solving skills. The nature of multimedia projects means that learners can develop a wider range of skills than traditionally available in core subjects, and the exciting context for this learning is highly motivating for learners.

Writing to develop projects: creative and divergent skills

There are many aspects of development which education in school cannot address in depth, especially those which are difficult to measure and assess. It is unfortunate that in a climate of high accountability, performance measurement is often focused on narrower convergent skills and measurable knowledge, rather than a broader range of creative and divergent skills (social, affective, philosophical). These accountability pressures force curriculum and pedagogy into increasingly narrow activities (sometimes called 'teaching to the test') in order to meet requirements of external monitoring. One means of addressing a lack of 'richness' in the academic curriculum in core subjects is to channel more diverse features into compelling cross-curricular projects through computing and other subjects.

So far, we have looked at multimedia projects and their potential to develop planning and strategic skills, and creative skills. Computing projects also pose novel problems to be resolved. Managing difficulty and responding to challenges with effective solutions is a key theme in computing, and multimedia projects bring with them novel problems for learners to resolve, such as:

How can we make our character 'fly'?

How do we get rid of the background noise?

How can we make the inside of a volcano sound hot?

What parts of the story can we cut out of our retelling without spoiling it?

This multi-aspect problem solving is an understated but great learning opportunity in such projects. In exploring the next example of podcasting, think about the kinds of challenges you would expect to arise from such a project, and then do the project and see how many challenges you could not predict.

Example: Podcasts

A podcast is an audio recording that is hosted as a downloadable file online – essentially a radio programme that is available at any time. Podcasts can be recorded with very simple tools and, once edited, these can be embedded into school websites as effective examples of pupils' work. Equipment needed is a microphone connected to a laptop or pc and some editing software (free software like *Audacity* is remarkably effective).

Podcasting offers many opportunities for activities, including making radio programmes, plays, poems, news reports about recent events, school trip reports, or even interviews. The planning and script-writing of podcasts are vital components in the project (it is amazing how quickly people run out of things to say when presented with a microphone), so time and effort should be spent developing scripts before attempting a recording – a perfect invitation for writing.

Risks

Confidentiality and anonymity of pupils may be a concern, as are potential issues which may be controversial; hosting podcasts on the school website may also need careful thought. It may be necessary to host the podcast elsewhere and offer a link. However, this might be seen as an endorsement of the associated website and company, so does need discussion with school leaders.

Benefits

Podcasting can be a free resource that can showcase your talented pupils, which is simple to use and embed into practice and is also unlikely to disrupt your classroom practice. Writing scripts and scenarios allows pupils to link their writing to speech and drama, and using a podcast means they can return to their work again and again.

Tips and tricks

Noisy environments are really bad for recording. Creating or finding a sound-proof (dampening) space will improve the sound quality of your podcast and reduce the need for fancy editing – demonstrate the difference to your pupils before serious podcast recording begins and they will be much more willing to ask for and support a 'live recording silence'.

Key points

Writing can be a highly creative process once basic skills are acquired, but there are pressures on classroom time and curricular focus, which means that sometimes there is less space for creative work. Multimedia projects like podcasting allow children to channel their creative writing skills into exciting and innovative works which they can be really proud of.

Writing to evaluate and assess

Evaluation and reflection are important parts of the learning process; if we don't learn from our errors, we are likely to repeat them. Indeed, it is also useful to identify the positive elements of a piece of work or project to confirm or maintain positive practices. Learners need to know what they are getting right and what to keep working on. Constructivist and social constructivist approaches emphasise the role of meaningful feedback to support the evaluation and learning process. In computing there are many opportunities to gain immediate, task-focused and context-relevant feedback, from the construction of simple programs which run correctly, incorrectly or not at all, to creating projects which can be shared with a global audience. A valuable experience in developing writing is the process of drafting and redrafting to improve the work (Lacina and Griffith, 2012). Sometimes this can be a difficult process, and the following example offers one way to share this experience of evaluation and assessment of work and its gradual improvement.

Example: Wikis

A wiki is an information text hosted online, which is collaboratively authored and edited to continuously 'improve' the information in the text. The most famous example of this is Wikipedia. You can write your own wikis using a web platform such as Wikispaces for education. This is a simple framework for the content to be written, edited and updated using on-screen buttons (usually edit, discuss, history and restore). Wiki writing is a really good opportunity to demonstrate drafting and redrafting to improve written work, and also to encourage constructive feedback and evaluation of written work, which is somewhat less personal as it is a multi-author work. Pupils can produce wikis in a range of relevant topics. Subjects for wikis might include fictional character biographies where major characters in a work are the subject of a wiki page each. This is also a useful way of approaching figures from history or information about scientific topics such as the planets.

Risks

A public audience for written work offers both opportunities for authentic feedback but also the risks of unsupportive or malicious feedback. To avoid this, you might set up moderated edits and monitor updates as a precaution. It is also worth offering clear guidance about permissible content and what constitutes a good source of information or evidence in developing wikis.

Benefits

Wikis allow us to write collaboratively with the purpose of creating informative texts. They give us the opportunity to read and improve our own and other people's writing. Learners can develop their editing skills, and think as a critical reader and constructive writer.

Key ideas

Evaluation and assessment is a vital part of the learning process. Writing in drafts demonstrates improvements with each iteration. Social media such as blogs and wikis can be used to develop writing skills, and wikis, in particular, provide opportunities to improve each iteration.

Writing to communicate

It is clear that literacy is a key requirement in social functioning and lack of literacy has major negative consequences. Developing writing as communication with our learners is therefore a critically important part of our role as teachers. One advantage that computing offers is the opportunity to communicate with more global, diverse and wide-reaching audiences than ever before, through a variety of platforms. Along with the advantages of reaching authentic audiences, there are also particular opportunities for developing writing skills that are associated with each platform. However, we also need to be aware that there are potential risks in offering our pupils an online platform (Poore, 2016 offers a detailed discussion of this, which is very helpful).

Social media offers both a range of formats for writing to communicate with others and a range of purposes and audiences. For this reason, effective writing for communication can be approached in a range of ways (O'Byrne and Murell, 2014).

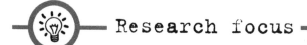 **Research focus**

Multimodal writing

O'Byrne and Murell (2014) and Lenhart et al. (2008) looked at the way learners read and write online; they point out that the relationship between text and pictures, icon symbols (for example, emojis) and videos is very different from the way we read and write text in school. These different platforms are sometimes called modes, so online writing is multimodal (O'Byrne and Murell, 2014). Another big difference is interactivity: that audiences are expected to access and respond to texts in different ways - and are encouraged to do so by the design of materials. This means that rather than just being 'readers' or 'writers', we have 'users' and 'creators' of multimodal content. Baker (2010) encourages us to think about the multimodal literacy skills being developed by learners when we use online platforms for writing and how we can address these in our curricula and practices in education.

Example: blogs

Blogs (short for weblog) are written text in the form of an online diary, report, article or opinion piece on an issue. Anyone can write a blog and there are many millions to be found online. Blogs are hosted on websites such as *WordPress* or *Kidblog* which are free (or relatively cheap). Blogs tend to be grouped by author or theme. The text of a blog tends to have the option for audience comments (optional), though the main purpose of a blog is a monologue rather than a discussion. Blogs can be a useful platform to get pupils writing about current events or issues which matter to them. The most effective blogs prompt the audience to engage and reflect too, so simply replacing an essay with a blog misses the point.

Risks

Before launching a blog site for school pupils, a code of conduct and the ethics of publishing online must be considered. Parents' views and permission should also be sought, particularly if pupils wish to use their own first names. Rather than establishing individual blogs for each pupil, consider a class or school blog which can be an efficient way to manage the content in the blog.

Benefits

Blogs offer an amazing opportunity to be an author who is read by the world.

Tips and tricks

Before launching the blog, prepare several articles of guidance about the aims, themes and purpose of the blog. A code of conduct, or guidance for how to constructively comment on the work, is also recommended. Using a moderation system so that comments are monitored before being posted online alongside the blog is important when hosting learners' work. The blog should also be launched with several pre-written blogs so that your audience has a chance to assess how the blog works. Look at other class blogs – use quadblog or partner up with other schools who are using blogging to offer audience feedback on each other's writing.

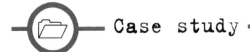 Case study

Writing a blog

Mikhaal's Year 5 class were learning about the water cycle, and during research several students became interested and concerned with issues of water pollution, global warming and the lack of safe drinking water in developing countries. He asked them to prepare a blog about the issues they thought most important (including some key facts and data, and why others should be concerned). Mikhaal was anxious about allowing the pupils on social media – so he asked the computing coordinator at school to find a safe platform to share the work. They agreed that the school website was an ideal place to host the pupil pages as it is carefully monitored, and parents and pupils could find it without too much difficulty. Mikhaal's class blog now regularly features discussions of 'big issues' and he plans to continue blogging with his learners next year.

Research focus

Bridging the gap

Lenhart et al. (2008) examined the role of technology and writing in the lives of teens in the USA. Their work identified that young people used lots of technology to communicate, but did not view the text-based elements for their technology use as 'real' writing. Their report offers many suggestions for developing teaching approaches which bridge the gap between what they call 'social' writing and writing in school. Two of Lenhart's key findings were that teens were motivated to write by having some choice in the topic of their writing, and also: *Teens also found it motivating when their writing could have broader impact through being publicly shared in class, in person, in print or on the Internet. In fact, many teens commented on the positive push publishing or presenting to a formal audience provided for their writing* (Lenhart et al., 2008, p70). This research finding fits in well with the self-determination theory of learning motivation. Deci and Ryan (2000) argued that for learning tasks to be effective they need to be linked to the learner's interest (i.e. personal competence), offer some level of autonomy, and be related to context (i.e. be real and engage with a real audience), and we can see many examples of this throughout this book.

Case study

Using Twitter

Jill (a Year 3 teacher) used the 140-character format of Twitter to encourage children to compose 'tweets' (short written summaries) of the class-shared reading of Anne Fine's *Diary of a Killer Cat*. After each reading session, a pair of learners wrote a 'tweet' about the story so far to be displayed on the classroom display wall. As the class progressed through the story, the Twitter display board gradually filled up (like a Twitter feed). The school Twitter account regularly posts updates about the focus of each class's learning, and parents respond to Jill's weekly class tweets with questions and comments about the story. This additional level of engagement with the class reading and writing has fostered a sense of excitement about learning in Jill's class.

Example: Twitter

Twitter is a social media platform where individuals or organisations can share crisp, clear messages with the world (more specifically, those who follow their tweets). In order to start tweeting, individuals or organisations must join Twitter and agree to abide by the terms and share certain information about themselves (there are age restrictions). Tweets must be 140 characters long and no more, and this is one reason why it is a good tool to use when approaching writing. If a school Twitter account is used, classes can be offered the (moderated) platform in turns to share their snappy book reviews, or e-safety messages, or reminders about school events. Pupils will find writing brief punchy texts a refreshing style of writing. The idea of Twitter is that it functions as a conversation with a broad audience, so tweeting questions, or responses to their work, to authors can be very rewarding.

Risks

The terms of use of Twitter do not allow minors to have their own accounts. Organisations such as schools can hold Twitter accounts, but care must be taken with the privacy settings. Schools wishing to use Twitter and publish learners' tweets might set their privacy levels so that they can moderate their audience rather than sending them to the mass public.

Benefits

Tweets offer a really meaningful context for writing concise texts and can be a great way to connect with teachers, learners, authors and others who wouldn't ordinarily be accessible.

Key ideas

A main purpose of writing is to communicate with the world, and social media allows our learners to connect with broader audiences than ever before. With careful planning social media (like blogging) can offer learners a global audience for their written work.

Conclusion

In this chapter we considered whether the greater focus on computer science and problem solving in the UK primary National Curriculum narrows opportunities for using computing and writing together. We looked at five aspects of computing which enhance opportunities for writing: developing logical thinking through organising thoughts and organising activities, developing imaginative and creative projects, and the practice of evaluating and reflecting on work as part of the learning process, as well as opportunities to communicate with broad and authentic audiences. The discussion also offered a number of examples for practitioners, which develop learner skills that are complementary to both their writing and developing understanding in computing. These examples and opportunities to develop skills demonstrate that the new curriculum provides a broad range of opportunities for our students to develop their writing.

━━ Resources ━━

Audacity – www.audacityteam.org

iMotion – free app by fingerlab

Kidblog – www.kidblog.org

Quadblog – quadblogging.net/

Scratch – https://scratch.mit.edu/

Wikispaces – www.wikispaces.com

Wix – www.wix.com

Wordpress – www.wordpress.com

References

Baker, E.A. (ed.) (2010) *The New Literacies: Multiple Perspectives on Research and Practice*. London: Guildford Press.

Deci, E.L. and Ryan, R.M. (2000) Self-determination theory and the facilitation of intrinsic motivation, social development and wellbeing. American Psychologist, 55(1): 68–78.

Department for Education (DfE) (2013) *National Curriculum in England: Computing Programmes of Study* (DFE-00171-2013). London. Available from: www.gov.uk/government/publications/national-curriculum-in-england-computing-programmes-of-study.

Fine, A. (1994) *The Diary of a Killer Cat*. London: Puffin.

Hutchison, A., Nadolny, L. and Estapa, A. (2015) Using coding apps to support literacy instruction and develop coding literacy. *The Reading Teacher*, 69(5): 493–503.

Lacina, J. and Griffith, R. (2012) Blogging as a means of crafting writing. *The Reading Teacher*, 66(4): 316–20. DOI:10.1002/TRTR.01128

Lenhart, A., Arafeh, S., Smith, A. and Macgill, A.R. (2008) *Writing, Technology and Teens*. Available from: www.perinternet.org/

Mayer, R.E. (ed.) (2010) *The Cambridge Handbook of Multimedia Learning*. Cambridge: Cambridge University Press.

O'Byrne, B. and Murrell, S. (2014) Evaluating multimodal literacies in student blogs. *British Journal of Educational Technology*; 45(5): 926–40. DOI:10.1111/bjet.12093

Plass, J.L., Moreno, R. and Brunken, R. (eds) (2010) *Cognitive Load Theory* (1st edn). Cambridge: Cambridge University Press.

Poore, M. (2016) *Using Social Media in the Classroom: A Best Practice Guide* (2nd edn). London: Sage.

Vygotsky, L. (1978 *Mind in Society: The Development of Higher Psychological Processes*. Cambridge, MA: Harvard University Press.

8
Writing in history
Andrew Joyce-Gibbons

Teachers' Standards

Standard 3 - Demonstrate good subject and curriculum knowledge

- have a secure knowledge of the relevant subject(s) and curriculum areas, foster and maintain pupils' interest in the subject, and address misunderstandings
- demonstrate a critical understanding of developments in the subject and curriculum areas, and promote the value of scholarship
- demonstrate an understanding of and take responsibility for promoting high standards of literacy, articulacy and the correct use of standard English, whatever the teacher's specialist subject

Standard 4 - Plan and teach well-structured lessons

- impart knowledge and develop understanding through effective use of lesson time
- promote a love of learning and children's intellectual curiosity

Key questions

- What is history and what is it that historians do?
- How do we support learners to articulate their historical ideas?
- How can we teach in a way in which historical skills and evidence are used to actively develop literacy skills rather than passively provide context?

Introduction

History is a complex and fascinating area of study. The teaching and learning of history is the subject of many books and journal articles already. This chapter focuses on a few key areas which can help stimulate and create meaningful historical writing.

The first sections consider what history is and what it is not. If teachers are unaware of the point of history, they will be unable to communicate this to learners and certainly unable to form a clear idea of the kind of writing they wish to elicit from their students. This chapter begins with a summary of the role of history in the moral and social development of all of us. We will then consider what makes a meaningful history lesson and just as importantly what does not. Too often, history is merely context for English or mathematics. While it can add inspiration and creative contexts in which to explore other disciplines, this is not the same as focusing on the subject explicitly. To do this requires teachers and learners to look in detail at the requirements of the National Curriculum – there are some exciting developments since 2014 in inclusive world history and an increased coherence surrounding the chronological narrative of human habitation of the island now called 'Britain' in our culture. However, the main thrust of the curriculum is on learners becoming historians, using skills of enquiry or evaluation and crucially to *communicate their explanations arising from this enquiry*.

The next area explores writing to develop chronological awareness – a key skill of the new curriculum and perhaps the best opportunity to develop truly cross-curricular history and English lessons. This is followed by an examination of developing understanding of significance by counter-factual thought experiments. This situates writing as part of the process of developing historical understanding. Writing in history is more than simply notes, storyboards and narrative reports. Each piece of writing is part of an iterative process: each time thought is articulated into written form, understanding is developed within the learner. It is a means by which collaboration can be captured and historical perspective assessed. The final section explores ideas of scaffolding in the context of progression; the level of scaffolding a teacher needs to put in place is a highly personal and professional decision.

History matters: democracy and the demise of the 'fact'

The study of history, perhaps more than any other, has a moral imperative which transcends all the quotidian demands of the classroom. It is through history that learners experience the best and worst in human endeavour: the imagination and drive within all of us which led some of our species to set foot on the moon and led others to develop the smart phone. These same qualities also lead to desperate wars in the twenty-first century. History is focused on the act of choosing an explanation out of the multiplicity available, based on the imperfect but available evidence of past human behaviour and relate these to the greater debates which take place throughout our social discourse. Why and how did people go to the moon? Was this a 'giant leap for mankind'? What is the significance of an iPhone – did it 'change everything' as it originally claimed? Why and how did migrants from war zones in Africa and Asia travel to Europe only to die along its offshore waters?

However, the obligation of the primary classroom teacher is not to the past, an unknowable country, but to the future, an undiscovered one. The key disposition which must be developed through the teaching and learning of history is *historical perspective*.

What historians do

Historians gather and interpret evidence in order to answer questions about the past. Evidence takes two forms:

1. primary – objects or documents contemporary with the time under consideration;

2. secondary – already existing interpretations of the past by historians. Interpretation of evidence requires two processes:

   • analysing the evidence to understand the limits of what can be inferred from this evidence in relation to the wider totality of historical knowledge;

   • evaluating this evidence as part of a coherent answer to a historical question.

The key attribute for a historian is a curiosity-driven imagination with which to ask and then to answer historical questions. Given that the past, including our own recent past, is entirely unknowable, in a sense all history is a work of the imagination. According to Neil Gaiman (2013, p 249), *There are no personal absolute truths because they are coloured by memory and feeling and point of view.*

The aims of the National Curriculum in Key Stage 1 and Key Stage 2

Introduced in 2014, the new National Curriculum in History focuses on five key aims which all build up to the final one:

1. chronological understanding;

2. understanding of the wider world;

3. historical terms;

4. conceptual understanding;

5. historical enquiry.

All these aims contribute to the learner developing the sixth key aim, a historical perspective to ensure that children develop into free-thinking adults able to function in a democratic society.

When teachers invite writing in history they must do so in furtherance of these aims, Without a clear focus on one of these five aims you are not teaching history. You may be teaching another subject using a historical context. That's fine, but it is *not* a history lesson. Teachers must be clear when they are teaching history, not using it. The test for this is that they are able to show which of the five key areas they are developing, how this is progressing from previous lessons and how they are going to assess that progress.

 **Case study**

Meaningless cross-curricular history

Aaron was teaching diary writing as part of a cross-curricular topic on the Second World War. The Year 5 class have spent a literacy lesson reading *The Diary of Anne Frank*. They have used this as a basis for writing their own diary entries having first looked at the key features of a diary which the teacher elicited during a whole class 'discussion' on diary writing (in practice, this was a series of didactic questions and answers). The children began working on drafting a diary entry. In the plenary, the teacher led a recap of Anne's story up to this point. Afterwards, they very quickly tidied away in preparation for their music lesson. This began with a lusty rendition of their class of the song, 'Who do you think you are kidding, Mr Hitler?'

While history provided the context for these lessons, neither could be considered lessons which involved the teaching and learning of history. The key requirement of effective planning and teaching in history is a thorough knowledge of the subject area. If the teacher had researched more thoroughly, he would have realised that this song was written in 1968 as the theme tune of the sitcom *Dad's Army*. In both cases, history is merely a vehicle for another subject – English and music. However, a segue from emotionally challenging experiences of a young diarist to a jaunty pastiche only belittles the former.

Writing for chronology

Perhaps the most straightforward place to start is with chronology. Learners must be able to express the sequence of events in the history of the British Isles from the Stone Age to 1066. More generally, they must be able to express ideas about the passage of time. Depending on your perspective, some events are relatively recent, others relatively distant. For Reception children, looking forward from one Christmas to the next requires them to wait for perhaps a quarter of their life so far. This fraction is much reduced for their teacher and therefore it may seem to approach much more closely.

We think of Cleopatra as a celebrity of the classical world. However, her lifetime is a period roughly equidistant between the writing of the epic of Gilgamesh (2150–2030BC) and the advent of the iPhone (2007AD). There is a particular challenge when we are dealing with the transition between periods, say between Roman Britain and Anglo-Saxon England. Sometimes there are key dates associated with these transitions – Roman armies leaving Britain after Honorius' letter in 410AD or the Battle of Hastings in 1066. However, the extent to which military or political events affected the lives and culture of ordinary people is frequently a matter for debate among professional historians.

 **Activity**

Timelines

Key Stage 1 - Socks and shoes

Reception and Year 1 children can be asked to construct a timeline of their own growth and development using sources brought from home (socks and shoes, showing growth and progression, at what age they were worn, what they might have done with them). These can be augmented with pictures of themselves growing up.

Writing timelines provides an opportunity for practising basic time connectives in response to questions such as:

First, my socks were small. Next they will be bigger. Last of all, they will be even larger.

Key Stage 2 - Large-scale timeline

There are lots of interesting ways to create large-scale timelines for Years 3 and 4: trundle wheels and chalk in the playground; plain wallpaper; toilet roll; a tabarded line of children. The key issue is to define your scale - 1cm = 1 year? One sheet = 10 years? One child = a century?

Once you have constructed your timeline, they can be described in increasingly complex written ways by adding specific events, key people and places, etc.

Target ideas - simultaneous actions/increasing and decreasing trends over time/causes and consequences

---

Writing is part of a process

All too often, when writing, history is relegated to little more than the context for literacy work – writing becomes useful only as an end in itself. True, the ability to communicate one's ideas is an essential part of the continual debate and reformation of historical discourse. However, writing is far from an end in itself. Writing is an essential component from the outset. Notes are needed to record unstructured thoughts and important details; written summaries are needed of the views in secondary sources, and historical questions are addressed through a range of genres. Factual narratives inform readers about events. Conflicting interpretations give rise to debate, which focuses on historical controversy, presenting both sides of an argument before drawing conclusions supported by evidence (Nichol, 2014, p 22).

Writing provides a record of reasoning and students should be encouraged to make notes and express themselves through writing wherever appropriate. These do not have to be in exercise books to begin with. Photographs of whiteboard notes, screen shots of iPad jottings, emails, tweets, blog posts are all relevant. Written records come in many forms, but only need to be analysed for the quality of their content – do they provide evidence of any of the key aims of the History National Curriculum at Key Stage 1 and Key Stage 2?

 Activity

Counterfactual narrative

A genre of writing which is perhaps unique to history in the primary curriculum is counterfactual narrative. Where narrative gives an account of events based on available evidence, counterfactual narrative uses the same available evidence to demonstrate the significance of events which are supported by the evidence by highlighting alternative futures had these not happened. This throws these events into relief. It is a technique frequently found in historical fiction: *Fatherland* by Robert Harris or *The Man in the High Castle* by Philip K. Dick are examples of counterfactual narratives centred around the principle that Nazi Germany was victorious in the Second World War.

A counterfactual narrative might form part of the exploration of a topic. It would invite learners to explore new vocabulary and alternative interpretations of evidence which could be expressed in a variety of textual forms. However, it seems to lend itself very well to a newspaper narrative report which requires some detail and gives scope for first-hand accounts based on evidence. For example, a Year 2 newspaper report praising the alert thinking of a baker and his housemaid who acted swiftly to extinguish a potentially deadly fire on Pudding Lane with supporting quotes from Samuel Pepys and other frightened Londoners who were thankful that no one was harmed. Alternatively, a Year 4 newspaper report exploring the visit of peaceful tourist Hernán Cortez to the vibrant city of Tenochtitlán, complete with expressions of welcome and hope for further co-operation between civilizations by Aztec leader Montezuma II.

 Case study

A Year 6 class preparing for writing – teacher questioning

A Year 6 class was learning about the Viking raid on the Holy Island of Lindisfarne.

The teacher, Liam, had set up a murder mystery scenario. A torso was wearing a monk's habit and had two arrows sticking out of the body.

The children gathered around the 'body' and were asked, 'Who is this? Why were they killed and by whom?'

(Continued)

(Continued)

Children discussed the possibilities and answers were shared. The children knew that this must have taken place in the past. They knew that the body had been moved. They also knew that the body wasn't real.

After discussions involving Robin Hood and Henry VIII, it was finally established that this was a monk and that Vikings had killed him. Liam asked the class why this would have happened. There was a debate and they finally concluded that it was for money.

The above study contains a brief example of different modes of teacher questioning. These are important as they produce very different answers and structure learners' thinking (expressed orally or in writing) very differently. There are two main types of question: closed and open. Closed questions have only one right answer and it is a single piece of information. Sinclair and Coulthard (1979, p 50) have termed this an *IRF* question. *Initiation* is by the teacher, who poses a question. The learner gives a *response*, an answer. The teacher finally gives *feedback* as to whether this is correct or incorrect. There has been much discussion of the IRF sequence; however, in its basic form it is the most common interaction in a classroom and one which has little or nothing to do with learning and much more to do with power, or classroom management. When framed as a *yes* or *no* question it is not an invitation to express a view so much as to work out what the teacher wishes to hear and tell it to them. Teachers ask these questions for a variety of reasons: to regain the attention of wandering eyes at the back of the class, to hurry along those not working at the desired pace, to hold accountable those who transgress the rules of the classroom. All of these may be valid reasons to employ an IRF sequence, but should not be confused with modelling thinking.

At its best, questioning can scaffold the reasoning processes necessary to produce high-quality writing. To get learners to think historically, they must be invited to choose in order to construct their own narrative. And to choose they must be asked open questions. These are questions which do not have one right answer; that have answers which must be justified and distinguished from the other possibilities by the articulation of reasoning processes. Many teachers will automatically recognise the form which such open questions take as those beginning with the six interrogatives – *What, Who, Where, When, Why* and *How*. However, what gives learners the crucial invitation to think for themselves is the addition of a modal verb: *What might … Why could … ;* closed questions deal in certainties; open ones deal in possibilities. For a discipline where learners should be invited to create their own interpretation of the past, the latter are more appropriate.

 Case study

Writing to communicate enquiry

A Year 5 class were conducting a study into their local area, a former mining community. The learners were all born after the final demolition of the mine and so had no memory of it or any architectural evidence of its existence. They were then set homework to ask grandparents about their memories of the colliery and note the answers.

Two children returned with identical stories about their grandfathers. Up until this point they were unaware that they knew each other. The story centred around an accident underground. One of the men injured his hand, the other assisted him. The class shared all their stories and it was agreed by consensus that this was the best story for the class to then base drama on. In groups, the class role-played, then drafted play scripts which focused on the two men: Albert and Ernie.

Each of the play scripts was acted by the groups which had written it and the best one, chosen by class consensus, was performed for recording, with the two grandsons leading the cast. The boys were then given CDs containing the recording to take to their grandfathers. An excerpt is presented below.

Narrator: The two men were putting a chain on a thread to pull the coal. The chain was also attached to the high tension apparatus.

Ernie: This is a very 'eavy chain.

Albert: Aye! Whadya think they're deein' makin' us pull this git heavy chain?

Narrator: Then the two men pulled on the chain, their hands were red raw, their backs aching.

Narrator: The links in the chain were huge, each one was about the size of a grown man's head but weighed much more.

Albert: Whoa!

Narrator: He screamed as the chain sprang backwards. Albert let go of the chain, but Ernie was too slow.

Ernie: Ay-ah!

Narrator: Albert turned around to see his friend's hand wedged in the chain as it moved towards the high tension apparatus.

Albert: Don't worry marra, I'll see you're all right.

While the class used high-level literacy skills to develop several versions of this play, culminating in the one from which these extracts are taken, the focus of the project had a strong history element. Authenticity is a key motivating factor driving the production of these stories. The teacher reported that the children enjoyed adding details which they had been told (such as 'high-tension apparatus'). They particularly enjoyed using the vernacular. The community in former mining village in the North of England where these children were based had a very strong accent and many words rooted in local dialect. Using words like 'git' meaning 'very' or 'marra' meaning 'friend' gave the dialogue a very familiar feel for the children and also gave them some authority as their teacher did not know how to pronounce these, and spellings were negotiated with reference to the group's knowledge of standard phonemes. The children had licence to talk and write in a way which felt more natural than Standard English, a way that linked them with the past of their immediate surroundings.

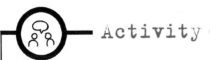

Activity

Exploring local history through digital storytelling

When communicating historical ideas, it is important for the learner to be aware of who is their audience at any given time. This will determine the tenor, mode and register which are chosen to communicate. They should be invited to consider the power relationship between them and their reader, the gaps in the readers' knowledge or understanding.

In the above example a play was an effective way to bring to life a narrative account of the accident. If the purpose of the account was changed, then so would the writing style. If the teacher had developed the activity beyond narrative to a persuasive activity, newspaper reports could be used for the learners to develop persuasive arguments; for example, that the colliery was at fault and that the injured man deserved compensation. Further evidence could be gathered of other injuries to miners (www.dmm.org.uk/names/index_18.htm) and non-chronological reports used to set the story of Ernie and Albert in wider coal-safety context.

Scaffolding for progression

It is a myth that Ofsted wish to see only one kind of history lesson. Although there is a belief based on their experiences among some inspectors that single subject teaching of history leads to better subject knowledge and skills development, this is not in any way enforced and schools remain at liberty to adopt their own teaching practices. What Ofsted really care about is current evidence of meaningful progress being made by every child in the class in the subject. This means teachers have to think carefully about how they support that progress for children. The notion of scaffolding children's activity is a hugely important one; the metaphor is useful as the activity of scaffolding can address multiple needs of learners at once.

> [Scaffolding is] an interactive system of exchange in which the tutor operates with an implicit theory of the learner's acts in order to recruit his attention, reduces degrees of freedom in the task to manageable limits, maintains 'direction' in the problem solving, marks critical features, controls frustration and demonstrates solutions when the learner can recognize them.
>
> (Wood et al., 1976, p 99)

However, frequently teachers do not recognise the description of scaffolding when presented with what Wood et al. originally intended. It is not synonymous with differentiation. It is a dynamic process where attention is recruited, motivation is crucial, and freedom is reduced. In this sense, it is initially freedom to fail by confining the learner's focus to the particular topic or skill identified as the focus of the lesson. Some of these elements take place prior to the lesson; scaffolding through differentiated planning and activity design. Some elements take place during the presentation of key input – a crucial part of scaffolding is teacher modelling of thought processes through verbalisation or shared writing. Other elements take place during independent or group collaborative work where the teacher monitors and interacts with the learners based on their assessment of their needs, for example, to control frustration or improve collaborative working where necessary (Joyce-Gibbons, 2016).

Finally, the teacher summarises – note that the plenary is not intended just as an 'answers session' where the teacher simply gives the answers to the children. Rather, answers are related to the teacher's judgement of the learners' readiness to hear them. In the case of open-ended historical enquiry, it must be made clear that there is no 'right' answer to a question, only interpretations which are better or less well supported by the evidence. Teachers may model their own enquiry processes when deriving their preferred explanation, but this does not make all other interpretations 'wrong' and this one 'right'.

But scaffolding is a recurring process, not just a writing frame. Yes, key vocabulary prompts, storyboards or other tools to structure thought as it is articulated into writing are all very important. But of themselves they will have little impact. Progression is a process of demonstrating that learners can do things independently which they were unable to do without help before, or where they demonstrate that they are able to attempt tasks which have a greater level of challenge while receiving a similar level of support to that which they had in the past. To gauge their progress, teachers must do two things.

1. Provide tasks which give children the opportunity to show they have internalised previously unlearned capabilities: this could be in the form of a task which they complete with less scaffolding than previously or one in which they show adaptation or transferability in a skill they have acquired.

2. Continue to provide scaffolding, but now use this to complete more advanced challenges.

 **Case study**

Reception class finding out about knights

Isla, a Reception teacher, had her class gathered on the carpet. They had been learning about a child-led topic of Knights, Castles and Princesses. In this lesson, Isla explained to the class that they would be learning about the colours that knights wore. She said that the word that describes the colours was 'heraldry'. The class repeated this word to their teacher, each other and their teacher again.

Isla told the children the ten main colours of heraldic design. She wrote these on the interactive whiteboard. They were red, white, blue, green, yellow, brown, purple, orange, black and pink.

She then told them the meaning of each colour and gave the children an action to perform for the meanings. Isla explained that:

* red meant strength and the children gave a growl as they flexed their muscles;

* white meant peace and the children sang a high-pitched chord as they put their hands together as if they were saying a prayer;

* blue meant friendship and the children said 'hello' to each other as they shook hands;

* green meant hope and the children said 'please' as they crossed their fingers;

(Continued)

(Continued)

- yellow meant kindness and the children said 'there you go' as they pretended to offer a gift to one another;

- brown meant a winner and the children said 'I win!' as they fist pumped the air;

- purple meant fairness and the children said 'fair play' as they nodded to each other;

- orange meant the best and the children said 'me' as they pointed to themselves;

- black meant sadness and the children said 'awww' as they pulled a sad face;

- pink meant love and the children said 'oh la la' as they made a love heart with their hands.

Isla then asked the children what each colour meant. She pointed to the colours she had written on the board and wrote the correct meanings as they were given by the children.

The class were then asked which three colours they would choose that best represented them. They shared their chosen colours with each other.

Isla then gave the class a sheet with the outline of a non-gender specific knight on and the children coloured it with their three chosen colours. The more able added labels of colours and meanings.

 **Activity**

Visual character studies

In the case study above the Reception class created a personal character study by using colours. Portraits of historical characters often contain lots of symbolism through colour and objects.

- Choose a painting such as *The Field of the Cloth of Gold* by an unknown artist.

- Why is there a dragon in the sky above Henry VIII?

- What colours does the artist use to show wealth and power?

- Who are the most important people in the painting? Why?

- Could you choose another painting and study it in the same way?

- What writing opportunities does this offer?

Conclusion

The one who does not remember History is bound to live through it again.

(George Santayana)

Santayana's quotation can be found at the entrance to Block 5 of the Auschwitz I camp, the block which displays 'material evidence'. If you have been, then you do not, need an explanation of what this place contains. If you have not then no amount of ink on paper will do it justice. To list the mounds of shoes, the suitcases piled high or the twisted wire of old glasses frames just cheapens the experience of something which must be experienced, if not through primary sources then through less sterile secondary ones than those made of ink and paper. Primary school teachers must take a small but profound share in the responsibility for ensuring their students are not prisoners to their history, but that they are able to shed the shackles of our species' past tragedies. The means by which this is accomplished is through the development of a historical perspective.

The challenge in writing in history is to enable the articulation of balanced and evidence-based explanations of the past: explanations which use the language of possibility, of chronology and of compromise. This will enable children to write and to think in more complex and flexible ways. In doing so, they will be better able to express how they deal with the challenges they face in a complex world.

Recommended texts and websites

Cooper, H. (2014) *Writing History 7–11: Historical Writing in Different Genres*. Abingdon: Routledge.

An excellent work with thought-provoking and technical chapters on genre and oracy. If a learner cannot say it, then they cannot think it, nor can they write it.

Comprehensive sites – covering all curriculum areas and key stages

BBC Schools Age 4–11 – www.bbc.co.uk/schools/websites/4_11/site/history.shtml

Excellent range of multi-media resources for teaching and learning as well as for improving teacher subject knowledge in all history curriculum areas.

British Library Images on Flickr – www.flickr.com/photos/britishlibrary/

A colossal number of digital images covering a vast array of topics.

The British Museum – www.britishmuseum.org/learning/schools_and_teachers/resources.aspx

Excellent site with high-quality resources for the classroom divided by culture and key stage.

Heritage Explorer from Historic England – www.heritage-explorer.co.uk/web/he/default.aspx

A free searchable archive of historic images from throughout British history.

Historical Association – www.history.org.uk/resources/primary_resources_129.html

Perhaps the largest and most relevant resource available on the teaching and learning of history. An excellent organisation to which schools would do well to affiliate to take advantage of publications and resources.

The National Archives – www.nationalarchives.gov.uk/education/

This is a massive site with huge amounts of resources for Key Stage 2 onwards. The thematic collections are particularly impressive. For example, their resources for Crime and Punishment would make the backbone of a thematic study, post-1066.

The Schools History Project – www.schoolshistoryproject.org.uk/Teaching/index.htm

A large number of free resources for all key stages.

Archaeology resources

Canterbury Archaeological Trust – www.canterburytrust.co.uk/learning/schools/

A site with numerous activities for archaeology in the classroom.

Museum of London – www.museumoflondon.org.uk/schools/classroom-homework-resources/

Many archaeological resources for the classroom with relevance outside London.

Wessex Archaeology – www.wessexarch.co.uk/learning

A site with a relevance to school archaeology outside the region. Large number of ideas and in particular a large number of photographic resources for classrooms.

Blogs

And All That – www.andallthat.co.uk/

This UK blog focuses on history teaching in the secondary school. Has an active twitter presence.

Clio et cetera – https://clioetcetera.com/

Michael Fordham's influential and interesting blog covers a wide range of history teaching policy and practice. Has an active Twitter presence.

References

Gaiman, N. (2013) *The Ocean at the End of the Lane*. London: Headline Publishing Group.

Joyce-Gibbons, A (2016) Observe, interact and act: teachers' initiation of mini-plenaries to scaffold small-group collaboration. *Technology, Pedagogy and Education*. DOI: 10.1080/1475939X.2016.1173089

Nichol, J. (2014) Genre and children writing history: reflective and discursive learning and writing. In: Cooper, H. (ed.) *Writing History 7–11: Historical Writing in Different Genres*. Abingdon: Routledge.

Sinclair, J. and Coulthard, M. (1975) *Towards an Analysis of Discourse*. Oxford: Oxford University Press.

Wood, D., Bruner, J.S. and Ross, G. (1976) The role of tutoring in problem solving. *Journal of Child Psychology and Psychiatry*, 17(2): 89–100.

9

writing in music

Adam Bushnell with Heather Jarvis, Emma Anyan and Mark Anyan

Teachers' Standards

Standard 3 - Demonstrate good subject and curriculum knowledge

- have a secure knowledge of the relevant subject(s) and curriculum areas, foster and maintain pupils' interest in the subject, and address misunderstandings
- demonstrate a critical understanding of developments in the subject and curriculum areas, and promote the value of scholarship
- demonstrate an understanding of and take responsibility for promoting high standards of literacy, articulacy and the correct use of standard English, whatever the teacher's specialist subject

Standard 4 - Plan and teach well-structured lessons

- impart knowledge and develop understanding through effective use of lesson time
- promote a love of learning and children's intellectual curiosity

Key questions

- How can music stimulate writing?
- What forms of writing can be created through music?
- How can we ensure quality writing is maintained in cross-curricular subjects?

Introduction

Maintaining high-quality writing across the curriculum is a constant target for teachers. Music can play a significant part in achieving this. As Kenneth Guilmartin, the founder of Music Together, an early childhood music programme, maintains in an online article by Laura Lewis Brown (2016), entitled The Benefits of Music Education (2016): Music learning supports all learning.

Music is a subject that does not have to be limited to specialist teachers. It is a creative subject that can naturally lead to quality creative writing. But a lot of teachers lack confidence in teaching music. Do you enjoy teaching music? Are you a good singer? Teaching music is not just about being able to sing well. Being a good singer does not necessarily make you good at teaching music. Teaching music is more about being able to appreciate what we hear. Teaching music is allowing children to interpret these sounds and create new sounds in their own way either through their voices, hands, feet, musical instruments or any object at all. Children make sounds with their bodies, sticks, toys, bricks – indeed almost anything. They do this confidently and experimentally. We, as teachers, should encourage this and develop the sounds that children are able to create as this can lead to improvement of language and literacy skills.

This chapter will at not only the benefits of teaching music in innovative and creative ways, but also look at the varied writing opportunities that can arise during these lessons.

Picture books or song books?

The Lambton Worm is a legend from the north-east of England. It tells the tale of a boy called John Lambton who went fishing and caught a tiny yet monstrous worm from the River Wear. He threw it down a well and then later went to fight in the Crusades. The worm then grew into a legless dragon and terrorised the local area until Lambton returned and slew the creature.

The worm's name comes from the Saxon word 'wyrm' and the German word 'wurm', both of which mean dragon. It is obviously a fictitious story but it is a legend rather than a myth as it does contain some historical truth. Indeed, the Lambton family are still living in the region to this day. John Lambton was a real Hospitalier Knight of Rhodes in the fifteenth century. But it is not the story that is most famous for locals to the area; rather, it is the traditional folk song.

The reason the story became a song is down to the invention of the pantomime during the Victorian era. The Lambton Worm was performed at the Sunderland Empire with great success.

Lewis Carroll was so inspired by the performance on a visit to Sunderland that many think that the *Jabberwocky* was based on the *Lambton Worm*. (See Brian Talbot's book *Alice in Sunderland* for a detailed study on the subject.)

The *Lambton Worm* is a story and a song. Songs and stories are often interlinked. Many texts, particularly in Early Years and Key Stage 1, are picture books such as *The Gruffalo,* which reads like a song complete with verses and chorus. *We're Going on a Bear Hunt* has all the rhythm, rhyme and sounds of a song for young children.

It is not just Julia Donaldson's and Michael Rosen's books that are like songs either; Giles Andreae, Claire Freedman and Jez Alborough all follow that sing-song style of text. They are written to be read aloud in order to encourage children to join in with them. They are also a good way to promote links between music and literacy. There are alternative versions of *The Gruffalo* available too. Versions are translated into other languages, including Arabic and even Latin. *The Gruffalo in Scots* is also available. Other Scottish versions of famous books include books by Roald Dahl and David Walliams such as *Billionaire Bairn* (Billionaire Boy) and *The Eejits* (The Twits). These are all fascinating examples when looking at dialect and accent, but they are also useful when exploring rhythm and pace in music lessons. The words are changed but the very structure of the story is not. It still *sounds* the same.

Changing the words but keeping the rhythm is a useful skill to teach in writing. It offers children scaffolding for their work but allows them to be creative with what they insert into the framework.

The *Lambton Worm* can be listened to on YouTube. Rather than reading a picture book, this song could be shared with children in the classroom. Alternatively, on the *Traditional Music Library* website, there is a vast collection of songs to choose from. These songs can be used for many writing opportunities not only to change lyrics and study rhythm but also to use for retelling the stories from the songs, inspire new pieces of writing with similar themes or look at language development.

In the case study below the teacher begins with a picture book during a lesson on science, but then goes on to develop children's knowledge using music as the stimulus. All of this culminates in independent writing from the children. It is important that we use books, websites, objects and a range of resources to engage children, and essential that all of this is working towards independent work.

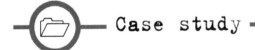 Case study

Year 2 class learning about the life cycle of a butterfly in science

Lorna, a Year 2 teacher, began the lesson discussing *The Very Hungry Caterpillar* by Eric Carle that they had read the previous day. She then read *The Crunching Munching Caterpillar* by Sheridan Cain. The children were encouraged to join in with the story as much as possible with actions and words. They knew the story well and the classroom became very animated. They discussed daily observations previously made in the classroom as they had been keeping real caterpillars in a small, netted tank. Three days earlier the chrysalises had changed into butterflies. Each member of the class had kept a labelled pictorial log of each step from egg to caterpillar to chrysalis to butterfly.

Lorna next played a clip from the *Melody* section of the Cbeebies website entitled *Little Blue Butterfly* to introduce music as an additional stimulus. The clip uses *Rhapsody in Blue* by George Gershwin. Lorna then asked the children what they thought they were going to do next. They all successfully guessed that they were going to release the butterflies, as this is what happens during the clip. Lorna took the class outside and they released the butterflies together.

Once back in the classroom, Lorna asked the children to close their eyes and to recall the moment when the class butterflies were released. The children listened to the music again, but this time without the visual aspect of the clip and then discussed the instruments used and the effect they had. They talked about the volume, intensity and speed of the music and how these elements would perhaps reflect the butterflies' movements after release. Indeed, the butterflies had started slowly and moved faster, just as the music did. She played the music a third time while the children recorded words on to a mind map to describe the flight of the butterflies.

They finally shared these ideas on the carpet. Lorna asked the class first to share any verbs that they may have included and then any adjectives. She wrote these into two labelled columns of the board. The verbs included fluttering, flitting, soaring, hovering, whirling and flapping, and the adjectives included majestic, colourful, beautiful, inspiring, free, happy, unique, fragile and symmetrical. The words were read out and then removed from the board.

The children were given a template in the shape of a butterfly and in one wing asked to write verbs and in the other wing to write adjectives. These could be taken from their own mind maps, from memory or from their own imaginations.

Finally, the lists of verbs and adjectives that the children had written were shared in small groups on the carpet while *Rhapsody in Blue* played in the background. The groups also added new words as they thought of them while the music played on.

 Activity

The case study began with a picture book relevant to the lesson and ended with music that was intended to enhance it. The sharing of the verbs and adjectives in small groups was certainly enhanced by the playing of the music. The children later imagined where their butterflies had gone. This led to a short narrative piece of writing the following morning during a literacy lesson on what happened next to the class butterflies. This was stimulated by questions such as 'Where did they go?', 'Who did they meet?', 'What did they do?'.

- What other writing opportunities could be explored with this class?
- What differentiation could have been used?
- Could the stories be performed with the music as an accompaniment?
- What else could help with the stories' performance?
- What other picture books could have been used?
- How could these activities be adapted for a different topic and a different class?
- How could independent writing be encouraged and developed in this way?

Research focus

Independent writers

In the case study above the teacher removed the words from the board when the children were writing so that they did not simply copy them. In order to help children become independent writers, we need to encourage them to rely less on structures and frameworks. Indeed, the National Strategy in *Primary Support for Writing* (2008, p1) in the *Narrative Fiction* section states.

> *Effective writers are not constrained by predictable narrative structure. Authors and storytellers often modify or adapt a generic structure, e.g. changing chronology by not telling the events in order (time shifts, flashbacks, backtracking). Children can add these less predictable narrative structures to their own writing repertoires.*

However, in the same document, on the same page, it goes on to recommend that, in order to do this, we, as teachers, should *Use some strategies to connect with the reader/listener e.g. use repetition of the same phrase or the same language pattern.*

So, we are recommended to use repetition but less predictable structures. This seems contradictory, but it is not. To help children become independent writers who move away from generic structures that we provide, we should first give them these same structures in order to increase confidence and understanding of narrative stories. Once well versed in working within these frameworks, they will be ready to move away from them and produce more independent and individual pieces of writing.

The poetry of lyrics

In the primary school we can lift the mood of a classroom with a song, and when we encourage children to sing along, then we are helping them to remember the lyrics, thus developing memory. Singing is said to be directly linked with memory as it accesses the pattern recognition part of the right side of the brain. This also stimulates and boosts acetylcholine, a chemical released by nerve cells to send signals to other cells, which also helps with memory retention. According to *The Psychology Encyclopaedia* (2016), *The right hemisphere of the brain neurologically controls the left side of the body and is thought to control spatial tasks, musical and artistic endeavors, body control and awareness, and creativity and imagination.*

By singing lyrics with your class you are helping them to develop their memories but also encourage feelings of positivity. The Alzheimer's Foundation of America has an entire web page dedicated to music therapy in Alzheimer's patients. They say in their article on *Education and Care* (Clair, 2016), that *When used appropriately, music can shift mood, manage stress-induced agitation, stimulate positive interactions, facilitate cognitive function and coordinate motor movements."*

Teachers may feel self-conscious about singing, but the more we do this with children, the more our confidence will grow.

Using popular music can be a useful tool. Websites like azlyrics.com have the lyrics to most modern songs listed alphabetically. Some songs contain some beautiful and poetic language. Songs such as Hozier's *Take Me to Church,* Adele's *Rolling in the Deep* and 2Pac's *Dear Mama* are highly recommended. Lyrics like these can be used as a structure where the children rewrite the song using the same framework, but make changes to nouns, verbs and adjectives. They could also alter the figurative language by making changes to the similes, metaphors, hyperbole, etc.

Modern music is vast and varied, and a popular genre is rap music. Using raps can be a useful writing tool, as the rhymes are not as strict as standard forms of poetry. Rap music contains a lot of half rhymes or alliteration. The theme tune to *The Fresh Prince of Bel-Air* works well for children to write about their own home and school life. They could compare their own lives to that of Will Smith's character.

Writing raps in this way is an opportunity for children to express themselves in a creative way and enhances performance skills.

Finding meanings within lyrics is also good for developing comprehension techniques. Difficult subject areas can be studied by looking at rap songs like Lowkey and Logic's *Relatives*. This song tells the story of the war in Iraq from two very different perspectives. Also, Lowkey's *Long Live Palestine* is another song that looks at a challenging subject area. This song is about the conflicts between Muslims and Jews in the Holy Land.

It is important to remember that the lyrics are the rapper's points of view. A lot of rap music contains swearing, so teacher discretion needs to be used when finding an appropriate song to use with your class.

The lyrics of songs can be a useful writing tool but instrumentals can be equally as rewarding as can be seen in the case study below.

 Case study

A mixed Year 3 and 4 class extending their vocabulary through music with no lyrics

A mixed Year 3 and 4 class had been struggling to use more adventurous vocabulary in their independent writing. David, their teacher, decided to teach creative writing using instrumental music as a stimulus. The focus of the lesson was part of their geography topic of weather. In this particular lesson they were looking at storms.

David wanted his class to fulfil the National Curriculum requirement of *to draft and write by composing and rehearsing sentences orally, progressively building a varied and rich vocabulary and an increasing range of sentence structures* (2014, p29).

David began by introducing a piece of music to the class called *Storm Interlude* by Benjamin Britten explaining that it is from an opera called *Peter Grimes*, which is set in a Suffolk coastal

(Continued)

(Continued)

village. He played the music, encouraging children to close their eyes as they listened. At the end of the piece, he asked the children what instruments were used and why; how the music made them feel; how the music changed as the piece progressed and how this reflected the development of the storm. The children were then provided with a picture of a storm in the centre of an A3 piece of paper as a visual stimulus and were asked, in pairs initially and then independently, to record nouns, verbs and adjectives to describe the storm.

The music played again as they did this. Some of the suggestions were given by David, including lightning, thunder, hail, rain and wind for nouns; boom, thunder, rumble, roar and deafen for verbs; and angry, dark, thundery, violent and loud for adjectives.

The children were then encouraged to use their own ideas and labelled around the picture to create a word mat. These were later used to write descriptive sentences individually. During both writing activities, the labelling and the sentence making, the music played throughout. Most children wrote about a storm at sea, and a few children imagined a storm in their street or town and came up with appropriate words. The music helped the children to become immersed in what they were writing. The improvement in the quality of the vocabulary they used was evident in their independent writing of descriptive sentences.

Classroom ideas for writing opportunities through instrumental music

Vanessa Mae's *Vivaldi Techno* rendition of *Storm* would be a perfect piece of dramatic music to complement writing like that in the case study above, but it could easily be appropriate for writing about tsunamis, earthquakes, volcanoes, etc.

Movie soundtracks from the *Harry Potter, Pirates of the Caribbean* and *Lord of the Rings* series are dramatic and exciting pieces of music that can lead to equally dramatic and exciting writing. James Carter, in his article *Music for Creative Writing* (2016), says, *Playing instrumental tracks as children write will free their minds to wander down some unexpected and creative avenues … Music, like no other stimulus, allows children to get into an unconscious writing state, one in which they don't even realise they are writing as they are so absorbed in the magical process of writing.*

The Literacy Shed website contains a great many animated short films and these can be used for just the audio aspect rather than the visual. We can *listen* to the animations rather than watch them. This has an impact on how we interpret the clip. The short animation *Alma* can be found on the Ghostly Shed and tells the tale of a terrifying doll shop that traps children. The music to complement this narrative begins with the upbeat soundtrack to Disney Pixar's *Up*, then descends into eerie sounds and finishes with the *Up* piece of music once again. Asking children to write what they think the storyline is using only the audio aspect will result in vast and varied responses. Often, when we use an animation or read a story on which the children base their writing, we end up with a whole class set of similar if not even identical storylines. By planning a story through only what they can hear, children will create their own unique narrative stories because they will interpret the sounds in their own way.

Activity

Instrumental music can produce rich and varied writing. From non-fiction descriptions, as with the *Storm Interlude* piece of music, to narrative stories as with *Alma*, the opportunities are vast.

- Which piece of music could you use to complement a writing lesson?

- How will you present the music?

- Will you listen to it only once or will the piece be played several times?

- Will the children write while the music is playing? If so, why?

- What writing do you want to achieve in your lesson?

- What other types of writing could instrumental music complement and enhance?

Case study

Year 5/6 class developing creative writing skills

Sanjay, a teacher of a Year 5/6 class, was looking for a wider range of opportunities to inspire his class to write creatively. The outcome he wanted was a stand-alone piece of writing that would build their confidence in this area. He encouraged children to use their imagination and demonstrate an independent application of skills already taught.

Previously, children had listened to a variety of classical music and discussed how it made them feel and what it made them think of. Answers always varied greatly, which allowed for some truly independent and creative thinking and discussion.

In this lesson Sanjay began by playing Debussy's *Clair du Lune* while the children closed their eyes. After the music had finished, the children talked in pairs about the piece. Sanjay mentioned the beginning, which was slow and lyrical, and then facilitated a discussion about the mood of the piece. The children mostly felt that the mood was solemn at the beginning, although some disagreed, leading to an interesting discussion. The class then tracked the mood of the piece using something similar to an emotions graph, describing the mood at different points of the music as the line of the graph changed. This was a whole class graph that was displayed on the board for all to see. Sanjay asked the children to infer what could be happening if this were a soundtrack to a film. He also asked what the film would be about. This began to give the children an idea for a story. The music would be the soundtrack to their own tale.

Sanjay asked the children who their characters would be and what would they be doing. The whole class began to take notes, recording their ideas on whiteboards. Sanjay next asked how the

(Continued)

(Continued)

characters knew each other and how they felt about each other. More notes were taken. Children began to share ideas about settings and what objects might be important in the story. All the time, the music played on a loop. The answers varied from somebody being ill and being looked after in hospital, to two soldiers preparing their equipment to leave for the Second World War, to a journey to an alien planet. Sanjay modelled his own storyline with characters, setting, objects and a plot to weave these three elements together. After Sanjay had modelled the planning, the children were encouraged to think of their own plot to accompany their own plans. The plot was to follow the changes of mood within the music. Children used the graph on the board to support this and planned their own story. They then wrote independently, using the graph to ensure the plot linked as closely to the music as possible. The results were 30 individual and creative pieces of narrative.

In this case study the teacher was searching for strategies to help his class to write in a more creative way. Ideally, we want children to do this instinctively and independently. Independent writing is something we strive for in the classroom. Shonette Bason's *Squiggle Whilst You Wiggle* is a strategy for the Early Years that involves mark making, letter formation and early writing development, all through music. The children listen to music and respond in their own way. There are some examples of sessions on YouTube that show the strategy in action. If we start using music as a stimulus in the Early Years and continue this throughout the primary school, as in the case study above with a Year 5/6 class, then this will result in more independent and original pieces of writing being produced on a more regular basis.

Research focus

Essential music

The DfE states in the National Literacy Strategy document *Developing Early Writing* (2001, p151) that *some children find drawing patterns in time to music helpful. Arches can be formed to slow, relaxed music and the tempo can be changed to a marching rhythm and children encouraged to produce angled movements.*

The strategy goes on to state: *In early Foundation Stage, while children are working at step 1 of Progression in phonics (learning to listen to, and discriminate between, sounds in their environment, in music and in rhyme) they will also be developing the three basic handwriting movements using gross and fine motor control* (p153).

In the Early Years, music is an essential partner to writing. It helps children to develop their literacy and language skills in a creative way. According to Laura Lewis Brown in her article on The benefits of music education (2016), the effect of music education on language development can be seen in the brain.

> 'Recent studies have clearly indicated that musical training physically develops the part of the left side of the brain known to be involved with processing language, and can actually wire the brain's circuits in specific ways. Linking familiar songs to new information can also help imprint information on young minds'.

Mary Luehrisen, executive director of the National Association of Music Merchants (NAMM) Foundation, agrees with this link between music and language and is quoted in Brown's same article (2016).

> A music-rich experience for children of singing, listening and moving is really bringing a very serious benefit to children as they progress into more formal learning ... When you look at children ages two to nine, one of the breakthroughs in that area is music's benefit for language development, which is so important at that stage.

Music in myths from all over the world

The Aztecs believed that Quetzacoatl, the feathered snake, was the god responsible for bringing music to the world. According to the myth, the world was once utterly silent. Quetzocoatl stole music from the sun god and filled the world with every sound that we now hear, from the wind in the trees to the lapping of waves to the roar of thunder. The animals heard this music and copied the sounds, interpreting it in their own way. The story states that the god also taught people to listen to this music from both nature and the animals. He taught men and women to mimic the sounds in their own way through singing. He then taught people to make musical instruments using the natural world around them. Branches became flutes, shells became blow horns, skins became drums and seed pods became shakers. So the Aztecs celebrated this gift to the world and made music as often as they could.

If we were to ask children to create musical instruments out of what was around them then they would not necessarily use the same sources at the Aztecs did. They would most likely use bottles, cans, boxes, elastic bands and a whole range of recycled materials.

Using instruments to complement their writing can produce effective results; for example, when characters are travelling in a narrative story this could be accompanied by the strumming of a home-made guitar. When a witch cackles in a character description there could be screeching from a recycled box violin. If a volcano explodes in a non-chronological report, then a plastic drum could boom. When children are describing a product they have designed with persuasive language there could be a noise from a shaker every time the product's name is mentioned. This technique can be applied to all genres of writing.

Myths like this Aztec one have inspired composers to create new pieces of music. The Russian composer Mussorgsky wrote *A Night on the Bare Mountain,* based on the folklore around the witch Baba-Yaga Bony Legs. His piece *The Hut on Fowl's Legs* is inspired by the witch's home. In the myths Baba Yaga lives in a triangular-shaped hut that stands upon giant chicken legs. If the witch is in danger, then she hides inside her house, which then runs away

Children could design their own house inspired by this myth accompanied by the music inspired by it. There could be cottages with birds' wings, blocks of flats covered in scales, or houses with eyes. They could also design Hallowe'en houses based upon the Baba Yaga house.

Another piece of music that would complement some scary writing is the French composer Saint-Saëns' *Danse Macabre*. Children could imagine skeletons dancing with one another while the music plays and then try to describe the dance of the dead. This music could be compared to the carnival music from South America during the Day of the Dead celebrations. The children could watch the opening to the James Bond film *Spectre* to give a visually rich example of this. *Danse Macabre* is quite an upbeat dramatic piece that conjures images of twirling dancers moving in a very balletic style, whereas the carnival music for the Day of the Dead contains fast-paced percussion, blazing whistles and blasting trumpets. The overall effect is a quite different one from the French piece; therefore, the style of writing that can be produced from each will be just as varied.

Offenbach's *Orpheus in the Underworld* overture is based on the classical Greek myth. It tells the story of a musician who travels to the Underworld to get back his recently deceased bride from Hades, the god of the dead. The music is sombre, reflecting the sad story that unfolds. Listening to this would certainly not result in stories with happy endings. It is a tragic tale of bereavement and loss, and the writing that children will produce by using this will be of a similar style. Whatever writing you want as the outcome, the music has to match the mood.

The Nutcracker, a Russian Christmas story by Tchaikovsky, is a two-act ballet with a very magical feel to it. The music can lead to stories with an equally magical theme as can be seen in the case study below.

 Case study

The Nutcracker with a Reception class

Grace read the story of *The Nutcracker* by Jane Ray to her class. The illustrations were shared on each page and the story discussed as key parts occurred. In it, a nutcracker toy is magically brought to life to rescue a young girl from a swarming colony of rats that try to attack her. It was almost time to break up for the Christmas holidays, so Grace had timed her festive story very well. It was met with great enthusiasm.

They then listened to Tchaikovsky's *Dance of the Sugar Plum Fairy* from the *Nutcracker Suite*. Grace asked if they knew which part of the story the music came from. After several answers, the class guessed it was the dance in the magical land towards the end of the story.

Grace then asked her class what their favourite part of the story was and the resounding answer was the part when the nutcracker saved the girl. She then showed them a stuffed elephant and explained that this was her toy from childhood. She next asked if the children slept with a cuddly toy. The children shared their answers, which mainly involved cuddly bears and other such animals. She then asked the class if they would like their toy to come to life as the nutcracker had in the story. All of the class agreed that this would be fun, with only some of the children saying that they wanted their toys to come to life for a little while as they might get eaten by dinosaurs, crocodiles or tigers.

Grace also told the class that her elephant sometimes came to life and did lots of crazy things. The class did not believe her, so Grace showed them a short computer-generated television advert from France called *Idents* from the advert shed on the Literacy Shed website. She kept it muted so the children could only see the visual and not hear the audio. It began with elephants sky diving and Grace said that this was her cuddly toy playing with his friends. The advert then went on to show a tortoise at a skate park, ostriches on a roller-coaster ride, and other animals doing crazy things. This was met with a lot of laughter.

Grace asked her class to draw pictures of their own cuddly toys doing similar activities. There were bears with jet packs, dragons playing musical instruments and football-playing fishes. The children were then asked to label their pictures with sounds that the animals would be making. Grace told the class that they should use their phonic knowledge to sound out the noises. There were labels like 'weeeeee', 'whooooooosh' and 'brrrrrrrrrrrmmmm'. She brought the class to the carpet and the sounds and pictures were shared. She asked if these sounds were loud or quiet and all of the children agreed that these were loud sounds. She drew an exclamation mark on the board and some of the children recognised it. She explained that this was to show something exciting that happens in a book, but also to indicate that something was said loudly. The class added exclamation marks to their own sounds and the more able turned these into sentences. *Dance of the Sugar Plum Fairy* played in the background throughout. The class finally shared their work with each other and begged Grace to show them the advert once again.

Activity

The lesson in the case study above used a mixture of storytelling, animation and music to inspire a phonics-based activity. This could then be extended using storyboards to plan and develop a narrative story in the first person about what happens when toys come to life. The children could have planned a beginning, middle and end, both pictorially and with words. The storyboards could then have been used to support individual writing differentiated as appropriate by the teacher.

- What story could you use in a similar way that is linked to a piece of music?

- How can you adapt the approach in the case study to meet the needs of your children?

- What visual literacy could be linked to the story and the music?

- How will you differentiate to meet the needs of all of the children?

Research focus

Motivation and confidence

Michael Morpurgo was a teacher before his career developed into being an award-winning author and British Children's Laureate. In Louise Holden's article Wicked writing lessons for children in the Irish Times (2013) Morpurgo states: *I think I picked up very early on in my career as a teacher that the two most important things to get children writing are motivation and confidence - seeing that their work is being treated with respect.*

If children know that we, as teachers, think that their writing has value and is important, then they will believe it too. Building up plans for writing in a structured way that works towards a piece

(Continued)

(Continued)

of writing is key. By giving children a stimulus, such as music or animation, to aid their writing, step by step, then eventually we build their confidence. They can be successful step by step. As they progress through the school and see that they are making progress in their writing, this will naturally develop their confidence in this area. The DfE (2012) maintains that we should *scaffold the process, enabling children to concentrate on certain aspects of writing without having to deal with all the others simultaneously, and work effectively towards independent writing* (p12). It goes on to state: *Children's confidence in writing will grow from aiming for and achieving success* (p20).

Strategies such as those examined in this chapter will help children achieve this success and feel proud of their writing.

Conclusion

Music is all around us, from adverts on television to soundtracks on films. It is played in shops, in lifts, in shopping centres, in waiting rooms, in coffee shops and restaurants. According to the Aztecs, it can be heard in nature, at all times. Children experience music in their lives on a daily basis. As such, it is impossible to ignore and can lead to vast and varied writing opportunities. As primary teachers we need to embrace every opportunity to make high-quality writing a habit in our classrooms. Music can help us to do this. Whether you think of yourself as a musician or singer should not affect whether you use music as a stimulus for writing in the classroom. Music is indeed all around us and we can use it to our and our children's advantage.

━━ Recommended websites ━━

A – Z Lyrics – www.azlyrics.com

Alma – www.literacyshed.com/the-ghostly-shed.html

Idents advert – www.literacyshed.com/the-advert-shed.html

The Little Blue Butterfly – www.bbc.co.uk/cbeebies/shows/melody

Squiggle Whilst You Wiggle – www.youtube.com/watch?v=2_33d5Vtx1Y

━━ References ━━

Carter, J. (2016) *Music for Creative Writing*. Available from: www.teachprimary.com/learning_resources/view/music-for-creative-writing

Clair, A. (2016) *Education and Care*. Alzheimer's Foundation of America. Available from: www.alzfdn.org/EducationandCare/musictherapy.html

Dahl, R. (2008) *The Eejits*. Edinburgh: Itchy Coo.

DfE (2001) *Developing Early Writing*. London: DfE.

DfE (2008) *The National Strategies: Primary Support for Writing*. London: DfE.

Donaldson, J. (2012) *The Gruffalo in Scots*. Edinburgh: Itchy Coo.

Holden, L. (2013) *Wicked Writing Lessons for Children*. Available from: www.irishtimes.com/news/education/wicked-writing-lessons-for-children-1.1565879

Lewis Brown, L. *The Benefits of Music Education*. Available from: www.pbs.org/parents/education/music-arts/the-benefits-of-music-education/

Right brain hemisphere. (2016) *Right Brain Hemisphere*. Available from: http://psychology.jrank.org/pages/545/Right-Brain-Hemisphere.html

Ray, J. (2015) *The Nutcracker*. London: Orchard Books.

Talbot, B. (2007) *Alice in Sunderland*. London: Random House.

Walliams, D. (2015) *Billionaire Bairn*. Edinburgh: Itchy Coo.

10
writing in physical education
Jonathan Doherty

Teachers' Standards

Standard 3 - Demonstrate good subject and curriculum knowledge

- have a secure knowledge of the relevant subject(s) and curriculum areas, foster and maintain pupils' interest in the subject, and address misunderstandings
- demonstrate a critical understanding of developments in the subject and curriculum areas, and promote the value of scholarship
- demonstrate an understanding of and take responsibility for promoting high standards of literacy, articulacy and the correct use of standard English, whatever the teacher's specialist subject

Standard 4 - Plan and teach well-structured lessons

- impart knowledge and develop understanding through effective use of lesson time
- promote a love of learning and children's intellectual curiosity

 **Key questions**

- How do we show children that writing is a tool to support thinking and learning in physical education?
- In what ways can we inspire children to want to write during PE lessons?
- How can we include writing in PE without taking time away from children being physically active?

Introduction: physical education in the lives of children

There can be no doubt as to the significance of movement, health and physical education in the lives of children. Being physical is the first expression of how children play. Physical competency is an important feature in social acceptance for all ages, and around the world every culture engages in spontaneous and rule-governed physical activity (Bailey, 1999). It provides real contexts to learn about fairness, competition and sportsmanship. Its emphasis on the body and how it moves increases strength, speed, stamina and physical responsiveness. It provides content knowledge about how to be fit and active, and have good mental and physical health. PE develops skills which are not only physical, such as problem-solving, decision-making, creative thinking, strategising and evaluating (Doherty, 2003), but it also fosters qualities of independence, tolerance, empathy and coping strategies to deal with success and failure.

In short, PE is about what children can do, what they know and what they understand (Doherty and Brennan, 2008).

The aims of PE in the National Curriculum (DfE, 2013b) are to:

- *develop competence to excel in a broad range of physical activities*
- *be physically active for sustained periods of time*
- *engage in competitive sports and activities*
- *lead healthy, active lives.*

(DfE, 2013b, p1)

PE is a learning-focused subject. It is the only curriculum subject that focuses on the body and allows children to learn *in* and *about* the physical. Children move to learn and learn to move through taught PE experiences. It provides opportunities to apply their knowledge and skills in a variety of activities and learning situations. Pickup (2012) argues that certain aspects of physical education are unique. It provides unique challenges, and the environments of the hall, the playground, the school fields and the swimming pool create interactive learning environments for dynamic, multi-sensory learning. PE has a valuable contribution to make to cross-curricular learning, through subjects such as ICT, mathematics and science. But can the experiences for children to be active, to interact with others and to solve problems through movement provide opportunities for classroom writing? They certainly can.

Writing in PE

Of all the subjects in the curriculum, PE may seem the least likely to provide opportunities for children's writing. Traditionally, teachers may not have included writing in PE lessons, perhaps seeing it as a practical 'doing' subject. Teachers already use speaking and listening to good effect in PE lessons (Wyatt-Smith and Gunn, 2007). For example, to give instructions: 'Stand still. Freeze'. To give feedback and praise: 'Well done, Imran, that was such a great attacking shot to play. Great follow through'. When teaching a new skill: 'Today in Athletics we are going to learn two ways of jumping for height', or when making a valuable teaching point to support learning: 'Keep your toes straight, please at the end of that balance, Kari'. Opportunities for discussion, for planning and making observation judgements, to give encouragement to a teammate, very commonly involve children in speaking and listening. Is the same true for writing in PE? Author of *Writing in the Physical Education Class*, Edward Behrman (2004), offers plenty of possible genres for writing in physical education.

diaries journals letters editorials summaries descriptions explanations critiques problem-solving predictions various forms of creative writing advertisements brochures visual displays analysis argumentation

Activities to get children writing in PE

- Keep a journal for half a term on how you are improving in games.
- Have a class competition to write a paragraph on why it is important to act fairly when playing sport.
- Describe how much effort you put into your athletics lesson today and how it made you feel.
- Search the Internet for a piece of news on keeping healthy and describe this.
- Work with a partner. List three ideas to improve each other's performance in gymnastics.
- Write about the dance composition you performed in today's lesson.
- Create an information leaflet on why PE and sport is good for you.
- Write the fixture list for the netball team's matches and post on the school noticeboard.
- Do a diary entry for a month on your training for a running race.
- Post a 'question for the class' on a health- or sport-related issue.
- Research a sport and create a small information booklet about it.
- Email a friend in another school and have a discussion about a sports event you are going to be both involved in.

- For homework, choose one physical activity in the outdoors and write about how you can keep yourself and others safe in it.

- Create a set of Task Cards for gymnastics that illustrate a set of balances you are practising and add teaching points to perform it well.

- Reflect on how your team co-operated well in games this week.

- Write out the rules and scoring of Kwik Cricket.

- Use an ICT package to design certificates of participation for sports events to take home.

- Design health and nutrition word searches.

- Devise a poster with a written commentary to market a game of your choice.

- Groups design orienteering courses around the school grounds writing fitness words as markers. Try out each other's courses.

- Use graphical organisers to structure thinking about tactics and strategies in games. One good idea is the K–W–L chart where children write what they know in the first column K; what they want to know in the second column W, and what they have learned after teaching in the third column L.

- Watch a DVD and analyse a top athlete in competition and make notes on an iPad.

- Create a termly newsletter for parents on PE and sports.

Literacy and PE go together

Literacy and PE are two words that have been separate for too long. Given the importance of literacy in the curriculum, it makes complete sense to connect literacy and PE. The importance of literacy as a life skill is captured by UNESCO (2004) who described literacy as the ability to identify, understand, interpret, create, communicate, compute and use printed words in different contexts. Literacy is the glue that binds so much of the primary curriculum together and we see it across the subjects in the curriculum. Neither is it a static concept reserved for English. Literacy offers multiple experiences and many subjects (for example, digital literacy in ICT) already demonstrate their connection to literacy. Physical education is no exception.

 ─── Research focus ───────────

Physical literacy

Physical literacy can be described as the motivation, confidence, physical competence, knowledge and understanding to value and take responsibility for engagement in physical activities for life (Whitehead, 2016). Fundamental movements such as running, jumping, kicking, throwing and climbing are developed in the activity areas of PE, along with knowledge and understanding of these activities

(Continued)

(Continued)

across the primary age phase. School PE is further supported by parents and carers, by coaches and involvement in extra-curricular clubs in school and sports clubs in the community. The Youth Sport Trust (2013) describe it as the motivation, confidence, physical competence, knowledge and understanding that gives children the foundation for moving and joining in physical activities as competent and healthy movers for life. Their framework has been designed to support sport provision in schools. It is not a programme but an outcome of any structured PE and school sport provision. Physical literacy in Key Stage 1 is about creating movement experiences as a foundation to underpin lifelong participation in physical activity as confident movers. In Key Stage 2 it is about adapted physical activities to develop and apply skills in different contexts to enhance social and creative thinking skills.

Games dominate the PE curriculum. The idea of 'games literacy' has emerged (Mandigo and Holt, 2004) and this offers much potential for children's writing. Being literate in games is about understanding a wide range of games and knowing their rules, tactics with levels of skill to enable successful play. This approach takes a much more holistic view of games. Normally, this is introduced thematically across the genre of games in PE of striking/fielding, net/wall and invasion. Understanding is key here and teachers can use this approach not only to teach a new game but also to assess children's understanding of it. One approach is to take this further and set the task of having children devising their own games. You can then ask the children to write about their game and describe the aims, rules, equipment needed and scoring, etc. In the case study below we meet Gemma who links games to instructional writing.

 Case study

Inventing games

Gemma wanted her Year 5 class to devise games which involved limited amounts of apparatus and in doing so to create opportunities for cooperative learning and talk. She divided the 30 children into six groups of five and provided each with different apparatus, including posts, hoops, large or small balls, bats, poles and beanbags. She asked the children to use their pieces of equipment to make up a game which would involve everyone in the group and which could be played competitively.

The children were allowed a short time to discuss possibilities and then were urged to try out their games and agree on rules as the need arose. Once they had played a game and established some basic rules, they were paired with another group and took turns to explain their games to each other. The groups then swapped apparatus and tried to play each other's games. Sometimes Gemma stopped the class and asked groups to get together again to explain rules or agree to change them if their partner group had found flaws or had ideas for improvement. Back in the classroom, after the PE lesson, Gemma asked each group to discuss their games and then write a list of instructions for playing and devising a scoring system. She explained that in the next PE lesson the rules would be given to groups who had not yet tried the games and they would use them to learn how to play. She emphasised that it was important to be clear and concise if other groups were to understand and be able to play properly.

In the next lesson, groups were asked to get out the pieces of apparatus they had used for their games and set them up ready for another group to play. An enlarged copy of the instructions and rules was provided and the groups moved to a set of equipment and were given five minutes to read and discuss the instructions before attempting the games. Once they had played for ten minutes, they were paired with groups who had played each other's games and were asked to feed back on the quality of the instructions and make suggestions on how to make them clearer and improve the games.

Throughout the school year, Gemma used some series of PE lessons in this way and found that children became increasingly conscious of the features of good instructional writing as well as enjoying creating increasingly imaginative and complex games.

Getting physically ready to write

The marks that children make and their first scribbles are the beginnings of the essentials they need in order to write (Bruce and Spratt, 2008). Getting ready to write is very much part of children's physical development, but if children are required to 'write' formally before developmental processes of bone differentiation and the necessary growth of the wrists and fingers take place, the result is frustration and inhibition in achievement (Maude, 2001).

Writing involves a number of physical and perceptual skills. Some of these might not appear immediately obvious such as oculomotor functioning and visual-motor integration, which are needed to track words and follow print on a page (these are the same skills needed in reading). Good posture is important to support the writing position and stability to maintain a controlled core. Muscle development of the shoulder girdle, along with development of the wrists, hands and fingers, are essential in order to write. Physical growth proceeds from the centre of the body outwards, called proximo-distal development, and is followed by later development of the smaller extremities like the hands and fingers (Doherty and Hughes, 2009).

 Research focus

Writing is as easy as ABCDE

This stands for A = Attention; B = Balance; C = Coordination; D = Developmental Readiness for Education. Research suggests that many as half of primary children have an underlying problem with undeveloped physical skills, which are linked to academic underachievement. Sally Goddard Blythe's work (2009) confirms the variations in the ages at which children are developmentally and neurologically ready to write. Boys are often later than girls in developing fine motor and language skills and the ability to sit still. Children born prematurely or those who are summer-born can be between 9 and 12 months younger than their peers in terms of neurological development. Children who are delayed in their physical development need more time in general physical activities before being ready to integrate fine motor and visual integration tasks. In other words, they may not be quite ready to read and write. Teachers will be very aware of the visible signs of development difficulties when children are writing; for example, difficulties in paying and

(Continued)

(Continued)

sustaining attention and sitting still. Their receptive and expressive language is behind expectations. They may use an immature grip to hold their pencil. Body awareness and coordination is poor. Blythe's research shows that children who walked late and usually did not pass through the crawling on their front stage had difficulties in writing and copying. Crossing the midline means that the hand is able to spontaneously move over to the other side of the body to work there, as is needed in writing. Crossing the midline is essential in transferring information across the body to coordinate learning and movement. Goddard's intervention work on the INPP Schools' Programme 2000-2005, which involved over 1,000 children, resulted in significant improvements in children's physical skills, including writing, and in behaviour, concentration and self-confidence. She is a strong advocate for movement experiences and daily physical education for all children.

Classroom ideas for supporting early writing

Teachers can support early writing using ideas like the following.

- Use Doodle Sticks and Wiggle Sticks with young children to increase kinaesthetic proficiency.
- In gymnastics, create apparatus layouts to facilitate children's crawling movements using large boxes, tunnels and soft play equipment.
- Develop upper body strength through increased opportunities to hang and climb on apparatus.
- Increase grip strength and finger dexterity by offering a range of malleable materials like plasticine, clay and dough to play with.
- Squeeze sponges to help grip strength.
- Include baking activities with whisking, stirring and mixing to develop fine motor strength.
- Improve the pincer grip through use of pegs, chopsticks and squirty bottles.
- Playing with padlocks, pegboards, laces and buttons improves fine motor control.
- Let children play with sock puppets to increase their wrist dexterity.
- Building blocks, jigsaws, threading and weaving develop hand–eye coordination.
- Provide opportunities for finger painting and writing in sand to develop finger isolation.

Writing and movement

Movement is highly important to children in PE through the areas of *stability* (e.g. balancing, bending, rolling, turning, swinging); *manipulation* (e.g. handling, throwing and catching, kicking, volleying) and *locomotion* (e.g. running, hopping, sliding, bouncing, jumping and skipping). In PE, movement is the key to all learning. It integrates the brain and body and anchors information into the brain's neural networks. It is a choreography of our neurobiological systems and involves memory, cognition, attention, fine and gross movement systems, balance and sensory-motor systems (Jensen, 2000). Movement provides an immediate sense of pleasure and through it we can express feelings.

Physical education is ideally placed to allow children to explore movement and develop a repertoire of movements like a range of different writing styles, whether holding a balance on one leg in gymnastics or feeling the rush of propelling oneself through water while swimming.

Hannaford (1995) believes movement is an indispensable part of learning and thinking. She sees each movement as a sensory-motor event that is linked to learning and develops what she calls an *action encyclopedia* (1995, p107). Each letter and number has movement attached where shapes are imprinted in our muscle memory so they can be repeated and elaborated upon. It is through movement that we put thinking creatively into words and actions. An excellent way for children to link the two is through *Write Dance*. Developed originally in Holland, this programme uses music and movement to introduce handwriting to children. Write Dance movements are designed to help children feel happy with their bodies, improve their motor skills and provide a strong foundation for writing. Read how one teacher took this on board with his class.

 **Case study**

Write Dance with Reception

Tom is in his second year of teaching Reception. He was keen to develop early writing with his class, but had observed that a number of children had very poor writing skills and seemed to lack motivation when it came to mark-making. He heard about Write Dance and was keen to try it out. In a geography-based theme the children had learnt about volcanoes. Before the planned lessons, his Teaching Assistant, Tina, gathered together the music CD and the ribbons and scarves the children would need to move with. She collected shaving foam, gloop and paints to further encourage their creativity and mark-making In addition, she collected chalks and crayons to 'scrimble' with on large pieces of A1 paper. (Scrimbling are the doodle and scribble marks in Write Dance the children experiment with while they listen to the music).

In the first lesson, Tom played some music to set the tone and fire the children's imagination. The children joined in and made exciting movements in the air with their arms and waved their scarves or ribbons about. They experimented with different actions here, bending and swirling with their bodies to show the volcano beginning to erupt. The best bit was the eruption when they threw their arms about in all directions to symbolise the lava

In the next lesson, Tom read them a short story about volcanoes which had finger actions for the children to do, and gave out the paper for them to scrimble on. They repeated the large movements from before, but this time on paper using crayons and chalks as they listened to the music again. The children had made a host of semi-circles, wavy lines and straight long and short lines to capture the volcano building to eruption. In the third lesson, Tom and Tina gave the children choice of paints and large paper again and by the end of the lesson the sheets were covered in an array of colourful volcanoes with straight and curvy lines, dashes and dots. This was PE in the classroom and the beginnings of writing.

Write Dance is an easy and enjoyable way to motivate children to write. The patterns children make in the air can be used in a number of other ways to build essential pathways in their brains to help with writing. Here are some more ideas.

Classroom ideas for writing and movement

- Play the *Alphabet Soup Game*. The teacher holds up a picture of a letter. Children say the letter and mimic its shape with arm movements, e.g. M, Z, A, X, C.

- Play *Mirror Me*. Two children face each other and copy each other's arm movements slowly and accurately.

- *Ringer Aerobics*. Sit beside a partner at a desk. Spread both hands on the table in front. Take turns to lift different fingers off and leave the others where they are. Do it in sequences, bending and stretching fingers.

- Choose speech marks and punctuation. Select physical gestures to accompany them. Extend this to the teacher reading a story as the class listen and add the punctuation physically to accompany.

- Trace letters in the air: one finger; one finger of each hand simultaneously; right arm; left arm; both hands together.

- Individually trace the key words of a lesson in the air as above.

- Write the key words of a lesson on a partner's back with one finger. Guess the word!

- Air write different letters and say their names aloud.

- Play *What's in a Name*? Stand in a circle and write your first name in the air with your elbow. Your middle name with the other elbow, and your last name with the foot and mum or dad's name with your head.

From the spoken to the written word

Communicating language through movement is a key element of physical education. Its effectiveness is seen in linking language with action. Hopper et al. (2003) agree that the rich potential of PE for developing children's understanding and use of language should be exploited. They recommend this happening through children's own descriptions of their work and judging others, feedback given, questions they ask, and through planning and evaluating. All of these are opportunities to develop spoken and written language.

Maude (2001) introduced us to the language-movement triangle of early movement, language and PE. She argues that language is an important factor in becoming physically educated and that PE is an important medium for language enhancement. There are at least nine categories of vocabulary that contribute to language and PE development:

Body awareness vocabulary – e.g. legs, arms, ankles, feet

Environment vocabulary – e.g. hall, gym, pitch, court, track, pool

Resource/apparatus – e.g. beanbag, ball, quoit, javelin, bat

Spatial vocabulary – e.g. over, under, above, beside, through

Temporal vocabulary – e.g. slowly, accelerate, pause, stop

Motor skills vocabulary – e.g. climb, vault, dive, traverse, float

Movement quality – e.g. fluently, lightly, with extension

PE vocabulary – e.g. skill, apply, evaluate, improve

PE activity-specific – e.g. teams, inversion, sequence, choreography.

Dance and gymnastics are fine examples of this because both focus on the skills of body management. Children's use of movement language in both provide excellent opportunities for writing. Identification and naming of body parts, describing actions, commenting upon performance and reflecting on one's own performance are examples of writing to use in these two areas of PE.

In gymnastics, movement activities build upon the fundamental and natural movements of childhood and centre around basic actions of travelling, balancing, jumping, rolling, turning, hanging, swinging and climbing activities. Work is progressed by taking the actions on the floor on to apparatus or performing the same skills with more quality or an extension, such as performing a handstand with legs apart or joining several movements together in a sequence. Much PE-specific language learning happens through teachers' talk, and this is a good way for children to hear and later use and write language specifically related to gymnastics. Much task-setting uses directional language, 'Put the mat here, Jodi'; spatial language: 'Use the space around the wall-bars too, Ben', and temporal language: 'How many ways of rolling can you find in 20 seconds?' All of these are useful precursors to children using this vocabulary in their writing.

High-quality gymnastics is about movement performance and understanding how to improve, and here there is an excellent opportunity to develop the precise language of observation and assessment in writing. When children understand about movement, they are much better equipped to be able to analyse it. Gymnastics provides a super medium for children to write their own self-assessments. Here is an example of Mark's writing about his gymnastics learning on a unit of work on Flight Year 4.

> *I liked doing Flight. I learnt how to jump up and land safe. I did well. My teacher said it was good because I kept my legs straight. And I landed quietly. I am working on getting better at this. I liked going through the air. It was cool.*

Children's written observations are often accompanied by illustrations and, as their spoken and movement vocabulary increases, the quality of their assessment improves. Teachers might find it helpful to provide a template for older children to focus their writing. Something along the lines as that provided by Maude (2001, p80) for Robert aged 11 is useful and is shown below.

Dance draws upon the creative aspect of movement and Action Words like those shown below can be used as a stimulus for dancing.

creep	expand	crumble	push	spread	zig-zag
crawl	explode	slither	stamp	pounce	twist
shake	dart	flop	whip	shrivel	sway
leap	pause	dive	drag	burst	hover

Table 10.1 *My gymnastics assessment on linking and sequences*

What I was taught	What I achieved	What I will try to learn next
To link gymnastic actions	Linking jumps, rolls, balances and travel	To include unusual twists as links
To make a sequence of 6 linked actions	Jump half turn (1), lower to sit to shoulder balance (2), fish flop to front lie, dish roll (3), press up to front support jump to feet, kettle stand (4), 3 travelling bunny jumps, forward roll (5), run and leap (6), lower to end in crouch	To make my sequence more dynamic and exciting by going from high to low twice and by balancing upside down on my hands
To include contrast in speed, direction, body shape and levels in sequence	I included fast and slow, high and low, forwards and backwards	I need to include more asymmetry in my body shapes
To teach my partner	To watch my partner and say it was good	Learn how to help my partner to link more smoothly
To assess my own work to improve it	I learnt to listen to my landings and make them quieter and to keep my sequence going	I need to make each action perfect as well as keeping my sequence flowing

Such a list of action words could be given to children on flashcards to choose up to three and then compose a short dance form. Young children might write one word and perform that action individually. Older children enjoy writing their own list of words. Try the following activity. Link together a short dance motif from the words *Stretch Roll, Explode*. Combining two contrasting words often results in quite dynamic movement responses. Get children to devise these and write them for themselves before performing them; for example, *Run and Balance; Slither and Explode*. Try *Tip-toe and Freeze*. Action words can be extended to action phrases and these can be written. A typical such phrase might be, 'I can jump high, curl up small and then roll slowly'. Here we not only have the action words but also describing words about the action and how it is being performed. This helps to build a movement vocabulary in exactly the same way as the spoken word. Movement categories combine Action (what the body is doing); Dynamics (how it is moving); Space (where it is moving) and Relationships (who it is moving with), which are common to both gymnastics and dance.

Obvious extensions are longer texts. Poetry is often used as a stimulus for dance. Children can write their own poems and develop movement content ideas into phrases to perform. Poems often contain vivid language and children enjoy collecting their own anthologies that they have written and performed in PE. Stories can be made up from movement words and when children's imaginations are encouraged might involve dragons, pirates, magic kingdoms and so on. In history, the Greek myths provide a rich source of material for story-writing, as the case study with a Year 2 class describes.

 **Case study**

Year 2 class telling a story through physical activity

Greek myths such as Perseus and Medusa or Theseus and the Minotaur have been captivating people for centuries. They follow clear structures and frequently use triadic rules for characters, objects and settings. Teachers often use them for retelling opportunities. By using actions in the telling it can help children to remember the key points in the story, so making the retelling that much easier.

Julie, a Year 2 teacher, read her class a version of the story of Medusa by Anthony Horowitz in the hall during a PE lesson. The children sat on mats while their teacher sat on a storytelling chair. After each main event in the story, the teacher paused and got the children to use physical action to re-enact what had just happened. When Perseus met the three Grey Sisters the children scrabbled and crawled around the hall. When he sailed across the sea, they rowed imaginary boats. When he flew, they pretended to fly. When he slashed with his sword, they did the same. Each major part of the story was given a different action. The whole of the hall was used.

The story has many potential actions. Julie broke the story into around 12 distinct sections. After each section, the children returned to the story space created by the chair and the mats.

The children then recorded the story using a storyboard. This was differentiated in three ways.

1. The less able recorded their story through six images and labelled them with six actions they performed.

2. The middle ability groups used both pictures and more complete sentences over nine boxes.

3. The more able wrote in sentences to retell the story using all 12 actions as prompts for their writing.

Just as this story inspired this Year 2 class to write, sport is highly motivating for many children and an excellent stimulus for writing. The Olympic Games provides such a stimulus with a Year 6 class.

 **Case study**

Year 6 class writing about the Olympic Games

A Year 6 class had been studying the Olympics both past and present. They had researched, using laptops and books, the type of sport that is included now and what is no longer included, such as rope climbing, horse long jump, live pigeon shooting, etc. Kit, a Year 6 teacher, took the children outside for PE and gave the children two sports to participate in that are no longer included in

(Continued)

(Continued)

the Olympic Games and two that are still included. The children first played cricket in two teams and then tug of war as a class, for the sports no longer included. They then all did a 100m sprint followed by a game of football for the sports that are included. The teacher did a running commentary like a sports news reporter throughout all four games.

They returned to the classroom and were read the story of *The Three Little Pigs*. The bemused class sat politely and listened to the story, exchanging raised eyebrows and a few giggles. Kit then asked the class if they knew any other fairy tale characters, and a comprehensive list was made on the whiteboard. Most of their knowledge came from the *Shrek* films. The children were then given a list of Olympic Games sports both currently included and no longer included. They were asked to match fairy tale characters to appropriate sports. So, Ariel the mermaid was given water polo, Puss in Boots was given fencing, Robin Hood was given archery, etc. After some discussion and sharing of these characters with their paired sports, the children then wrote about the Fairy Tale Olympics.

The style of writing was that of a commentary, as Kit had done outside. To finish, there was a plenary where some children shared their writing with the class before everyone worked in 'talk partners' to share their writing with one another.

Concluding thoughts

Being literate is vitally important to children, schools and society. In this chapter, it has been argued that literacy is for all subjects and that children should: be able to write and be given opportunities to write in all subjects. Physical Education has so much to offer writing and vice versa. Writing enhances learning in PE and knowledge and skills of writing from PE transfer across to the other subject areas of the primary curriculum. A number of practical strategies were given to help introduce writing for different audiences, different purposes and in different formats to encourage children to view writing as integral to their learning and achievement in PE.

━━ References ━━

Bailey, R. (1999) Physical education: action, play and movement. In: J. Riley and R. Prentice (eds) *The Curriculum for 7–11 Year Olds*. London: Paul Chapman Publishing.

Behrman, E.H. (2004) Writing in the physical education class. *Journal of Physical Education, Recreation & Dance*, 75 (8).

Bruce, T. and Spratt, J. (2008) *Essentials of Literacy from 0–7*. London: Sage.

DfE (2013a) *Teachers' Standards: Guidance for School Leaders, School Staff and Governing Bodies*. London: DfE.

DfE (2013b) *Physical Education Programmes of Study: Key Stages 1 and 2 National Curriculum in England*. London: DfE.

Doherty, J. (2003) Extending learning in physical education: a framework for promoting thinking skills across the key stages. *British Journal of Teaching Physical Education*, Autumn, 34(3).

Doherty, J. and Brennan, P. (2008) *Physical Education and Development 3–11: A Guide for Teachers.* London: Routledge.

Doherty, J. and Hughes, M. (2009) *Child Development: Theory and Practice 0–11* (2nd edition). Harlow: Pearson.

Goddard Blythe, S. (2009) *Attention, Balance and Coordination. The A.B.C. of Learning Success.* Oxford: Wiley-Blackwell.

Hannaford, C. (2009) *Smart Moves: Why Learning is Not All in your Head.* Arlington, VA: Great Ocean Publishers.

Hopper, B., Grey, J. and Maude, T. (2003) *Teaching Physical Education in the Primary School.* London: RoutledgeFalmer.

Jensen, E. (2000) *Learning with the Body in Mind.* San Diego, CA: The Brain Store.

Mandigo, J.L. and Holt, N.L (2004) Reading the game: introducing the notion of games literacy. *Physical and Health Education.* Autumn.

Maude, T. (2001) *Physical Children, Active Teaching.* Buckingham: Open University Press.

OFSTED (2013) *Beyond 2012 – Outstanding Physical Education for All: Physical Education in Schools 2008–12.* Manchester: Ofsted.

Oussoren, R.A. (2010) *Write Dance* (2nd edition) London: Sage.

Pickup, I. (2012) The importance of primary physical education. In: G. Griggs (ed.) *An Introduction to Primary Physical Education.* London: Routledge.

Unesco Education Sector (2004). The plurality of literacy and its implications for policies and programs: position paper. Paris: United National Educational, Scientific and Cultural Organization.

Whitehead, M. (2016) International Physical Literacy Association. Available from: www.physical-literacy.org.uk (accessed 20 August 2016).

Wyatt-Smith, C.M. and Gunn, S. (2007) *Evidence-based Research for Expert Literacy Teaching.* Melbourne: Department of Education and Early Childhood Development. Education Policy and Research Division, Office for Education Policy and Innovation

Youth Sport Trust (2013) *Primary School Physical Literacy Framework.* Loughborough: YST/Sport England.

Writing in geography

Angela Gill

Teachers' Standards

Standard 3 - Demonstrate good subject and curriculum knowledge

- have a secure knowledge of the relevant subject(s) and curriculum areas, foster and maintain pupils' interest in the subject, and address misunderstandings
- demonstrate a critical understanding of developments in the subject and curriculum areas, and promote the value of scholarship
- demonstrate an understanding of and take responsibility for promoting high standards of literacy, articulacy and the correct use of standard English, whatever the teacher's specialist subject

Standard 4 - Plan and teach well-structured lessons

- impart knowledge and develop understanding through effective use of lesson time
- promote a love of learning and children's intellectual curiosity

Key questions

- How can we inspire children to want to write during geography lessons?
- What steps lead to effective writing based around geography?
- How can we maintain high quality writing in geogrpahy?

Introduction

Everywhere's been where it is ever since it was first put there. It's called geography.

(Terry Pratchett (1988) *Wyrd Sisters*, from the Discworld series)

The aims of the Geography National Curriculum Programme of Study (DfE (2013), p214) are to develop children who are competent in the geographical skills to:

- *Collect, analyse* and *communicate* with a range of data gathered through experience of fieldwork that deepen their understanding of geographical processes

- *Interpret* a range of sources of geographical *information*, including maps, diagrams, globes, aerial photographs and Geographical Information Systems

- *Communicate* geographical information in a variety of ways, including through maps, numerical and quantitative skills and *writing at length*.

As you can see from the text in bold font, there are many opportunities for children to develop their writing skills, alongside their geographical ones. If we consider the aims of the English Programme of Study we will see similar possibilities.

The National Curriculum Programme of Study for Writing (2013), with particular reference to those related to the geography curriculum, state that pupils should be taught as follows.

Year 1

- Spell the days of the week.

- Use capital letters for the names of places and the days of the week.

Year 2

Develop positive attitudes towards and stamina for writing by engaging in the following.

- Write about personal experiences.

- Write about real events.

- Write for different purposes.

Year 3/4

- Wse simple organisational devices.
- Have opportunities to write for a range of real purposes as part of their work across the curriculum.

Year 5/6

- Identify the purpose of writing.
- Use further organisational and presentation devices.
- Be clear about what standard of handwriting is appropriate for a particular task, e.g. an unjoined style for labelling.

In this chapter, we will explore the ways in which children can develop writing through their geographical enquiry, and will consider those types of writing that are appropriate to the geography curriculum: notes from fieldwork, symbols on maps, or perhaps a persuasive piece about land use. Geographical vocabulary will be explored in terms of origin and subject-specific terminology. We will see how illustrations and descriptions from picture books and fiction texts can be used as a stimulus for writing around geographical themes, such as the detailed illustrations of Max's journey and the Wild Island by Maurice Sendak in *Where the Wild Things Are,* and the powerful descriptions of the contrasting places that Willie Beech lives, as written by Michelle Magorian in *Goodnight Mister Tom.* We will consider how writing skills can be used to organise and communicate geographical ideas and findings. Case studies will provide examples of effective teaching and suggest successful ideas for writing through the geography curriculum.

Geographical vocabulary

What is the capital city of Venezuela?

Which is the longest river in the world?

What are cirrus and altostratus types of?

How well would you do in the geography round of a pub quiz? Could you write questions for your own geography quiz? Could you confidently spell the geographical terms mentioned in the questions and answers? The capital city of Venezuela is Caracas, cirrus and altostratus are types of clouds and the debate continues as to whether the Nile or the Amazon is the longest river. The geography curriculum has a large amount of specialist content, and with that an array of subject-specific vocabulary that children need to be able to both read and spell.

Many geographical words are thought of as 'tricky' words by both teachers and children. They might be considered 'common exception words', as referred to in the National Curriculum Programme of Study for English. They often contain an unusual grapheme-phoneme correspondence – some of the letters don't sound the way we would usually expect them to. Examples include the words *ocean, biomes* and *Asia.*

Let's consider the etymology (origins) of some geographical terms. Scoffham (2004) points out that if we look at the word *geography* itself, and trace it back to its Greek linguistic roots, we can see two key aspects of the subject: *geo* meaning *earth* and *graphia* meaning *writing.* The names of many villages, towns and cities in the United Kingdom are derived from the type of location in which they were established. Examples of these include *borough*, as in *Scarborough* and *Knaresborough*, which means a fortified place and *ham*, as in *Durham* and *Birmingham*, meaning a farm or homestead.

What about the morphology (structure) of geographical vocabulary? Many terms have the same root; for example, *geo* is contained in *geology, geometrics* and *geomorphology* and *topography, photography* and *cartography* all have the root *-graphy*. Many terms have roots with similar meanings. The cloud, *cumulus,* has the same root as *accumulate;* both are a collection of sorts. The word *tributary* has the same root as the word *contribute*; a tributary contributes water to another river.

By exploring the etymology and morphology of geographical terms when children are engaged in writing, it will help them begin to understand how words work, that there are many similarities between these words, and that they can successfully write several words by learning the root of one.

Children use geographical vocabulary in many aspects of their writing. Lewis (2004) explains that children need to use technical and scientific language to explain places, features and processes. She goes on to state that children also use descriptive, visual and emotive language when they express responses to places or issues. With this in mind, let's look back at the pub quiz questions at the start of this section. Those types of questions require some simple recall of knowledge to be able to answer them, but limited use of the different types of language that Lewis describes. Children's involvement in geography does not stop at knowledge recall, and geographical enquiry is key to developing a greater understanding of place and issues. Questions that are more suitable for promoting enquiry might include the following.

What is it like to live in the shadow of a volcano?

Where in the world has a higher rainfall each year than the United Kingdom?

Should farmers be able to grow the crops they choose?

When engaged in geographical enquiry, children need to be confident in using specific geographical terms in their writing and need to develop a language that is rich in description and emotion.

 Case study

How do we know what a place is like if we've never been? – developing geographical enquiry in Key Stage 1

As part of their understanding about human features, as indicated in the National Curriculum Programme of Study for Geography, children in Key Stage 1 need to know about factories.

When discussing with her Year 2 class what they knew about a factory, Sarah realised that the children had never visited one, didn't know anyone who worked in one, and had limited knowledge about what factories looked like or what their purpose is. She understood that the children had not yet developed a sense of place in relation to factories.

(Continued)

(Continued)

Sarah wanted to use the children's enquiry into factories as an opportunity to explore creative writing. Sarah started by using role play and hot seating and took on the role as a factory manager, and after some initial discussion about what might happen in her factory, she showed the children a video of her factory in action. This was actually the Skoda car advert, entitled 'Cake', which showed the Skoda Fabia being made out of cake and other sweet treats, accompanied by the song *A Few of My Favourite Things*, taken from the soundtrack of *The Sound of Music*, performed by Julie Andrews.

Figure 11.1 Images courtesy of Skoda UK

The children then took on the role of factory manager and chose their own 'magical' product to make. Writing outcomes from this stimulus included:

- drawing and labelling plans of the factory;
- making a simple timeline of production, using organisational features such as arrows and boxed text;
- designing a poster to advertise the product;
- writing customer reviews of the product.

The children were so engaged by the activities that they were keen to actually make the products that they had chosen for their imaginary factory. Although not an easy task, Sarah asked the children to bring the materials they would need from home, and enlisted some extra adult helpers to spend a day making the vast array of products. The products and writing that the children produced made a very effective display.

Sarah and the children wanted to continue the topic, and Sarah saw opportunities to include other types of writing. She created a factory role-play area in the classroom, with a variety of construction and modelling activities, and opportunities to write lists and complete orders. The children used photographs, videos and products to explore 'real' factories. Sarah invited visitors who work in factories to talk to the children about their role and, in preparation for this, the children wrote questions to ask in the style of an informal interview. The children visited a local factory, where they took photographs and made notes that helped them to write a recount once they had returned to school.

 Activity

Think of six different writing opportunities that could be explored through studying one of the human features suggested in the National Curriculum Programme of Study for Geography for KS1: *city, town, village, factory, farm, house, office, port, harbour and shop.*

In the case study above, the children in Sarah's class were able to develop a sense of a place that was close by and yet unfamiliar to them. The National Curriculum Programme of Study for Geography states that children should have knowledge of places that are not in the children's locality: the similarities and differences of human and physical geography of an area of a non-European country (Key Stage 1) and of an area of a European country and a region of North or South America (Key Stage 2). Barnes (2015) discusses the benefits of making global connections and developing links with schools in other parts of the world. As part of this, meaningful writing opportunities could be created, such as emailing children from the linked school with questions about their locality, answering questions about their own local area, exchanging annotated photographs, maps and weather reports, and discussing local issues.

Locational vocabulary and mapping

In the very popular 1980s comedy series *Blackadder II*, Edmund Blackadder was about to set sail on a voyage on behalf of Queen Elizabeth I.

Lord Melchett: Farewell, Blackadder. The foremost cartographers of this land have prepared this for you; it's a map of the area that you'll be traversing.

(Blackadder opens up the parchment and sees that it's blank.)

Lord Melchett: They'll be very grateful if you could just fill it in as you go along.

Edmund Blackadder was asked to do what children are expected to do: make maps. Starting with a blank piece of paper can be as daunting for children as it was for Blackadder. But in doing so, children are also developing specific language and writing skills that are appropriate to the task, such as designing symbols and using organisational devices. As part of the geography curriculum children should use maps, symbols and keys, that children in Key Stage 1 should be able to use locational language and that children in Key Stage 2 should be able to use grid references. Bridge (2004) explains that the need to record, revisit and pass on information to others is important and that one of the most effective ways of achieving these things is by making and using maps.

Lewis (2004) considers using maps with children and suggests that expressing position begins with the gradual acquisition of place language and progresses towards sophisticated knowledge of mapping conventions and the ability to define location. Children can begin developing their concept of location and position by drawing maps and plans of familiar places; perhaps their bedroom, the classroom or a place they have recently visited. They can then develop their knowledge of mapping conventions by adding their own symbols and labels. Scoffham (2004) notes that children often choose to draw and write about familiar, special and significant places. He suggests that they might make postcards depicting these places, or draw and describe a snapshot of a place, as if it's a view from a window. More creative maps, perhaps those that record different emotions, sounds and smells of a particular place, can be used to develop poetry or descriptive writing.

Maps from children's fiction can be used as a stimulus for developing mapping skills and for creative writing. Examples include the map of the Hundred Acre wood in the *Winnie the Pooh* books, the maps of the semi-fictitious Scottish island of Struay in the *Katie Morag* books and the map of *Treasure Island*. As Tanner (2004) points out, picture books and fiction offer many opportunities for developing a sense of place, and for exploring feeling about places and issues. Maps can also be an effective way of recording children's knowledge about texts. Children might draw a plan, after reading the texts, of the Three Bears' house from *Goldilocks* or a map of Hogwarts from *Harry Potter and the Philosopher's Stone*. Lewis (2004) also suggests that by encouraging children to invent settings and make imaginary maps their story writing might be enhanced and that, in turn, this can support children's ability to visualise sequenced events.

Directional vocabulary and routes

Through planning, drawing, describing and following routes children are engaged in geographical activity that is sequential. The National Curriculum Programme of Study for Geography states that children should describe routes and use compass directions.

As we have already discussed in relation to locational vocabulary and mapping, children might begin by drawing and annotating routes that represent a familiar journey: the walk from the classroom to the playground, the car journey from home to a grandparent's house or perhaps the route around the play spaces in their favourite park. They might also represent what they have read in stories with a route; the journey from Little Red Riding Hood's house to Grandma's, Harry's route through the Forbidden Forest in *Harry Potter and the Chamber of Secrets* or the path that Rosie took in *Rosie's Walk*.

Once children have developed their mapping skills and are comfortable with sequencing, symbols and written representations of place and direction, they may then record less familiar routes, such as the bus trip to a school visit or the train journey to a holiday destination.

Developing understanding of location and direction through story

How might children represent location and direction in written form? Hamel and Langley-Hamel (2006) suggest that story seems to be an appropriate starting point to help children develop their understanding and sense of place. Young children make sense of their experiences and of the world in which they live through narrative. They can then develop the vocabulary that they need to explain this understanding and use it in their writing. Scoffham (2004) points out that many EYFS and Key Stage 1 teachers already create pictures, and encourage their children to do the same, to show the journeys associated with stories and fairy tales.

We can see a link between routes and narrative with the notion of a beginning, middle and end. We can see the relationship between maps and narrative in respect of turning ideas into visual representations (Chamberlain with Kerrigan-Draper, 2016). As part of the planning process when writing stories, children might draw a 'story route' to plan the introduction, action and adventure and conclusion of their writing.

Poetry can also be used to represent location and direction. Children might use a journey stick, which they carry with them collecting objects as they go. Once back in the classroom children draw the route that they followed, make maps of where they found the objects and use the objects and drawings to write poetry and descriptive pieces. Barnes (2015) suggests other ways of creating poems, for example, by compiling scenes collected through a viewfinder, and by composing 'fridge magnet poems'. Fridge magnet poems are created when visiting a chosen place: children stop at intervals, record a word that describes what they can see, hear, smell and touch, and then on returning to the classroom the children rearrange and edit the words to create a poem.

 Case study

How can we use fiction as a stimulus in geography? – developing knowledge and understanding of mapping and routes in Key Stage 1

Joe's Year 1 class were discussing their route to the assembly hall, which was in a different building from their classroom, on the other side of the playground. The children were able to talk about the things that they passed on their short journey, but Joe quickly realised that they were having difficulty sequencing the landmarks in the correct order to form an accurate route. The children's misconceptions and lack of knowledge were confirmed when Joe asked them to draw a route map of the same short journey; their sequencing and mapping skills were limited.

Joe understood that the children needed to be able to talk about a journey following the correct sequence, and accurately represent direction and location in written form. He decided to capitalise on

(Continued)

(Continued)

the children's great love of story; reading and writing stories is a daily occurrence in their classroom. Starting with traditional tales such as *The Three Little Pigs* and *Little Red Riding Hood*, the children began by sequencing pictures and objects from the story. They then drew simple symbols to replace the objects and added those to route maps, with labels to show the way to Grandma's house or the third Little Pig's cottage. They used chalk, skipping ropes, cones and other props to make a large-scale route map on the playground, complete with road signs. The children worked in groups to write simple directions, using the large map, for their friends to follow.

Joe then moved on to less familiar tales. The children made maps of Harry's journey to and from Grandad's house in the country, from the picture book *Harry's Home*. They rehearsed, then performed *We're Going on a Bear Hunt* during an assembly – a story in which a family travels through lots of different natural elements, such as long grass and a swirling, whirling snowstorm, looking for a bear.

Joe wanted to extend the children's learning beyond using story maps, to consolidate what they had learned and to use their newly acquired skills in other contexts. He wanted to use the opportunity to introduce other writing outcomes. So, referring back to the initial stimulus of the journey to their assembly hall, the children went on to study their school grounds, engaging in simple fieldwork and making observations. Writing outcomes from this stimulus included:

- making simple labelled drawings and field notes at different locations;
- using aerial photographs of the school to identify landmarks, give friends instruction directions and make a representation as a map;
- drawing and printing a map of the school, complete with symbols, labels and a key, noting important locations for visitors to the school;
- planning and designing a new nature area for an unused corner of the school field; producing plans, leaflets and posters to promote their idea.

 Activity

Identify six children's fiction texts that contain descriptions or illustrations of places or journeys, which could be used as a stimulus for writing activities involving mapping and routes. Are the texts suitable for children in KS1 or KS2? What different kinds of writing outcomes would you expect to achieve from using the texts?

In the case study above, the children in Joe's class were able to use traditional tales, picture books and fiction as a way of understanding and using simple maps and routes. Story and poetry can also be used to explore place and culture, and creative writing can be produced as a result. *Elephant Dance* is a story about life in India, in particular the reverence given to elephants during Diwali, and is suitable for children in EYFS and KS1. The *Great Kapok Tree* explored the rainforests and the issues about cutting down precious trees. KS2 children can find out about life and conditions in the Arctic through the book *Island*, in which an urban teenager moves to an Arctic island with his research scientist mother. Fictional places depicted in books, images and films can be an effective stimulus for writing, such as the fictitious planet Pandora, in the film *Avatar*.

Organising writing in geography

The National Curriculum Programme of Study for English states that children should use organisational devices in their writing, and the geography curriculum presents many opportunities for this to happen. When learning about the water cycle, children could use text boxes and arrows to make a visual representation of the process. As part of their study of a UK river, children may learn that an unjoined style of handwriting is appropriate when writing labels. When collecting information about the distribution of natural resources in a chosen area, children can use tables, charts and graphs to record and present their information. While watching video clips of physical feature in North America, children might make notes, using organisational devices such as bullet points.

Children may also engage in taking field notes, recording observations while out of the classroom. They might use digital devices to record their findings, taking photographs that can be annotated, or using note-taking apps. They will learn to understand that their standard of handwriting while making notes is expected to be different from the standard when presenting their findings. They will understand that capitalisation is needed for place names in a written report and for the days of the week in a weather forecast.

Case study

Where in the world is it colder than the UK? – an enquiry into weather and climate zones in lower Key Stage 2

As part of the geography curriculum, children in Key Stage 2 need to know about climate zones and the significance of the hemispheres, tropics, Arctic and Antarctic. They have learned about daily and seasonal weather in the UK in Key Stage 1.

Ben's Year 4 class demonstrated a good understanding of the weather in the UK. They were able to make simple forecasts based on the current weather and seasonal norms, use symbols to represent what the weather was like in visual form and use devices, such as apps, to find out weather information.

Ben wanted to extend the children's understanding by using fieldwork skills to collect weather data and by comparing the climate in the UK to the climate in the Antarctic zone. The children were engaged in activities that not only promoted their geographical knowledge and understanding, but also developed their writing skills. The writing tasks that the children were involved in included:

- collecting weather information in the school grounds, for example, using rain gauges and anemometers to gather data, making notes in the field and using tables and charts to record and present results;

- observing and recording the weather in their local area over a period of time, using notes to record observations;

- using digital devices and online forecasts to make observations about the weather in the Antarctic, and make comparisons between the two climate zones being observed;

(Continued)

(Continued)

- designing weather symbols and maps for both climate zones;

- writing, presenting and recording weather forecasts for both their local area and the Antarctic;

- describing simple patterns in the weather, in both climate zones, and making simple predictions, e.g. *'I think the weather tomorrow will be ... because ...'.*

Many of the skills, both geographical and writing, that the children developed through this topic are transferable, and can be developed further through other areas of the geography curriculum.

 Activity

A lower Key Stage 2 class will be studying the topics of mountains. Choose three types of writing outcomes that might be appropriate for this topic. Which different ways of organising their writing could you plan for the children to develop? What types of organisational devices might they use to research and present their work?

More opportunities to write through geography

Simply leaving the classroom, and engaging in fieldwork, can provide the stimulus for writing. Chamberlain with Kerrigan-Draper (2016) suggests that any activity that involves children leaving the classroom and experiencing an event ensures that they have something to write about, and consequently they will write better. Poems, recounts and reports, illustrated with sketches and photographs, can be written after a visit to a local landmark or area of special interest.

Instructional and procedural texts might be written, perhaps directions to the local supermarket or a checklist of successful ways to collect rainwater. Writing questions for a friend or producing a simple quiz would demonstrate understanding of a particular topic.

Creating texts that are designed to explain what has been learned are often interesting writing outcomes; a newspaper report on deforestation in the Amazon, a leaflet about climate zones or a diary entry or blog describing the day the volcano erupted.

Texts designed to persuade, such as an interview about waste and land fill, and those that present an argument, such as debating land use in a region of South America, can be engaging and stimulating. Barnes (2015) notes that children often express an interest in 'green issues'. Topics such as deforestation and pollution are regularly highlighted in the media and in curriculum initiatives, and so these issues often lead to high-quality writing outcomes.

Writing outcomes with a geography focus do not have to take the form of long, written reports. Alcock (2004) suggests many activities that use and develop writing skills, but that are often quick to facilitate and limit writing output. One of the activities suggested is to make marks in different types of natural media such as sand, soil and shale. Another is to design a passport and pack a suitcase to travel to a destination with a particular climate and physical features – for example, a skiing trip in a mountainous area with a cold climate. Many simple games can be given a geographical twist: anagrams of capital cities, snap with mapping symbols, and crosswords with specific geographical vocabulary that has been recently introduced.

 Case study

Should fishing vessels be allowed to catch what they want? – understanding issues related to the distribution of natural resources in upper Key Stage 2

As part of their understanding about human features, as indicated in the National Curriculum Programme of Study for Geography, children in Key Stage 2 need to know about the distribution of natural resources, including food.

Surinder decided to introduce her Year 6 class to the idea of fishing quotas, and they began by discussing whether the fishing industry should be regulated and why. The children collected, analysed and presented simple data about fishing quotas in the North Sea. They used the Internet to research the industry, finding key facts and images to use in their writing. They watched clips of interviews with people in various roles in the fishing industry, offering different perspectives on the issue of imposed quotas.

Surinder was keen to plan some writing outcomes that developed the children's understanding of persuasion and argument, and to develop the skills to become persuasive communicators. These writing outcomes included:

- making notes while listening to, and watching clips of, media related to the fishing industry;

- finding and analysing media coverage related to the issue, e.g. newspaper headlines and the straplines from search engine results, then writing their own;

- developing key points to support one side of the argument, while a writing partner developed the opposing points;

- presenting their own side of the argument, justifying their reasons and responding to others' opinions;

- writing questions and carrying out a role-play interview, designed to question a particular person involved in the issue, for example, the captain of a fishing fleet, a supplier, a policy maker or a conservationist.

The children took ownership of their work and wanted a wider audience to see it. They filmed their interviews using iPads and shared their work with a neighbouring school. They published the articles they had written in their school newspaper.

Activity

Think of six questions, related to the National Curriculum Programme of Study for Geography, which could be used as a stimulus to develop argument and debate. These could include questions about deforestation, cash crops, water damming, waste management and pollution.

Conclusion

Writing through geography can be as simple as making marks in the snow, or as challenging as exploring the economic activity of Russia. It can produce outcomes such as a new mapping symbol for a local landmark, or a report debating and justifying opinions about opening a new mine near a settlement.

We use geography and writing as part of our everyday lives; drawing a map to guide someone to a place or, perhaps, checking and sharing the weather app on our devices.

At the beginning of this chapter we shared the aims of the geography curriculum. The key words that were highlighted in bold font can all be successfully addressed by the writing activities discussed in this chapter: *collect, analyse, interpret* and *communicate*. As we've seen in this chapter, the opportunities for writing through geography are diverse and extensive.

References

Alcock, K. (2004) Making geography fun. In: Scoffham, S. (ed.) *Primary Geography Handbook*. London: Geographical Association.

Anholt, C. and Anholt, L. (1999) *Harry's Home*. London: Orchard Books.

Barnes, J. (2015) *Cross-Curricular Learning 3–14*. London: Sage.

Blackadder II, episode 3 'Potato', BBC (1986) (TV episode).

Bridge, C. (2004) Mapwork skills. In: Scoffham, S (ed.) *Primary Geography Handbook*. London: Geographical Association.

Chamberlain, L. with Kerrigan-Draper, E. (2016) *Inspiring Writing in Primary Schools*. London: Sage.

Cherry, L. (1990) *The Great Kapok Tree*. London: Harcourt International,.

DfE (2013) *National Curriculum Programmes of Study for English; Key Stages 1 and 2*. London: DfE.

DfE (2013) *National Curriculum Programmes of Study for Geography; Key Stages 1 and 2*. London: DfE.

Hamel, K. and Langley-Hamel, K. (2006) How can geography make a significant contribution to a coherent and meaningful Key Stage 1 Curriculum? In: Cooper, H., Rowley, C. and Asquith, S. (eds) *Geography 3–11*. London: David Fulton.

Hedderwick, M. (1984) *Katie Morag Delivers the Mail*. London: Random House.

Heine, T. (2004) *Elephant Dance: Memories of India*. Oxford: Barefoot Books.

Hutchins, P. (1968) *Rosie's Walk*. London: Macmillan.

Lewis, L. (2004) Geography and language development. In: Scoffham, S. (ed.) *Primary Geography Handbook*. London: Geographical Association.

Magorian, M. (1981) *Goodnight Mister Tom*. London: Kestrel Books.

Pratchett, T (1988) *Wyrd Sisters* (from the Discworld series). London: Transworld.

Rosen, M. (2006) *We're Going on a Bear Hunt*. London: Walker Books.

Rowling, J.K. (1997) *Harry Potter and the Philosopher's Stone*. London: Bloomsbury.

Rowling, J.K. (1998) *Harry Potter and the Chamber of Secrets*. London: Bloomsbury.

Scoffham, S. (2004) *Primary Geography Handbook*. London: Geographical Association.

Sendak, M. (1968) *Where the Wild Things Are*. New York: Harper & Row.

Singer, N. (2015) *Island*. Bradford: Caboodle Books.

Tanner, J. (2004) Geography and the emotions. In: Scoffham, S (ed.) *Primary Geography Handbook*. London: Geographical Association.

12

writing in art and design

Adam Bushnell with staff of the Bowes Museum Education Team

Teachers' Standards

4. Plan and teach well-structured lessons

- impart knowledge and develop understanding through effective use of lesson time
- promote a love of learning and children's intellectual curiosity

Key questions

- How can writing be linked to art?
- What kind of art is best to promote a positive attitude towards writing in the classroom?
- What steps lead to effective writing based around art?
- How can we maintain high-quality writing when teaching children about art?

Introduction

Art is a subject that is often left for PPA lessons. It is a subject that some might consider less important than other curriculum areas and one that some teachers are uncomfortable about because they feel that they are not good at it themselves. If you were to ask a staffroom full of teachers 'who likes teaching art?', you would probably get a definite answer of a 'yes' or a resounding 'no'. This is usually down to a lack of confidence in the subject area. If you were to also ask the teachers who do not like teaching art why, their response is likely to be 'I can't draw, so I can't teach it.'

Yet, art is not about being able to draw well. It is an expression of emotion. It is how human beings have expressed themselves from the very beginning of our existence. There are Stone Age sculptures crafted from animal bones and tusks. There are ancient cave paintings. Before language was ever fully developed, people used art to communicate their experiences and stories. Art is as old as we are and it comes in many forms.

When children first begin to make marks, it is a visual communication that they use before they develop their written literacy skills. They use pictorial images to make sense of the world in chalk, crayon, pencil, Play-Doh, plasticine, clay, recycled junk, paint and even mud. But this confident artistic expression seems to slowly dwindle in some children as they progress through primary school. Why is this? Is it due to a lack of confidence in themselves or in us as their teachers? This chapter will examine some strategies that will boost the confidence in this subject area of both child and teacher. It will show how the written word can be stimulated by the beautiful and the grotesque through art.

Using art for retelling

Hamish Fulton describes himself as a walking artist. He transforms walks into works of art. In his 1988 piece entitled *Wall Painting* (Temple University, Philadelphia, USA) the canvas does not show a landscape in the form of an image, rather it is painted with words.

What Fulton is doing here is painting a picture inside our own imaginations. He does this with words rather than a paintbrush. This can be something that we can employ in the classroom, as seen in this case study below.

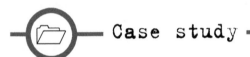

Figure 12.1 Wall Painting, *Hamish Fulton (1988)*

Case study

Year 5 class retelling their class novel *The Railway Children*

Michelle, a Year 5 teacher, had finished reading *The Railway Children* by Edith Nesbit to her class. They had read two chapters per week as part of a literacy unit of work. They had written poems based on the poem in Chapter 1, described railway stations using their five senses, made adverts persuading people to use a particular rail line of their own invention, researched what the railway was like in the 1900s, and used the 'How Stuff Works' website to find out how steam engines run. They wrote information texts based on their research.

In this particular lesson, Michelle was asking the children to retell what happened chapter by chapter. She showed them the image above by Fulton. She then asked them to work in talk partners with whiteboards and come up with four, four-letter words that would retell the first chapter. These were then shared and compared.

Next, the class were asked to repeat the process chapter by chapter. They continued to work in partners but there was much discussion between the whole class as to what happened in each part of the book. Michelle continually reminded them about the plot using key events that she wrote on the board.

Eventually, the children had a complete 14-chapter list written in four four-letter words on whiteboards. They then transferred this individually into their literacy books.

This is an example of one child's finished product:

THE RAILWAY CHILDREN
FIVE RICH FOUR MOVE
POOR WAVE GENT COLD
COAL SICK HELP GIFT

FURY MALE TALK USSR
STAY TYPE JAIL PRAY
PITY SLIP FLAG FALL
STOP TIME SAVE NEWS
FIND WIFE KIDS MEND
LOCO PRAM FULL BERT
RAGE KEPT CLIP PAPA
FIVE JAIL LOST HURT
TRIP WIRE HELP BOAT
LIFT HOME GENT HOME
JIM✓ LEFT 0915 LOTS
WAVE MAMA WALK NICE
1157 MIST PAPA FREE

The case study worked extremely well in creating a very visual piece of writing. The teacher demonstrated an excellent blend of art and literacy, using Fulton's example. This can be applied to all year groups, but perhaps changing the number of words and not limiting those words to four letters would work best for younger ages. If a Reception class was retelling *The Three Little Pigs*, they could simply use one word for each section of the story and not restrict the children to four-letter words alone. For example:

Mother, pigs, home, leave, build, straw, wolf, blow, down, build, sticks, wolf, blow, down, build, bricks, wolf, blow, chimney, fire, burn.

There is a series of books entitled 'Cosy Classics' that provides perfect examples of this form of retelling. *Moby Dick* is retold in twelve words. In the series, also retold in twelve words, are *Les Miserables*, *Jane Eyre*, *War and Peace* and many others.

Retelling using individual words as a stimulus is an effective classroom tool and can be a form of artwork in itself, as can be seen in the Fulton painting.

 Activity

Using four, four-letter words for retelling

Try using a short story or animation such as *Alma* (for upper Key Stage 2) or *Marshmallows* (for lower Key Stage 1) from the Literacy Shed.

- Could the children retell the narrative using just four-letter words?
- Are you going to ask the children to retell the whole thing once the story is shared, or are you going to break it down into sections?

(Continued)

(Continued)

- Are you going to ask them to work together or individually?

- The aim of the lesson above was purely as a retelling device. Can this be adapted for a new piece of writing following the same structure? Can the children perhaps make changes, such as to the characters, setting or objects featured?

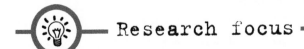

Research focus

Inspiring retelling

Retelling is something that the DfE (2001), in its report *Developing Early Writing*, states is essential. It lists retelling in its top three recommended strategies for writing: the first is reading, then retelling and finally sharing writing with peers. As can be seen in the case study, art, like Fullerton's painting, can be used to inspire retelling in ways that encourage writing.

In the National Strategies (2008) it states that it is essential that we as teachers allow children to express themselves creatively and imaginatively. This can be done both through art and the written word but also together. This is echoed by the United Kingdom Literacy Association (2004, p20) which states that it is good practice when teachers are *integrating the visual, whether film, DVD, still images or pupils' own drawings into units of work and continuing to use 3D stimulus, music and videos alongside books in the classroom for both fiction and non-fiction writing. It goes on to say; at Key Stage 2, there was evidence of pupils identifying characters' feelings and emotions from visual images but also closer reading of print text as more careful and attentive reading of visual text developed.*

So, it would seem that when we study art we learn to be able to also study the written word more closely too. We notice the detail in the visual and then the detail in the written word. In the next section, we will look at how to focus children's attention and look for detail, then apply this to their own writing.

The power of portraits

When children in the Early Years are asked to draw themselves, we frequently see images where limbs are emerging from heads. I remember my own first attempts at self-portraits looking like Humpty Dumpty, my arms and legs protruding from a head.

As is true with everything, it is only through practice that we get better.

In the Phaidon book of *500 Self-Portraits* we see a vast range of artistic styles and self-interpretation. There are sculptures, sketches, paintings and photographs all depicting how the artists see themselves. The results are startlingly varied.

There is another Phaidon book called *Fish Face*. In it, there are dozens of portrait-style photographs of fish faces. To see these creatures so close up makes for eerie viewing. There are beautiful colours, strange patterns and bizarre expressions.

The surrealist artist, Remedios Varo, uses nature and blends people and animals together as in her painting *The Creation of the Birds*. In this painting an owl-like figure is busy sewing together a bird, like some strange taxidermist, but instead of stuffing the bird with sawdust, she fills it with new life.

Asking children to create a self-portrait with a twist is a good way of feeding descriptive language. They could use all of the elements of portrait drawing such as proportion and comparison but with a surreal style twist by adding animal features. The children could add fish-like features copying elements of the images in *Fish Face* or bird-like features, copying elements from *The Creation of the Birds*. Or they could add any animal features, at all.

Also, the website www.buildyourwildself.com allows children to create avatars of themselves but then add animal features. This can be an excellent tool for teaching connectives: *First,* I grew deer antlers. *Next,* I had spider's legs; sheep's eyes. *After that,* I grew a kangaroo tail. *Then,* I had sheep eyes. *Afterwards,* I had cat's paws. *Finally,* I had a snake's tongue.

Alternatively, by looking at the work of Italian artist Giuseppe Arcimboldo, children could even blend human portraits not with animals but rather with fruit and vegetables, as can be seen in the case study below.

Case study

Reception class on the topic 'All About Me'

Mina's class had been studying healthy eating as part of their topic 'All About Me'. They had been learning about the benefits of eating healthily and knew that certain foods were better than others for growth and long life. The class were discussing which products contained calcium to help teeth and bones grow strong. They then listed fruits and vegetables that also keep them healthy. Mina explained which vitamins were in which fruit or vegetable and explained which part of the body benefited most. She held up images of broccoli and told the children that this made them strong as it contains a lot of iron. She showed an image of a carrot containing vitamin A for good eyesight and an image of strawberries containing vitamin C for a healthy immune system.

Mina then showed them the work of the nineteenth-century artist Arcimboldo. They looked at the four paintings entitled *Spring, Summer, Autumn* and *Winter*. The children thought that these portraits

(Continued)

(Continued)

were highly amusing as each face comprised the fruit and vegetables that are most available during that season. *Spring* contains lots of berries, *Summer* contains lots of fruit, *Autumn* contains lots of squashes and *Winter* contains lots of root vegetables.

Mina then gave the children cut-out pictures of fruits and vegetables. The children were asked to create their own self-portrait but using the template foods for eyes, nose, mouth, etc. These were stuck down on a blank face template. The children were then asked to label each fruit or vegetable with adjectives. The less able children used word mats to help them and the more able children used their phonics to sound out and spell words like *bright*, *tasty* and *colourful*.

The children then all showed their fruit faces to each other back on the carpet and read their adjectives.

Activity

Making healthy heroes

Take a look at Arcimboldo's four seasons portraits.

- What writing opportunities are created by using these portraits?
- Could the children use real fruits and vegetables? In what way and why would this be of more benefit?
- Could the children in your class design full body versions?
- Could the health benefits be elaborated further? How could this be recorded?
- Could the children design healthy fruit and vegetable super heroes?

The BBC TV advert Sprout Boy can be viewed on YouTube. This animation can support narrative writing of this kind or character descriptions for a class designing their own fruit or vegetable healthy hero.

A picture paints a thousand words?

We are extremely fortunate in the United Kingdom that we have a huge number of galleries and museums containing splendid and priceless works of art. A trip to any one of these places is an exciting and worthwhile opportunity. Viewing an image online is a very different experience from actually seeing it in real life. It is only when you come face to face with King Henry VIII at the National Portrait Gallery that his truly imposing nature is revealed.

Lots of Victorian artists like Daniel Maclise painted very detailed and character-heavy pictures. Show a class his painting of *Alfred the Saxon King Disguised as a Minstrel, in the Tent of Guthrum the Dane* – it has a rather long title but also an exciting story attached to it. This story tells how Alfred the Great defeated an invading Viking army by pretending to be a musician. He entertained the raiders with music and they drank a lot of ale while he did so. The king then waited for them to pass out and killed them in their sleep, thus saving England. But the painting itself is very open to interpretation as to what is going on. After discussing with the children what they think is happening in the painting, they could write their own interpretations of the story. They could then be told the actual story and compare this to their own. They could also research the original story and attempt to find out if it is based on true events.

Another storytelling artist to look at is the Dutch artist Hieronymus Bosch who painted lots of triptychs, which were three-part stories. For example, in the *Haywain Triptych*, the first panel tells the story of Adam and Eve, the middle section tells of life during the fifteenth century, and the third shows Hell on Earth. The artist was warning the world that if they were, to carry on as sinfully as they were then this is what would happen.

Pictures were used to tell stories long before then. Anglo-Saxon monks used carved crosses to tell the stories from the Bible to the illiterate pagans in order to convert them to Christianity. There are stone crosses all over the United Kingdom that look like comic strips. The images tell the stories. This has been a popular art form since the very first people.

Now, comic books and graphic novels are more popular than ever. At one time they were considered only for children, but now reach a far wider audience. Character creators like Stan Lee have made the superhero genre a global phenomenon. Websites such as www.cpbherofactory.com help children to create their own superhero characters to make up stories about them in the same tradition of Spiderman or Batman.

It doesn't just have to be a modern superhero that comic strip stories can be written about either. Heroes such as Perseus and Herakles (who had his Ancient Greek name changed to Hercules by the Romans) can also inspire creative writing, as is explained in the case study below.

 **Case study**

Year 4 class involved in a storytelling session as part of their topic on Ancient Greece

Using a large nineteenth-century bronze sculpture of Hercules as a focus, Amy, an Education Officer at the Bowes Museum, gathered a class of Year 4 children in the Silver and Metals gallery for a storytelling session.

Amy began the workshop by showing the children the sculpture and seeing if they recognised the character. The children were encouraged to look for details in the statue, such as Hercules' big muscles symbolising his strength and the lion's head tucked beneath his armpit representing the fabled twelve labours. Once the children were familiar with the character the story began.

(Continued)

(Continued)

The children read aloud the first sentence of the story from an A3 laminated sheet in order to involve and engage them from the beginning. Throughout the story, Amy encouraged the children to think about how characters might feel at key points. They were also asked to act out parts of the story or make sound effects, such as a knock at the door or the roar of the lion in order to continue to engage the group. The children particularly enjoyed the section of the story where Amy produced a story sack containing items gathered by Hercules during his twelve labours.

She was very animated in her storytelling, becoming characters from the myth, using voices and actions to bring the story to life.

At the end of the session the children were asked by Amy which characters were their favourite and why. The children enjoyed reliving key elements of the story by acting it out in small groups.

The children were asked to design their own heroic character like Hercules. They then had to design twelve difficult tasks for the hero to complete, such as wrestling crocodiles, climbing volcanoes or rescuing a prince from a dragon. These planning sheets were then followed up in class by turning the plan into narrative stories.

 ── **Activity**

Writing a narrative story using a space

In the case study the focus of attention was the bronze sculpture. The setting played an equally important role, though. Being in a space filled with beautiful and interesting objects can have an extremely positive effect on speaking and listening. According to Hattie (2003), the classroom environment is one of the most influential factors upon children's learning.

Where could you take your class linked to your art topic?

- Which objects will be your focus while you are there?
- What will need to be done before the trip?
- What creative writing opportunities will there be both during the trip and afterwards?

 ── **Research focus**

School visits

When we take children on a school trip to a museum or gallery, it can significantly increase the amount and quality of what they write. When children fully experience something themselves, this can fuel the words we want them to produce. According to Croker Costa (2008), what children experience visually affects their long-term and short-term memories. By giving children lots of visual and other auditory stimulus, we increase what they remember. By visiting locations full of visual stimulation, the children who usually say that they do not know what to write can use notes or sketches recorded on the trip to help them remember what happened and what to write in school.

The United Kingdom Literacy Association (2004) highly recommend the integration of visual approaches to learning that lead to writing as it is *successful in promoting marked and rapid improvements in standards of boys' writing.* They go on to say, *One of the key factors for those involved in the project was the powerful impact that using the visual had not only on the pupils' writing but also on their reading* (p37).

As well as the visual stimulation, visiting museums and galleries also stimulate the other senses. When we enter these places, tastes, sounds and texture flood our senses too. We can feel the hard floor or lush carpet beneath our feet. We can taste the musty scent lingering in the air. We can hear the creak of floorboards. But it is our sense of smell that is linked directly to our memory. According to the Fifth Sense (2015), a charity for those with smell and taste disorders, *The sense of smell is closely linked with memory, probably more so than any of our other senses. Those with full olfactory function may be able to think of smells that evoke particular memories; the scent of an orchard in blossom conjuring up recollections of a childhood picnic, for example* (www. fifthsense.org.uk/psychology-and-smell/).

This is echoed by air-freshener manufacturers Dale Air who have developed smell boxes for schools. Dale Air (www.daleair.com/dispensing/vortex-cubes-choose-4-aromas) say: *The Vortex Cube was designed to add another dimension to teaching, particularly as an aid for the visually impaired, for example. Introducing a new sense to teaching can help hold the attention of the class.* They sell Dinosaur, Battlefield, Fun Fair and Zoo presentation packs. Or you can choose your own scents from Chocolate to Penguin Sick. These smells do indeed help to fuel descriptive writing but taking the children to a place, such as a gallery, leads to the most effective writing as it floods *all* of the senses at once.

Interpreting art – what does it mean?

Have you ever been in a modern art gallery and wondered what you were looking at? Art can be interpreted in many different ways. Sometimes the artist does not want us to find any meaning in what we see, but rather wants us to just experience the art. Sometimes, they just want to provoke a reaction. They want us to feel something.

Artists like Damien Hirst can use quite shocking techniques, for example in his formaldehyde works or very humorous techniques, as in his *28 Tablets*. Frances Bacon used similar shock tactics in his paintings. The Spanish romantic painter Goya produced beautiful paintings that told tales of chivalry, yet his *Black Paintings* are deeply disturbing images portraying the artist's fear for humanity. Picasso's *Guernica* reflects the horrors of the Nazi bombing of the town of the same name during the Spanish Civil War.

Art can be beautiful and it can be grotesque, but it is still art. It is still an artist's expression. All art makes us react in some way and this can be positive or negative, but it is still a *reaction*. Children's reactions can be so profound that they *want* to write about the art that they have seen. A perfect example of this is the Harris Burdick charcoal illustrations by Chris Van Allsburg. There are 15 illustrations in total, each with a title and a sample sentence from a story. There is an explanation at the front of the book that outlines the story of Harris Burdick. He is a fictional character but the narrative reads as if he is real. It states that he was an author and illustrator who entered a publishing house in America in 1953 with 14 illustrations to pitch to the publishers. The illustrations were a hit and the publishers asked to see the accompanying stories. Harris Burdick told the publisher that he would return with the text the following day and left the illustrations with the publisher. But Harris Burdick was never seen again.

The story explains that the publishers went ahead and published the 14 images as an art book without the stories. But then the narrative goes on to say that in 1993 a fifteenth illustration was uncovered and the book *The Mysteries of Harris Burdick* was published along with this missing fifteenth illustration. The website www.houghtonmifflinbooks.com/features/harrisburdick/ outlines the story in more detail.

These illustrations are beautifully drawn and with the added introductory line at the bottom, they genuinely make you want to write the story that should accompany them. This is their great power; they make you *want* to write. They will make your class *want* to write. Indeed, they have made authors such as Stephen King, Louis Sachar, Lemony Snicket and many others want to write too. In the book *The Chronicles of Harris Burdick* these authors and twelve others have each submitted their own short story interpreting the illustrations in their own way. This highly recommended resource can be used in Early Years, Key Stage S1, Key Stage 2 and beyond.

There are countless other examples of images that can tell stories. In the case study below, based at an art gallery, the Education Officer uses children's own interpretation of the art to fuel words for a narrative story.

 **Case study**

Year 6 class involved in a creative writing workshop at the Bowes Museum

The session began in the fine art gallery where Julia, an Education Officer, introduced the children to the large portrait of Napoleon I in his coronation robes. Julia led a discussion, which encouraged the children to find out more about Napoleon by thinking about his clothing, facial expression, pose and posture, as well as the background and setting of the portrait. The children were then asked to choose another portrait in the gallery that interested them and were given 20 minutes to sketch and record clues and details they could see in their chosen portrait.

Throughout the session the children recorded their writing in a booklet and were encouraged to edit their work to improve their sentences and enhance descriptions by adding similes, alliteration, hyperbole and other figurative language techniques, and were supported by their teacher. Before the children began each activity, Julia modelled the task using the Napoleon portrait so they had a model that they could follow.

Julia continually asked questions about what the character was thinking about at the time they had their picture painted and what emotions the character was feeling. In their booklets, the children wrote in first person, filling a thought bubble (like in a comic) with their character's thoughts at the time of the painting. Julia then asked the children which five items would be found inside their character's bag or pocket. The children were encouraged to write detailed descriptions of the items so their peers could visualise the belongings.

As the activities were short and fast-paced, the children built up lots of information about their characters. The children clearly enjoyed the lesson as at the end of each activity they were keen to share their work with Julia, their teacher and their peers.

 Activity

Writing your own story based on a painting

In the case study above the children based their writing around a classical portrait. Now we move on to more abstract art. Looking at the dream-like landscape of artists such as Chagall, Kandinsky or Miro can also have great benefit when planning to write a story. Show your class a Salvador Dali landscape such as *Swans Reflecting Elephants* or *The Persistence of Memory*.

- Who will be the central character in your story? Is your story going to be in the first or third person? Will there be any other characters?

- Are there plants or animals in your setting? Are they harmless or dangerous? Are there any sounds in your setting?

- How will your characters move around? Are they on foot or perhaps riding in or on something?

- Is there going to be a problem in your story? How will you solve this?

- What will be the ending? Will your characters return home? How?

- How can the story be improved? What editing will take place?

 Research focus

Structured writing

Children often need structures to scaffold writing. Interspersing a writing session with detailed further instructions in order to expand what is being written, as in the case study, will develop the children's writing at a pace that the teacher can control. This is important, as some children will find it difficult to retain instructions if too many are given at once. The DfE (2012) stated, *boys (and girls) can benefit from a range of diverse interventions such as stepped instructions using mini plenaries and task cards; using visual organisers and frames to scaffold text structure* (p20).

(Continued)

(Continued)

We often lead writing lessons by asking the class to contribute ideas for a piece of writing that is done collaboratively by the class. The children share ideas and we scribe them using a structure that we first decide on and then lead. Roth and Guinee (2011) maintain that collaborative writing is to be recommended. They say that, *Interactive Writing focuses on multiple aspects of writing development simultaneously and allows teachers to support each learner in the class at his or her own level of language and literacy, it is a promising approach to instructing and engaging young writers* (p354).

Drawing can also add another dimension to structured writing. If children are able to sketch some ideas to aid their planning, then this can significantly affect the amount that they write. According to Norris (1998, pp69–74), *The students in the group which drew before writing tended to produce more words, more sentences and more idea units, and their overall writing performance was higher than the students who wrote without drawing. These findings were consistent for boys as well as girls.*

If children draw their ideas, then they have a visual prompt that can be a useful tool in promoting independent writing.

Art is free expression. Art is whatever we interpret it to be. But even in art we can find ideas that give children a framework for their writing, as can be seen in the case study and activity above.

Conclusion – art is everywhere

Art is not restricted to galleries or museums. There is art everywhere. Whatever your opinion of graffiti or of public art, like sculptures and statues, it is all around. It is in our schools on display boards. In every primary classroom there is art. There are also books: books on shelves, books in bags, in trays, on desks, in hands. Books all around Picture books such as *FArTHER* by Grahame Baker-Smith or *The Invention of Hugo Cabret* by Brian Selznick are undeniably works of art. The illustrations are what make the book in these cases. Also, books like *Journey* by Aaron Becker, which contain no words at all, can tell a story in just as compelling a way as descriptive books.

Art can be practical too. Clarice Cliff's pottery is a classic example of amazing art that has a practical use. With her use of colour, a bowl can become a masterpiece. There is art all around us at every moment. It is sometimes useful or sometimes simply to be admired. It is inescapable and we should celebrate that.

Art is a subject that has most teachers divided. Some love teaching it and others loathe it. As primary school teachers, we have a vast range of subjects to teach. We cannot be experts in them all. But as art *is* everywhere, it is a resource at our fingertips. We should take full advantage of that and use it to inspire some incredible writing.

■■ Recommended websites ■■■■

Alma Animation – www.literacyshed.com/the-ghostly-shed.html

Build Your Wild Self – www.buildyourwildself.com

Dale Air – www.daleair.com/dispensing/vortex-cubes/

Fifth Sense – www.fifthsense.org.uk/psychology-and-smell/

Hamish Fullerton – www.hamish-fulton.com/hamish_fulton_v01.htm

Harris Burdick – www.houghtonmifflinbooks.com/features/harrisburdick/

Hero Factory – cpbherofactory.com

How Stuff Works – www.howstuffworks.com

Marshmallows Animation – www.literacyshed.com/the-fun-shed.html

Scholastic Art and Writing Awards – www.artandwriting.org

Sprout Boy Animation – www.radiotimes.com/news/2015-12-01/meet-sprout-boy---the-christmas-character-loved-by-sherlock-doctor-who-and-luther

■■ References ■■■■

Baker-Smith, G. (2011) *FArTHER*. London: Templar Publishing.

Becker, A. (2014) *Journey*. London: Walker Books.

Bell, J. (2004) *500 Self-Portraits*. London: Phaidon Press.

Croker Costa, L-J. (2008) *Predictors of Students At-Risk for Writing Problems: The Development of Written Expression for Early Elementary School Children*. Chapel Hill, NC:. University of North Carolina.

DfE (2001) *Developing Early Writing*. London: Department for Education.

DfE (2008) *The National Strategies: Primary Support for Writing: Fiction*. London: Department for Education.

DfE (2012) *What is the Research Evidence on Writing?* London: Education Standards Research Team, Department for Education.

Doubilet, D. (2003) *Fish Face*. London: Phaidon Press.

Hattie, J. (2003) *Teachers Make a Difference: What is the Research Evidence?* Auckland: Auckland University Press.

Nesbit, E. (2016) *The Railway Children*. Oxford: Oxford University Press.

Norris, E. (1998) Children's use of drawing as a pre-writing strategy. *Journal of Research in Reading*, University of Texas.

Roth, K. and Guinee, K. (2011) Ten minutes a day: the impact of interactive writing instruction on first graders' independent writing. *Journal of Early Childhood Literacy*. London: Sage.

Selznick, B. (2007) *The Invention of Hugo Cabret*. London: Scholastic.

UKLA (2004) *Raising Boys' Achievement in Writing*. Hertfordshire: United Kingdom Literacy Association.

Van Allsburg, C. (2011) *The Mysteries of Harris Burdick*. London: Anderson Press.

Van Allsburg, C. (2013) *The Chronicles of Harris Burdick*. London: Anderson Press

Wang, J. and Wang, H. (2012) *Cozy Classics – Moby Dick*. Vancouver: Simply Read Books.

13

Writing in MFL

Tina Page with Nathalie Paris from Natta-lingo

Teachers' Standards

Standard 3 - Demonstrate good subject and curriculum knowledge

- have a secure knowledge of the relevant subject(s) and curriculum areas, foster and maintain pupils' interest in the subject, and address misunderstandings
- demonstrate a critical understanding of developments in the subject and curriculum areas, and promote the value of scholarship

Standard 4 - Plan and teach well-structured lessons

- impart knowledge and develop understanding through effective use of lesson time
- promote a love of learning and children's intellectual curiosity

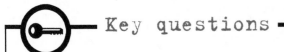

Key questions

- How do we introduce the skill of writing to early learners of a foreign language?
- How can we encourage early learners to write in a foreign language?
- What approaches can we use to develop writing in a foreign language?

Introduction

The purpose of this chapter is to provide a context for current primary practice in teaching a foreign language, and to explore how teaching the skill of writing in a foreign language to early learners consolidates and enhances their learning, in addition to being a creative and expressive element of their primary experience. Throughout their careers teachers develop a keen awareness of the relationship between child and language. In teaching a foreign language it is important for the teacher to

> have in mind that even monolingual children bring many languages with them before they enter a foreign language programme: a dialect, a secret code, the language of poems learned in their L1 (First Language) lessons

(Kubanek-German, 1998, p203)

Teaching writing is one of four important skills in language learning, all of which are integral to a balanced effective approach to teaching a foreign language. Primary school teachers are not necessarily language specialists. They teach a broad range of subjects across a wide ability range and resources for teaching a foreign language are vital to its delivery. Resources need to be up-to-date, easily accessible, relevant and appropriate, and carefully designed to cater for the age and ability range for which they are intended. Writing is an important communicative skill in a learner's first language and in a foreign language. As Newton (2016) states, it develops knowledge and is a valuable tool supporting lifelong learning.

Foreign language examples in this chapter have, where necessary, been translated into English so that the meaning is clear.

Statutory status

Research into the development of first language over 40 years ago suggested that young children were more receptive to language learning (Penfield and Roberts, 1959; Stern, 1963; Lennenberg, 1967). This did not, however, influence education policy as Burstall et al.'s research into the early learning of French in the 1960s and 1970s highlighted problems with over-assessment, and a lack of enjoyment in language learning (Burstall et al., 1974). This resulted in a declining interest in an early start to language learning. Subsequent initiatives in primary language learning, involving a variety of delivery arrangements such as after-school and lunchtime clubs in the 1990s, lacked impact on central government primary education policy as this was dominated by the National Literacy and Numeracy Strategies (Page, 2000, p76). The National Languages Strategy for England, Languages for All: Languages for Life did rekindle interest in early language learning and paved the way for an early start: all primary school pupils between the ages of seven and eleven in England would have an entitlement to learn a new language by 2010 (DfES, 2002). By 2009, almost all primary schools were offering languages at Key Stage 2, and fully meeting the entitlement to all year groups (Wade and Marshall, 2009, p1). Statutory status came into effect in September 2014.

The study of a foreign language is a compulsory subject at Key Stage 2. Its title is 'foreign language' and at Key Stage 3 it is 'modern foreign language'. The focus of study in teaching foreign languages is communication, and at Key Stage 2 the focus is on practical communication, with no specific language prescribed. Primary schools can choose to teach any modern foreign language (MFL) or an ancient language such as Latin or Greek where the emphasis is on reading comprehension and an appreciation of civilisation rather than practical communication. The Languages Programmes of Study: Key Stage 2 states that the teaching of a foreign language *should focus on enabling pupils to make substantial progress in one language* (DfE, 2013, p212). Almost all the schools participating in a recent survey on language teaching in primary schools, reported teaching a foreign language as part of their Key Stage 2 curriculum, and more than half had been teaching languages to primary-phase pupils for more than five years (Board and Tinsley, 2015, p35). Schools in England, according to the evidence, appear to be teaching French in the main, *although some do introduce a second language for a short time* (Driscoll et al., 2015, p235).

Why learn a language?

Delivering a 'high-quality' languages education, the purpose of studying a foreign language, according to the National Curriculum, not only deepens children's understanding of the world but also equips them to work in other countries. Perhaps the first sentence of the 'Purpose of study' for the Languages Programmes of Study: Key Stage 2 (National Curriculum in England) provides a better answer to the question title of this section: *Learning a foreign language is a liberation from insularity and provides an opening to other cultures* (DfE, 2013, p1).

Apart from the 'practical', the 'horizons broadening' and 'reading great literature in the original', which are very sound reasons for learning a language, another good reason for learning a language is its value in providing the learner with a new set of codes and skills. This enhances literacy and general intellectual development. Learning a language is essentially about communication. Teaching pupils to communicate in a foreign language is a main element of its purpose, and writing in a foreign language is an essential part of this: *The teaching should enable pupils to express their ideas and thoughts in another language and to understand and respond to its speakers, both in speech and in writing* (DfE, 2013, p193).

Responding to speakers of a foreign language in both speech and writing demands intercultural awareness. Primary schools celebrate other cultures in their lessons, for example, on world religions in their Religious Education (Bushnell, 2016). History and geography also provide opportunities for developing children's cultural awareness. Language learning extends the scope of this cultural awareness by giving them the opportunity to master a foreign language and gain a new perspective on their own language, and the lives and cultures of others.

Writing in a foreign language

Although communication is the main focus of foreign language learning, there is an increasing emphasis in the National Curriculum placed on the mastery of grammar. The Communicative Competence Approach, based on a range of communicative language strategies, and drawing on Krashen's target language input hypothesis (1982), has dominated language teaching in England for over 30 years with an emphasis on the skills of listening and speaking. Although for the teacher of a foreign language there has always been importance placed on balancing the four skill areas of listening, speaking, reading and writing, first steps in language learning, particularly for early learners, were generally made by listening and speaking. Writing might be the last skill to be introduced when the teacher was confident that the words or sentences would contain few errors. In the new primary curriculum and in order to achieve the outcomes below, teachers of a foreign language need to incorporate writing tasks at an early stage.

The primary national curriculum for languages has four aims:

* *understand and respond to spoken and written language from a variety of authentic sources;*

* *speak with increasing confidence, fluency and spontaneity, finding ways of communication what they want to say, including through discussion and asking questions, and continually improving the accuracy of their pronunciation and intonation;*

* *can write at varying length, for different purposes and audiences, using the variety of grammatical structures that they have learnt;*

* *discover and develop an appreciation of a range of writing in the language studied.*

(DfE, 2013, p193)

There are twelve areas stipulated in the primary national curriculum for foreign language subject content. Three areas relate directly to writing: Pupils should be taught to.

* *read carefully and show understanding of words, phrases and simple writing;*

* *write phrases from memory, and adapt these to create new sentences, to express ideas clearly;*

* *describe people, places, things and actions orally and in writing.*

(DfE, 2013, p194)

Teaching writing

Telling a story in a foreign language is a motivating way to prepare young children for the task of simple writing. It provides a good opportunity for listening to the sound of the language, to repeat words or phrases in preparation for the task of writing. In order to provide a stimulus for a writing task there is a wealth of foreign language reading resources easily accessible online. They include translations of all-time favourites such as *The Hungry Caterpillar* and *Stick Man*, and a plethora of authentic language books; for example, for teaching French, *Aboie Georges!* (Feiffer, 2000), for teaching Spanish, *Ardilla tiene hambre* (Kitamura, 1998). Natta-lingo provides online reading resources for teachers of a foreign language (www.natta-lingo.gihem.info). As primary teachers are engaged with teaching literacy skills to mixed ability classes, language provision *may improve, as learners have greater access to the creative cross-curricular potential of the written word and the wealth of opportunity offered by storybooks and the internet* (Driscoll et al., 2015, p238).

One of the main concerns for teachers in introducing a writing task into their language teaching, particularly for early learners, can be their level of accuracy in, for example, copying words or phrases. For some learners finding difficulty in writing in English, it is vital that the foreign language writing tasks are carefully designed and differentiated for all abilities. It is inevitable that errors will be made in writing in a foreign language, but as Hurrell points out:

> to deny the children access to the written word until such times as error is avoidable, is to deny them access to a cornucopia and to run counter to pedagogy in mother tongue acquisition … there is a creative impulse in all children and they will want to commit this creativity to the permanence of the written text.
>
> (Hurrell, 1999, p81, pp 83–4)

Storytelling is the impetus for the author's idea of 'word banks' in a foreign language. Posters are made by pupils illustrating a story setting, as in this example in French:

> Underneath the poster there are a range of 'pockets' … In the various 'pockets' language items such as 'devant' (in front of), 'le village'(village) and 'je vois' (I see) are placed. The children take one card from each 'pocket', make up a sentence, physically (for example, derrière la maison il y a un grand parc = behind the house there is a large park) and tangibly lay the sentence out in front of them, have it checked by the teacher, then write it into their jotter with an accompanying illustration.
>
> (Hurrell, 1999, p85, cited in Driscoll and Frost, 1999)

The following case studies amply illustrate how a story in a foreign language can provide a very good opportunity for the teacher to introduce a writing task by using the skills of reading, listening and speaking, in addition to encouraging early learners to be creative and imaginative in their work. In the first case study the teacher introduces a simple writing task in French to early learners in Year 3. In the second case study, Year 4 pupils who have been learning their foreign language for two years produce a mini book in Spanish.

 Case study

Introducing children to writing in French

Nathalie provided a writing task for Year 3 writing in French for the first time. Writing in French for the first time can be a daunting experience for the early learner of a foreign language. They may be struggling with writing in their own language and lacking in confidence with forming their letters and making sentences. Nathalie used a story to introduce her new pupils to the French language. This case study shows how Year 3 pupils were taught to write in this block of four half-hour language lessons.

(Continued)

(Continued)

Lesson 1: *Petit-Bleu et Petit-Jaune* (Little-Blue and Little-Yellow) by Leo Lionni provided the stimulus for writing. Nathalie planned a lesson reading half the book to her new pupils asking questions in English.

Lesson 2: The rest of the story was read to pupils with questions in English. Each pupil was given a copy of the book.

Lesson 3: Nathalie read the story again while pupils followed it in their book and kept a tally of the number of times the colours 'bleu' (blue) and 'jaune' (yellow) were mentioned.

Lesson 4: Pupils were given a French exercise book (they differ from English exercise books as they usually have squared paper rather than lined paper). Pupils were given their writing task, copying examples from the board, writing a phrase, for example, *Bonjour Petit-Bleu* (Hello Little-Blue), next to a coloured piece of paper representing the story-book characters, and sticking this into their exercise book.

Nathalie's first lesson was designed to involve her new pupils, and gain their interest by reading half of the story book. She chose easy, direct questions, for example: 'Who do you think this is?' and 'What do think the word "maison" (house) means?' and 'What do you think he will do next?' The pupils had time to think about the story, guess what would happen next, and start to enjoy hearing a new language. The story also provided an opportunity to introduce the greeting 'Bonjour' (Hello) as each character was introduced. Nathalie chose a 'cliff-hanging moment' to stop reading the book, and the children did not want her to stop.

The second lesson centred on reading and understanding the second half of the book. First, Nathalie used similar techniques, making use of questions in English to ensure pupils understood everything. Second, pupils were given their own personal copy of the story. They were fascinated and looked for words they could recognise immediately, for example, the names of the characters. This formed the basis for the third lesson when Nathalie re-read the story. Pupils were able to follow it in their own books. They also kept a tally of the number of times they heard the colours 'bleu' and 'jaune'. New colours were added to the pupils' vocabulary through the use of flashcards.

In addition to their own story book, pupils were given their own French exercise book. Nathalie prepared the first writing lesson by showing her new pupils a document on the board. This showed an example: a picture of the main character with the writing: 'Bonjour Petit-Bleu!' (Hello Little-Blue!) beside it. The name of the character was a different colour and there was a list of the main characters from the book underneath. The task was to copy the example then write 'Bonjour' (Hello) with the names of each character next to pieces of coloured paper which represented them. Then pupils could stick them in their books. The children really enjoyed the task. Some only managed to copy the example, while others asked to do extra characters and use more colours. Nathalie encouraged her new pupils to pay particular care to their use of capital letters and exclamation marks as well as their spellings of the key three French words.

This series of lessons provides an excellent illustration of how writing can be introduced to early learners of a foreign language. It shows in detail how writing can be successfully introduced using the three other skills of reading, listening and speaking. It also shows how carefully designed lessons geared to teaching writing in a foreign language can incorporate good opportunities for enhancing early learners' experience of a foreign language with new, different and interesting resources.

Research focus

Making links

Making links between English and a foreign language is a good exercise for the early language learner; for example, compound words which contain prefixes and suffixes. Datta and Pomphrey (2004) provide an example of how the teacher can ask children to collect and compare prefixes and suffixes in languages they know and how storytelling can be used to support their grammatical knowledge of, for example, the prefix 'un' in Hindi, which is like the English prefix 'un'.

> Sometimes a story can stimulate a discussion about linguistic features such as prefixes. For example the story in Hindi about an unthoughtful man in the village ek gaun ki ek unoochit aadmi ki kahani *(literally a village's unthoughtful man's story).*

> (Datta and Pomphrey, 2004, p63)

Cheater highlights the advantages of making links with 'Literacy' in teaching a foreign language: the new programmes of study in English and in learning a foreign language complement each other and help teachers to make links for their pupils. This can be found at www.networkforlanguageslondon. org.uk/blog/making-the-link-with-english-literacy. Concepts such as word, sentence, full stop, comma, capital letter, are familiar to primary pupils. When teaching French, Cheater (2014) illustrates how children love to read the page on which the wolf cries 'J'arrive!'

> Children adore giving the 'secret signal' to show they have recognised it. This in turn, provides an opportunity for children to share what they know about speech marks and the exclamation mark, and to notice similarities and differences between English and French punctuation – ah, intercultural understanding!

> (Cheater, 2014, on above website)

Activity

The skills of reading and writing are closely related, as Lambirth states: *reading experiences are integral to being able to write* (Lambirth, 2015, p14). One of the ways in which a teacher can start an interest in writing in a foreign language can be in providing a new 'foreign language' name for each pupil. This can be written by the teacher to be copied by the pupil. Depending on the ability of the pupils the teacher can provide a template so that pupils can try out writing their new name, for example, in French script. Each example below starts with the phrase 'My name is ... ':

Je m'appelle Marie-Christine

Je m'appelle Guillaume

(Continued)

(Continued)

This exercise can be useful in giving pupils an opportunity to discuss differences in writing and the teacher can easily provide examples from authentic sources. Some pupils may already have been to France on holiday and noticed how menus are often written on a chalk board in French writing.

Early learners can benefit from tracing words and letters with a finger using, for example, a story, poem or song. This is a very good way for children to hear the intonation, and cadences of a foreign language. Attention can be drawn to, for example, in German, the use of capital letters for all nouns, or in French, the accents, and in both languages the use of punctuation. The following examples of a well-known children's song in both German and French illustrate how children, learning either language, might trace the words and sing a song which is easily memorised by early beginners because of its brevity and repetitiveness.

Bruder Jakob, Bruder Jakob,	Frère Jacques, Frère Jacques,
Schläfst du noch, schläfst du noch?	Dormez-vous, Dormez-vous?
Hörst du nicht die Glocken?	Sonnez les matines!
Hörst du nicht die Glocken?	Sonnez les matines!
Ding ding dong, ding ding dong.	Ding ding dong, ding ding dong.

A follow-on activity can be designed when the song is committed to memory. Children can be given a sheet with some of the words from the song replaced with a picture, under which they can write the French or German word. A further activity for learners in Years 5 and 6 using the songs above can be in teaching grammar points; the 'negative' in German using 'nicht', and the 'vous' form of the verb in French. The song can also provide a template for pupils to write their own rhyme and put it to music.

Case study

Creative writing in Spanish

In this case study Year 4 pupils are writing in Spanish: they write their own versions of the story of *Los Quatros Amigos* (The Four Friends).

Grammar: Prior to writing their mini books, Year 4 pupils had been learning their colours and the names of animals in Spanish. They learnt that nouns can be 'masculine' or 'feminine' and the adjective must 'agree' with the noun, and that the word order is different. In Spanish, the adjective comes after the noun: for example, the word for horse in Spanish is masculine, 'el caballo', the word for sheep is feminine, 'la oveja'; the white horse = *el caballo blanco*; the white sheep = *la oveja blanca*.

Preparation for writing: The teacher and Year 4 pupils shared the story in Spanish of 'The Four Friends': four animals who call on each other for help to reach an apple at the top of a tree, together manage to grab it and share it.

Writing the mini book: The pupils' task was to design a mini book which would be a simplified version of the story in Spanish in which they had to change the names of the animals and the colours to make it their own.

Resources: Each pupil was given a sheet of A4 paper. They were shown how to fold and cut it to make it into a mini book. This provided them with a glossary of animals in English and Spanish and a simplified version of the story for them to adapt.

Method: When the Year 4 pupils had selected their four chosen animals in Spanish they designed their front cover. They were encouraged to add the words for colours, writing their version of the Spanish story at their own pace. Then they illustrated their story.

Differentiation: This happened by outcome as some of the pupils wrote little more than a line per page (not including colours) while others managed the whole story, including correct adjectival agreements.

This writing lesson in Spanish for Year 4 pupils is an excellent example of how writing in a foreign language can be a creative and enriching experience in self-expression. Adjectival agreements in Spanish had been taught in an enjoyable way using the names of animals and colours. A story was used to stimulate interest in the foreign language. As in the case above, a story provided an opportunity for the teacher to introduce a writing task using the three other skills of reading, listening and speaking. The Year 4 pupils who produced their own mini books in Spanish were so proud of their work they asked if they could take them home.

 Activity

Early learners, learning a foreign language for more than a year, are generally more able to write longer and more complex sentences than those who have just started a foreign language. The first step in writing a longer sentence can be to use commonly used connectives; for example, in French, German and Spanish: 'et', 'und', 'y' (and); 'mais', 'aber', 'pero' (but); 'avec', 'mit', 'con' (with). A simple writing task for early learners, which can be developed into a more complex one, is to provide children with a grid of words they know already on a topic and which they have practised relating to their likes and dislikes. They use the grid as a guide, copy the sentence and provide the connectives. The example below is in French: Emily likes rabbits (and) frogs, (but) she can't stand ants and wasps. Edward can't stand mice (and) tortoises (but) he likes dogs and cats.

| Emily | aime | les lapins | et | les grenouilles | mais | elle déteste | les fourmis | et | les guêpes |
| Edward | déteste | les souris | et | les tortues | mais | il aime | les chiens | et | les chats |

Years 5 and 6 will have two or three years of foreign language learning and will be using different tenses, subordinate and relative clauses, and adverbial phrases of place or time. To develop this task further the teacher can:

- replace words with pictures: children are asked to write the 'picture' words from memory;

- introduce 'likes' and 'dislikes' for everyday activities, for example, daily routine and sport;

- introduce reasons for likes and dislikes using the connective 'because';

- display a survey of 'likes and dislikes' written by children in the class.

Activity

Do a survey of the 'likes and dislikes' of children in the class. Divide the class into groups and use the grid above as a basis for an extended writing task, for example, each member of the group writes about the likes and dislikes of the rest of the group. More verbs can be introduced, for example, 'adorer' (to love). New grammar points can be introduced, for example, the *negative* which in French uses 'ne pas' (e.g. elle n'aime pas = she doesn't like). Longer sentences can be introduced by showing the class how to use the verb 'aimer' (to like) followed by another verb in the 'infinitive', for example, 'jouer' (to play). Early learners who have mastered how to write 'j'aime' (I like); 'je n'aime pas' (I don't like); 'il/elle aime' (he/she likes); 'il/elle n'aime pas' (he/she doesn't like), enjoy expanding their sentences. They are able to be more specific in describing what they and others like, or dislike, for example, in French, 'Je n'aime pas jouer au ping-pong. Harry adore jouer à cache-cache' (I don't like to play table tennis. Harry loves to play hide and seek). When each member of the class has several sentences for themselves and each member of their group, they can offer to present their 'research' to the whole class.

Research focus

Linguistic concepts

Cheater makes use of speaking and writing frames for Year 5 and 6 pupils. This enables them to 'understand the linguistic concepts' (www.networkforlanguageslondon.org.uk/blog/making-the-link-with-literacy). Taking this a step further, she encourages the use of a bilingual dictionary so that pupils can choose their own vocabulary and create longer sentences using a range of tenses (Cheater, 2014). Driscoll shows how using a dictionary helped children in Year 5 and 6 prepare compound sentences joining together short texts on an ecological theme (Driscoll et al., 2015).

Research by teaching school alliances highlights the need for good resources for teaching writing. One project at a primary school in the south-west of England focused on finding a methodology which would enhance confidence to learn and teach reading and writing in French. An important feature of the research was identifying skills and resources which could be easily transferred to non-specialist teachers. Whereas the story-telling method had been used previously to learn a story by heart, repeat and adapt for other writing, this research centred more on introducing a story using games and repetitive activities. Another new element was the introduction of a story map, produced as an 'aide-memoire', and where important words were included. Pupils then were able to create their own story map. This consolidated their learning and they were able to practise their story with the teacher leading less and less as pupils' confidence grew (Cross, 2013, in Churches, 2013). Another project on teaching a foreign language in a Special Education setting illustrates how Year 5 and Year 6 pupils enjoy reading simple French texts and love written language (Kelly, 2013, in Churches, 2013). One project investigated the use of interactive e-books with less able Key Stage 3 pupils illustrating how a *digilog*, which uses a page-turn with 3D effect, culminated in a written piece about a real or imagined holiday (Hall, 2013, in Churches, 2013).

Activity

Providing pupils with an opportunity to communicate with pupils of a similar age in the foreign country whose language they are learning is a wonderful way to encourage learning, especially if it can be arranged by teachers in the English and 'foreign language' primary schools. Writing to a friend, in class, or in school, is a meaningful task which can incorporate valuable lessons in sentence structure, grammar, punctuation and presentation. The different conventions we use in writing a short letter or post-card, and writing an email or text can be discussed with pupils and a display of the various means we use for communicating messages in a foreign language as well as in English is a good way to consolidate this work.

 Activity

One of the aims of the language programmes of study for Key Stage 2 is to ensure all pupils understand and respond to spoken and written language from a variety of authentic sources. Teachers can introduce an authentic source very effectively with early learners of a foreign language using poetry. It is essential to choose a poem which is attractive to early learners regarding content, length and sound, for example, the poem below in Spanish which is easily accessible on the 'Spanish Playground' website: www.spanishplayground.net. It is about a squirrel (*la ardilla*). It is a short poem and one that can easily be used to encourage pupils to write their own poems. 'La ardilla' by the Mexican poet, Amado Nervo, has several simple verbs and is easily committed to memory.

La ardilla corre,	the squirrel runs
La ardilla vuela,	the squirrel flys
La ardilla salta,	the squirrel jumps
Como locuela.	Like a madcap.
-Mamá, la ardilla	Mum, isn't the squirrel going to school?
¿No va a la escuela?	
Ven, ardillita,	Come here, little squirrel,
tengo una jaula	I have a cage
que es muy bonita.	which is very pretty.
No, yo prefiero	No, I prefer
mi tronco de árbol	my tree trunk
y mi agujero.	and my hole.

The poem can be read out loud by the teacher. Pupils can mime the actions before the whole class read the poem together. Oral questions on the text can help pupils to remember the sequence of

(Continued)

(Continued)

this little story. Pupils can be given the poem to trace words and read the poem with the teacher. When the poem is partially or fully memorised, pupils can start to use the poem to help them to write their own. They can do this by substituting words in the poem with vocabulary and verbs they have already learnt. When they are ready, pupils can read their poems to each other, and to the class. The poems can be illustrated and displayed in the class and/or in the school. They can also be linked to cross-curricular themes.

Conclusion

Writing in a foreign language is an excellent opportunity to provide early learners of a foreign language with an insight into the mechanics of a different language. It is a skill which does not have to be left until last, or attempted when the other skills are deemed to be sufficiently mastered. If it is the 'flip side' to reading, writing has its roots in listening and speaking. Storytelling, songs and poetry are good ways in which to introduce foreign language words. Building confidence is essential in teaching writing in a foreign language. Good lesson planning together with appropriate and relevant resources are key to building early learners' confidence in writing in a foreign language. The first steps will very likely be copying the foreign language word, and this can be closely followed by simple sentences as the case studies above have illustrated. Writing in a foreign language can be supported with a cross-curricular approach: all primary curriculum subjects can be reference points, for example, English can be used to consolidate understanding a foreign language story or poem; geography can supply a foreign language focus on an ecological theme; religious education can support a foreign language in intercultural awareness. Writing is a highly creative activity which complements the skill of writing in English, allowing pupils to step outside of their English literacy experience, and view it differently, through a 'foreign language' lens.

━━━ References ━━━

Board, K. and Tinsley, T. (2015) *Language Trends 2014/15: The State of Language Learning in Primary and Secondary Schools in England*. British Council CfBT Education Trust 2015. Available from: www.britishcouncil.org (accessed online 25/7/16).

Burstall, C., Jamieson, M., Cohen, S. and Hargreaves, M. (1974) *Primary French in the Balance*. Slough: National Foundation for Educational Research.

Carle, E. (1969) *The Hungry Caterpillar*. London: Penguin Putnam.

Cheater, C. (2014) Making the link with English literacy. *Network for Languages*. Available from: www.networkforlanguageslondon.org.uk/blog/making-the-link-with-english-literacy (accessed 15/7/16).

Churches, R. (ed.) (2013) *The Quiet Revolution: Transformational Languages Research by Teaching School Alliances*. CfBT Education Trust. Available from: www.educationdevelopmenttrust.com (accessed 15/7/16).

Cross, J. (2013) How non-specialist primary school teachers can use stories and extended texts to enhance teacher and pupil confidence in reading and writing skills. In: Churches, R. (ed.) (2013) *The Quiet Revolution: Transformational Languages Research by Teaching School Alliances.* CfBT Education Trust. Available from: www.educationdevelopmenttrust.com (accessed 15/7/16).

Datta, M. and Pomphrey, C. (2004) A world of language. *Young Pathfinder,*10. CILT The National Centre for Languages. Early Language Learning (ELL).

DfE (Department for Education) (2013) *National Curriculum in England: Primary Curriculum.* Available from: www.gov.uk (accessed 14/7/16).

DfES (2002) *Languages for All: Languages for Life. A Strategy for England.* London: DfES Publications.

Donaldson, J. and Scheffler, A. (2008) *Stick Man.* London: Scholastic.

Driscoll, P. and Frost, D. (eds) (1999) *The Teaching of Modern Foreign Languages in the Primary School.* London: Routledge.

Driscoll, P., Lambirth, A. and Roden, J. (eds) (2015) *The Primary Curriculum: A Creative Approach.* London: Sage.

Feiffer, J. (2000) *Aboie Georges!* Brussels: École des Loisirs.

Hall, K. (2013) Investigating the use of interactive books with less able pupils. In: Churches, R. (ed.) (2013) *The Quiet Revolution: Transformational Languages Research by Teaching School Alliances.* CfBT Education Trust. Available from: www.educationdevelopmenttrust.com (accessed 15/7/16).

Hurrell, A. (1999) The four language skills: the whole works! In: Driscoll, D. and Frost, D. (eds)*The Teaching of Modern Foreign Languages in the Primary School.* London: Routledge.

Kelly, K. (2013) What is the impact of modern foreign languages on engagement and communication of Autism Spectrum Disorder (ASD) Pupils in Key Stage 2? In: Churches, R. (ed.) (2013) *The Quiet Revolution: Transformational Languages Research by Teaching School Alliances.* CfBT Education Trust. Available from: www.educationdevelopmenttrust.com (accessed 15/7/16).

Kitamura, S. (1998) *Ardilla tiene hambre.* Mexico: Fondo de Cultura Económica.

Krashen, S. (1982) *Principles and Practice in Second Language Acquisition.* New York: Pergamon Press.

Kubanek-German, A. (1998) Primary Foreign Language Teaching in Europe – trends and issues. *Language Teaching,* 31 (04): 193–205.

Lambirth, A. (2015) An Introduction to English. In: Driscoll, P., Lambirth, A. and Roden, J. (eds) *The Primary Curriculum. A Creative Approach.* London: SAGE.

Lennenberg, D. (1967) *Biological Foundations of Language.* New York: John Wiley.

Lionni, L. (1997) *Petit-Bleu et Petit-Jaune.* Brussels: L'École des Loisirs.

Newton, (D.P.) (2016) Writing in Design & Technology. In: Bushnell, A. and Waugh, D. (eds) *Inviting Writing Across the Curriculum.* London: Learning Matters/Sage.

Page, T. (2000) A new era for primary foreign languages? University of Hull, unpublished.

Penfield, W. and Roberts, J. (1959) *Speech and Brain Mechanisms*. Princeton, NJ: Princeton University Press.

Stern, H.H. (ed.) (1963) *Foreign Languages in Primary Education*. London: Oxford University Press.

Wade, P. and Marshall, H., with O'Donnell, S. (2009) *Primary Modern Foreign Languages: Longitudinal Survey of Implementation of National Entitlement to Language Learning at Key Stage 2*. London: DCSF.

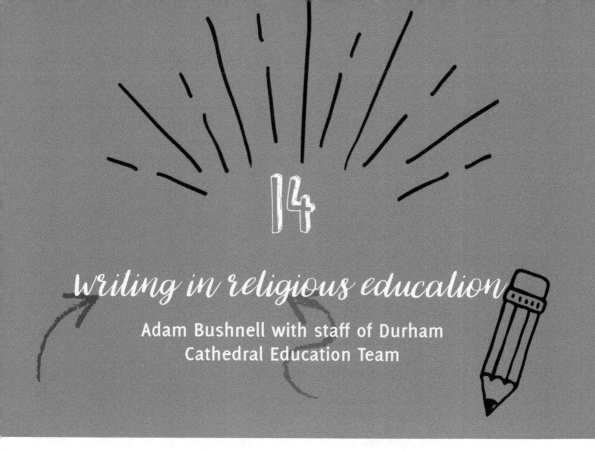

14
Writing in religious education

Adam Bushnell with staff of Durham
Cathedral Education Team

Teachers' Standards

Standard 3 – Demonstrate good subject and curriculum knowledge

- have a secure knowledge of the relevant subject(s) and curriculum areas, foster and maintain pupils' interest in the subject, and address misunderstandings
- demonstrate a critical understanding of developments in the subject and curriculum areas, and promote the value of scholarship
- demonstrate an understanding of and take responsibility for promoting high standards of literacy, articulacy and the correct use of standard English, whatever the teacher's specialist subject

Standard 4 – Plan and teach well-structured lessons

- impart knowledge and develop understanding through effective use of lesson time
- promote a love of learning and children's intellectual curiosity

---

⊙━━ `Key questions` ━━━━━━━━━━━━━━━━━━━━━━━━━━

- How can we inspire children to want to write during religious education lessons?
- What steps lead to effective writing based around religion?
- How can we maintain high-quality writing in religious education?

Introduction

If I were to ask you if I can steal your pen and you say yes, then is that stealing?

Is there really no such thing as a stupid question?

If you were to be reincarnated, would you come back as a dog?

These are questions that come from the website www.thunks.co.uk.

The heading at the top of the website bears the subheading 'questions to make your brain go ouch!', but they can be so much more than this.

Questions are essential in religious education (RE). Questions are designed to make you think. Thinking leads to wondering which leads to deciding, which leads to understanding, which leads to reflecting, which leads to knowing, which leads to giving opinions, which leads to concluding, which leads to justifying and finally arriving at effective learning.

Passionate arguments take place in the classroom during RE lessons. You might think that arguing in the classroom is inappropriate, but it is the *right* kind of arguing in this case. If children are arguing about something, it is because they care. When children care about something, they are more inclined to want to write about it. It is when children are disaffected from what they are writing about that leads to poor writing.

This chapter seeks to give practical examples of how RE can produce not only effective learning, but also enhanced thinking skills and ultimately high-quality writing. We will now explore how we can inspire children to *want* to write during RE lessons.

Belief systems of the world religions

As teachers or people working in education, we have very rewarding but also very stressful jobs. There are times when the children we work with can test our patience to its very limit. In all of the world religions, there is an element of addressing this.

All major religions have times of reflection, of clearing the mind, whether this is through meditation, retreat or prayer. This is essential for the classroom too, both for teachers and children. We all need to know that we make mistakes and that this is part of learning, especially when we are writing.

In Durham Cathedral the stonemasons who carved the intricate patterns on the columns were described as being able to produce perfect results. But this did not make them happy. In fact, it had quite the opposite effect. These artists started to put deliberate mistakes into their work, such as patterns that don't follow on from one another. They were trying to illustrate that they weren't perfect, that the only perfect being in the universe is God. Knowing that none of us is perfect and that we all make mistakes is essential for children.

Part of the biggest problem in writing is that children are so very hard on themselves. They believe that what they can produce is just never good enough, so some do not want to try in the first place. By teaching children this important life lesson, reflected by all of the world's religions, we can encourage them at least to attempt to write something, to at least have a go.

Carol Dweck (2000, p1) states:

> *You might think that students who were highly skilled would be the ones who relish a challenge and persevere in the face of setbacks. Instead, many of these students are the most worried about failure, and the most likely to question their ability and to wilt when they hit obstacles.*

It is children's belief in themselves that is the first step towards high-quality writing. We can teach children this through looking at any of the major religions. There is a clear message that runs through each of them: you as an individual are loved and are special. When children believe this then they can believe in themselves.

The World Health Organization (2001) states that there are four anchors of mental health. The first is being loved, the second is belief in something, the third is a sense of belonging and the fourth is routine. Primary schools offer all four of these anchors. It is these four anchors that not only lead to positive mental health, but also to high-quality writing.

So remember, don't let the stress of the job get to you or get to your children. Use the world religions as your guide. Take the advice of the great philosopher, Elsa, and *let it go!*

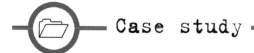 **Case study**

Year 6 class discussing Auschwitz as part of their topic on the Second World War

The Holocaust is one of the most tragic and saddening moments in the history of our world. To teach it in primary schools requires a great deal of understanding and sensitivity on the subject. Jane, a Year 6 teacher, read her class the picture book *Erika's Story* by Ruth Vander Zee. It is a heart-rending and moving book. There is a brief discussion about the story afterwards.

Jane had prepared some images that she had found on the Internet. These had been stapled together in the following order.

1. A busy train station in Nazi-occupied Poland

2. The carriages of the 'death trains'

(Continued)

(Continued)

3. The train station at Auschwitz

4. An empty dormitory

5. A dormitory filled with inmates

6. Children wearing the stripped uniform of Auschwitz standing behind barbed wire

7. A vast pile of wedding rings collected from a gas chamber

8. A vast pile of spectacles collected from a gas chamber

9. The Auschwitz orchestra

The children were shown each image one at a time and their teacher explained the history behind each one. Once all of the images had been revealed and discussed, the children worked in small groups to discuss all of what they could remember.

A question-and-answer session followed, led by the teacher.

Jane then asked the children to imagine what it would have been like in the dormitories. She asked them what they would have seen and heard. She explained that the uniforms would have been very thin. The beds would have had no blankets or pillows. The food would have been served in bowls and often there was not enough for everyone. She then asked the children what they would have felt both physically and emotionally. Smells and tastes that would have been in the air were then also discussed.

The children then wrote words and phrases on a sheet depicting five senses and emotions. Jane modelled three sentences using the children's word banks. The children then wrote their own sentences using the template they had been given. Each child was given the option of not using the template on the board and could make up their own sentences. All children then chose their favourite sentence that they had written and shared them with the class.

The case study contained a highly sensitive subject, but the teacher knew her subject well. It was a lesson focused on discussion and all of the children were highly engaged. This was reflected in the sentences that were shared. The writing contained vivid descriptions and a lot of factual detail. This process could be repeated looking at images from other periods of history.

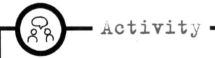

Activity

Discussing evil

The problem of evil in the world is something that all the world's religions have an opinion on. How can God allow bad things to happen to good people? Read through the case study above in which a teacher introduces a very sensitive topic through images in a chronological order. The aim of the lesson was to encourage children to take part in a class discussion that would lead to a piece of writing using all five senses.

Think of a different period of history that may lend itself to the discussion of the problem of evil in the world, such as war, famine, natural disaster, etc.

- What images could you use to introduce it? A before and after scene?

- What books or websites could you use to give information about your chosen topic? What other resources would get the children listening and engaged?

- Would you use a picture book like *Erika's Story*? There are suggested texts at the end of this chapter.

- What might you ask them to discuss? How would you manage this? How could you deal with the subject matter as sensitively as possible?

In planning such work, it is important both to know your subject before the lesson and be honest if you do not know the answer. Finding out information with a class of pupils can be extremely rewarding for all.

 Research focus

Research evidence on writing

The DfE (2012) in its report on *What is the Research Evidence on Writing?*, stated that we should encourage children to be self-motivated when writing. It recommended that teachers should do this is by setting goals created by the children themselves, encouraging personal target-setting and giving pupils writing tasks that include the use of enquiry skills. In other words, children need to *want* to write.

RE gives children huge opportunities to follow lines of enquiry. Asking fundamental questions about the way in which we behave as human beings can lead to some very philosophical writing. Some very profound statements have been written by primary school-aged children.

Berys and Morag Gaut (2013) state that discussions in the classroom like the one in the case study above are essential for developing key skills such as critical reasoning, creative thinking, concentration, listening, communication and social skills. Taking it one step further, in addition to all of these skills, it also makes children better writers because it motivates them to pick up the pen and express themselves through the written word.

All paths lead to God?

Picture a Nativity scene. A plastic baby lies in a crib surrounded by children in shop-bought costumes: kings, shepherds, donkeys, even camels. Standing above them all is the Angel Gabriel complete with golden tinsel as a halo. That is the image that children have of angels. Yet if you were to look at Hieronymus Bosch's *Haywain Triptych* we can see the Angel Gabriel standing seven feet tall over Adam and Eve in the Garden of Eden wielding a sword over the cowering pair. Consider also Gustav Doré *Angel of Death* slaying the first-born in Egypt with one swing of a flaming sword.

The angels described in the Bible are very different from the ones we see depicted annually in a school hall. These slightly scary winged messengers feature in Islam as well as in Judaism and Christianity. It is the Angel Jibreel (Gabriel) who reveals the Holy Quran to the Prophet Mohammed.

Angels such as Lucifer, Leviathan and Azazel feature across these three religions too. These are the fallen angels thrown out of Heaven by the Angel Michael in Judaism and Christianity or Angel Mikael in Islam. It is these fallen angels that are thought of as demons. In Islam they are known as the *djinn*, which gives us the word *genie*.

Demons seem to feature in all world religions, but they are not meant to be taken as literal monsters. Rather, they are more demons of the mind. In Sikhism there are five major mind monsters: Kaam (demon of lust), Krodth (demon of anger), Lobh (demon of greed), Moh (demon of possessions) and Ahankaar (demon of selfishness). These demons are more earthly distractions rather than actual real monsters that are inside each of us according to Guru teachings. We are advised to control these distractions in order to achieve clarity of mind.

Buddhists tell stories of Mara, the demon putting images of his beautiful daughters in Buddha's mind during meditation. The Buddha focused his mind on reaching Nirvana, thus defeating the demon. Mara is a character that tries to lure Buddhists away from anything spiritual.

All of this is great fuel for writing. Character descriptions, retellings, demon lair settings and many other writing opportunities can be gained, as we can see in the case study below.

 Case study

Year 1 class retelling the Nativity

On Angel Wings by Michael Morpurgo is a retelling of the Nativity from the perspective of a shepherd boy. Eamon, a Year 1 teacher, read the story to his class pausing at key moments to ask questions. He then asked the children to work in small groups to tell each other what they could remember about the story. They each drew a picture of their favourite part and added sounds to the picture.

A lot of children added whooshing and zooming sounds to reflect the part in the story where the angel raced across the sky. Some of the children added mooing and baaing to show the scene in the stable with the animals.

Eamon then gave the children a template outline of a person and asked the children to draw a picture of an angel. The children returned to the carpet and were asked for the definition of an adjective. Together they began to add adjectives to the whiteboard to describe an angel. Soon a whole word bank was on the board.

The children chose their favourite words and wrote them around their own angel character. The more able added new words not copied from the board.

Eamon then asked the children to return to the carpet area again, but to remain standing. He and the children pretended that they were angels and started to fly. Words like *flying, racing, zooming, flapping* and *soaring* were shared. The children were asked what kind of words these are and were then asked to sound out their own verbs. At the end of the lesson children were selected to read first their adjectives and then their verbs.

Many teachers say that they are happy with the standard of writing done by their class in the morning literacy lessons, but it is not maintained in cross-curricular writing, which is usually done in the afternoons. The afternoon is when children seem to be less motivated to write which is what leads to poor quality writing. The case study contained a lot of physical movement. The children were up and down then given short, snappy writing activities. It is this method of teaching, particularly with younger pupils, that leads to maintaining quality writing, especially in the afternoon. See Chapter 10 on physical education for further detail on this subject.

Writing opportunities through Lego

Brick Testament is a website and series of books that retell the Bible in Lego. Below is Mary's reaction to the news that she will be having a baby in the Nativity story.

It is a fantastic resource that children love for retelling Bible stories. But, warning! You do have to be rather careful with the website. It has abbreviations next to each story; N = nudity, S = sexual content, V = violence and S = cursing. A dubious resource but a very valuable one.

You need to copy and paste the appropriate images in advance of your lesson.

Using Lego in the classroom to retell any story from any of the major religions is an extremely effective way of cementing the story in the children's minds. The visual prop is something that can be a very useful tool. You could use Lego to tell any story scene. I have seen Lego retellings of *Krishna Steals the Butter* (Hindu), *The Milk and the Jasmine Flower* (Sikh), *The Temple Lamp* (Jewish) and *The Sound the Hare Heard* (Buddhist). The teacher read the stories from Anita Ganeri's *Stories from Faiths* series of books.

Figure 14.1 Mary learns she'll be having a baby

Retelling stories

Read through the case study above in which a teacher uses a story from Christianity to lead to a lesson on adjectives and verbs. The aim of the lesson was to build confidence in writing by scribing sounds, then relying on the teacher to write adjectives before the children are able to write down their own verbs that they have acted out. There were three activities in short succession during this one lesson. The children were up and down from the carpet; they wrote some words then moved around, wrote and moved, wrote and moved. In Early Years and Key Stage 1 it is important that children aren't just sitting all afternoon when a lot of cross-curricular writing occurs. The writing activities need to be short and snappy interspersed with changing the environment at short intervals.

Think of a different story from any world religion that you can use.

- Make a list of suitable stories for this activity.
- What type of vocabulary do you want to achieve from the children? What part of the story can you focus on to maximise this type of vocabulary?
- Are there any opportunities to use action and drama? Can part of the story be acted out by the children to aid vocabulary choices?
- How could you use Lego to enhance the retelling of the story?
- What digital media can be used?

 # Research focus

Modelling writing

Writing has to be interactive. Children need to be involved in the writing process when it is being modelled for them. They need to feel listened to, valued and that their ideas are necessary.

The DfE (2012) says that when modelling writing we should use *explicit, interactive, scaffolded instruction in planning* (p4). This is essential. Children need to feel part of the process of writing even when you are modelling the writing for them. They need to take ownership of it. They need to feel that they have contributed towards the process. This is the case for the teacher also. Teachers need to be writers.

In Cremin and Baker's report on 'Teachers as Writers' (2014) they state: *Other studies affirm this, suggesting teachers are neither as confident or as assured writers as they are readers, and that tensions exist between their perceptions of self as teachers and/or writers (Cremin, 2006; Gannon and Davies, 2007) with consequences for classroom practice* (p1).

In the classroom we all need to be involved together in the writing process to gain confidence in writing both as teacher and as a learner. It is important for children to know that we are all learning together.

As Cremin and Baker put it:

> *In taking a more consciously reflective role as writers, teachers often feel impelled to make changes to their pedagogy and practice and this can shape the children's views of their teachers as writers and their growing competence and confidence as young writers themselves (Bearne et al. 2011). A stronger community of writers can be built in the classroom if teachers and support staff are able to connect to and share their writing lives and enable children to recognise and celebrate the diversity of their own writing practices.*

(2004, p5)

Gods and monsters – play the game

In all the world religions there are some pretty awesome creatures, such as the mud-made servant Golem in Judaism. There is a seven-headed dragon in the book of Revelation in the Bible in Christianity, and Hanuman the flying monkey and son of the god of the wind, in Hinduism.

Children of all ages seem to love the stories that contain these amazing characters. Writing stories based on them is something that can be very effective.

Monkey Magic is a Buddhist character who can summon clouds to hop upon but go flying through the sky. He can also use his magical staff to create replicas of himself and can turn into almost anything. Some might even remember that he had his own TV series in the 1970s, and if you don't then take a look on YouTube. There's potential for Monkey Magic stories, poems, descriptions and all kinds of writing there. See Chapter 2 on Non-Fiction writing for further ideas too.

Some of the language for names of characters, places, objects, ceremonies, etc. can be difficult for children to remember when learning about any of the world's religions.

A way to place this vocabulary firmly in children's memory is by playing board games connected to the religion you are studying.

In order to create your religion board game, share a story from that particular religion, for example, the story of Diwali in Hinduism. Anita Ganeri's version of this is highly recommended. Ask the children to make a list of characters in the story. In this case we have Rama, Sita, Hanuman, Ravana, Dasaratha, Lakshman, etc. Then add a tick next to the character's name if they are a good character and a cross if they are bad.

Take a template of a board game and add the characters but spread out across the whole board leaving plenty of squares in between each character.

Write next to each character what happens in the original story and what happens in the board game. For example, if you land on Ravana, he kidnaps Sita, so go back to the start. Or, if you land on Rama, he kills the demon king, so have another go.

By the time the children have played the board game a few times, the vocabulary is firmly in their heads.

This can be applied to any story such as the story of Ibrahim and Ismail in Islam or the story of the Golem of Prague in Judaism.

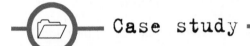

Case study

Year 3 class writing about a monster they have designed

A Year 3 class had been studying Hinduism. Gupreet, their teacher, told the class about the Naga, a serpent-like creature that was half-human and half-snake. They looked at images of these creatures. Gupreet explained that Nagas could be good creatures if treated with courtesy and respect.

The children then designed their own half-human and half-animal creatures. There were people with blob fish heads, scorpion-tailed boys, girls with unicorn horns. These were all labelled with similes and alliteration after being modelled by their teacher. The class were then read the *Origin of Snakes*, a Hindu Naga story that their teacher found online at: www.shraddhananda.com/Origin_of_snake_A_Hindu_mythology.html.

It tells the tale of how Lord Brahma gives snakes their own place in the world with people. They live side by side with humans and only hurt them if they are treated badly. The story ends with a warning that we should all treat snakes with respect.

The children were asked to create stories about their own characters. The stories have to end with 'and that is why we now have this animal in our world'.

The children clearly enjoyed the lesson in the case study. The boys, in particular, were extremely engaged when designing their monster. The story was short but this seemed to help the children to plan their own story. They used the same structure and made changes to ensure their own story followed the same pattern but contained their own ideas. There are hundreds of creation stories like the *Origin of Snakes* available online.

Writing creation stories

Some of the most ancient stories in the world are creation stories. These are tales told by the first people in order to make sense of the world. Rudyard Kipling in his *Just So Stories* brought this genre of story back to a modern audience. Now there are a vast number of them published all over the world, but they are often deeply spiritual in their original form.

Nordic stories such as *Why the Sea is Salt* or African myths about Ngai, who made all people from his home atop a mountain in Kenya, are from the very first religions.

We can use these examples to plan our own creation story in the same style.

The first step is to choose what the story will be about, perhaps using the colour of the sky or plants or the sea. You could choose weather, but a simple way to start is by choosing an animal.

You can ask the children to notice the most distinctive thing about that animal. If it's an elephant it might be its trunk. If it's a tortoise it might be its shell. If it's a tiger it might be its stripes.

The story begins with the animal looking very different from the way it does today. So, you have elephants with no trunks, tortoises with no shells and tigers with no stripes.

The end of the story has the animal looking the way we would normally see it today; elephants with trunks, tortoises with shells and tigers with stripes.

It is the middle part that requires the most thought. Creation stories, like most tales, begin with some sort of problem. The animal has some kind of difficulty, for example, an elephant with no trunk might not be able to drink or wash itself. A tortoise with no shell might be vulnerable. A tiger with no stripes cannot be camouflaged.

You need to ask the children what the problem will be in their story.

There is then a triadic structure to be followed. The animal (perhaps with the help of other characters) tries to fix the problem but it doesn't work. They try again, but once more it does not work. On the third attempt it does work and the animal is transformed into how we see it today. An example could be as follows.

1. The elephant has no trunk.

2. It is sad because it cannot reach the water in the lake. The elephant tries to reach the water and gets stuck in the squishy mud.

3. A monkey comes along and tries to pull the elephant out. It doesn't work.

4. A giraffe comes along to help, but it doesn't help.

5. A lion helps and it does work. The elephant is free from its muddy trap.

6. The elephant has a trunk. It can now reach the water in the lake easily.

 **Activity**

Writing your own creation story

Read through the case study and the section above about creation stories. These are two very different types of stories. Plan which kind you want your class to write. There are countless examples on the Internet, but Michael Rosen's *How the Animals Got Their Colours* and also *Margaret Mayo's The Orchard Book of Creation Stories* are superb.

(Continued)

(Continued)

- Are you planning a story about an animal or people? Who will be your characters?

- Is your story based around the environment or the weather? What will be the setting?

- What will be the problem? How will you solve it?

- Often, creation stories have a divine character in them. This character is usually the one to solve the problem in the end. Will your story have a god-like character?

- What will happen in your triadic structure? Will you have three other characters to go with these three major events?

- How can the writing be edited and improved? Can you include speech to reveal character?

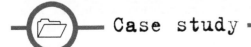 **Case study**

A Year 4 class visit Durham Cathedral to learn about the northern saints

The Education Team at Durham Cathedral deliver this session hundreds of times over an academic year to Key Stage 2 and have had a range of positive outcomes over the years. However, the common thread is that it offers learners an excellent opportunity to explore Christianity in an accessible way.

Several times, when time has allowed, they have adapted the session at the request of the teacher to specifically develop their learners' writing skills. The basis of the session remains the same but they extend opportunities for learners to break away from the standard interactive session.

A Learning Officer, Caroline, started the session by asking the class what they think the word *saint* means. She used the visual stimulus of a stained-glass window. The children worked in groups to discuss what they thought. These ideas were then shared and Caroline explained the definition.

The children were asked how they arrived at the cathedral that day. This was compared to how people used to travel to the cathedral on foot hundreds of years ago.

They then discussed the word pilgrimage. Caroline makes a link between the children and the pilgrims that have been visiting the cathedral for over one thousand years. It was explained that one of the main reasons for pilgrimage is to visit the tomb of saints like Cuthbert and Bede.

The children were taken to the shrine of St Cuthbert and told briefly his life story, including a tale about his body's journey from Lindisfarne to Durham. Caroline then took the children to the Education Department and into a classroom. Here the children explored replica artefacts connected to Cuthbert. These are displayed in a replica Anglo-Saxon coffin and include a cross, a comb and textiles. The children handled each object and discussed what it is and also questioned its significance.

They were then given a template of a coffin and labelled it with objects and explained why each artefact was placed in there. This was to be used for a non-chronological report to be written back at school later in the week.

Caroline then finished with another story about St Cuthbert and his connection to animals.

 **Research focus**

School trips

School trips to places like Durham Cathedral are essential to give children amazing experiences and also for the potential of something to write about. The Education Endowment Foundation in their report on *Improving Writing Quality* (2014) recommended that memorable experiences such as trips are a focus for writing lessons. They also state, *The Improving Writing Quality intervention (delivered and supported by CEP) encouraged and funded primary schools to provide memorable experiences for all pupils in Year 6 before the transition to Year 7* (p7).

The trips fuel the words, but also linger on in the memory as part of the whole primary school experience. Visits are what children will remember.

Conclusion

Religious education is one of those subjects that seem to get missed out of a lot of classrooms in the UK. Many teachers say that they just don't have time to teach it as often as they would like. Some teachers say that they don't have enough knowledge on the subject to be able to teach it well. Equally, lots of schools focus their attention on RE as much as they do the core curriculum subjects.

Writing based on RE can be heavenly. If we want to invite writing into our cross-curricular subjects, we need to embrace subjects like RE in the primary school. It has the power and the potential to lead to some unique creative writing that would be otherwise lost.

Recommended texts

For bereavement: Rosen, M. (2011) *The Sad Book*. London: Walker Books.

For death and bereavement: Stickney, D. (2004) *Water Bugs and Butterflies*. Ohio, OH. The Pilgrim Press. (note sp. Pilgrim)

For death: Varley, S. (2013) *Badger's Parting Gifts*. London: Anderson Press.

For discussion on souls: Snunit, M. (2010) *The Soul Bird*. London: Robinson Publishing.

For emotions: Foreman, K. (2001) *The Angel and the Wild Animal*. London: Anderson Books.

For friendship and sharing: Ray, J. (2003) *Can You Catch a Mermaid?* London: Orchard Books.

For multiculturalism: Cooling, W. (2004) *All the Colours of the Earth: A Multicultural Treasury*. London: Frances Lincoln Children's Books.

For self-confidence: Andreae, G. (2014) *Giraffes Can't Dance*. London: Orchard Books.

For the First World War: Huggins-Cooper, L. (2010) *One Boy's War*. London: Francis Lincoln Publishers.

For the Second World War: McEwan, I. (2004) *Rose Blanche*. London: Red Fox.

For worrying and problem-solving: Ironside, V. (2011) *Huge Bag of Worries*. London: Hodder Children's Books.

━━ References ━━

Cremin, T. and Baker, S. (2014) *Teachers As Writers; a PETAA occasional research paper.* Sydney: PETAA.

DfE (2012) *What is the Research Evidence on Writing?* London: Department for Education.

Dweck, C. (2000) *Self-theories: Their Role in Motivation, Personality, and Development (Essays in Social Psychology).* London: Psychology Press.

Education Endowment Foundation, (2014) *Improving Writing Quality.* Durham University and University of York. Available for download at: www.educationendowmentfoundation.org.uk.

Ganeri, A. (2002) *The Divali Story.* London: Evans Publishing Group.

Ganeri, A. (2008) *Krishna Steals the Butter.* London: QED Publishing Group.

Ganeri, A. (2008) *The Milk and the Jasmine Flower.* London: QED Publishing Group.

Ganeri, A. (2008) *The Temple Lamp.* London: QED Publishing Group.

Ganeri, A. (2008) *The Sound the Hare Heard.* London: QED Publishing Group.

Gaut, B. and Gaut, M .(2013) *Philosophy for Children: A Practical Guide.* Abingdon: Routledge.

Gilbert, I. (2007) *The Little Book of Thunks.* Carmarthen: Crown House Publishing.

Huggins-Cooper, L. (2010) *One Boy's War.* London: Frances Lincoln Children's Books.

Kipling, R. (2015) *Just So Stories.* County Durham: Aziloth Books.

McEwan, I (2004) *Rose Blanche.* London: Red Fox.

Mayo, M. (1995) *The Orchard Book of Creation Stories.* London: Orchard Books, Hachette Children's Group.

Morpurgo, M. (2006) *On Angel Wings.* London: Egmont Publishing.

Powell Smith, B. (2013) *The Brick Bible: The Complete Set.* New York: Skyhorse Publishing.

Rosen, M. (1992) *How the Animals Got Their Colours.* London: Harcourt.

Vander Zee, R. (2013) *Erika's Story.* Mankato: The Creative Company.

World Health Organization (WHO) (2001) *The World Health Report 2001 – Mental Health: New Understanding, New Hope.* Available for available at: www.who.int/whr/2001/en/

15

Writing in social, moral, spiritual and cultural education

Claire Patterson in association with Educate&Celebrate

Teachers' Standards

Personal and professional conduct

Teachers uphold public trust in the profession and maintain high standards of ethics and behaviour, within and outside school, by:

- treating pupils with dignity, building relationships rooted in mutual respect, and at all times observing proper boundaries appropriate to a teacher's professional position
- having regard for the need to safeguard pupils' well-being, in accordance with statutory provisions
- showing tolerance of and respect for the rights of others
- not undermining fundamental British values, including democracy, the rule of law, individual liberty and mutual respect, and tolerance of those with different faiths and beliefs
- ensuring that personal beliefs are not expressed in ways which exploit pupils' vulnerability or might lead them to break the law

```
┌─○─── Key questions ────────────────────
│
│  • How can we transform a predominantly discussion-based subject into one that produces high-
│    quality writing?
│  • How can we create a cross-curricular approach to teaching about equality?
│  • How can we embed SMSC into other subjects?
└─────────────────────────────────────────
```

Introduction

SMSC (Social, Moral, Spiritual and Cultural) is a predominantly discussion-based topic and one that might not immediately appear to lend itself to writing. Often it is lost in a curriculum that is bursting at the seams with ever-increasing demands, resulting in a circle time discussion being relegated to Friday afternoons. However, this subject is brimming with opportunities for writing that allows children to explore their own views and beliefs. Imagine finding real-life stimuli that will encourage those rich, passionate discussions, then transforming the dialogue into campaign letters, video scripts, adverts, diary entries and so much more.

Adults can very often underestimate the impact that children can have on the world. The children in our schools need to feel valued and most importantly listened to. An ethos must be established in the classroom where children understand their place in the world, the difference they can make and they should be encouraged to take their voices across the globe. The writing that takes place in SMSC doesn't belong in a closed exercise book where only a teacher will see it. It belongs on school blogs, in newspaper articles, in the websites of agencies that support the issue in question, to name but a few. As teachers we should actively encourage children to be as passionate as possible about their opinions. We should also give children the opportunity to discuss and write for real-life purposes and real-life audiences.

This chapter will explore not only the teaching of British values, which is now part of the curriculum, but also look at how children can be encouraged to become passionate about issues that are happening in the world they live in, including those surrounding LGBT+ (Lesbian, Gay, Bisexual, Transgender) equality. We will look at how we can encourage acceptance and a drive for justice within children and utilise this to create exceptional, relevant pieces of writing which can then be shared with the world via blogs and social media.

What to teach

It is important to understand what is required of us as teachers regarding the teaching of British values in our schools. Fundamental British values are:

- democracy;

- the rule of law;

- individual liberty;

- mutual respect for and tolerance of those with different faiths and beliefs, and for those without faith.

In its document, *Promoting Fundamental British Values as Part of SMSC in Schools* (2014) the Department for Education states that schools should:

- *enable students to develop their self-knowledge, self-esteem and self-confidence;*

- *enable students to distinguish right from wrong and to respect the civil and criminal law of England;*

- *encourage students to accept responsibility for their behaviour, show initiative, and to understand how they can contribute positively to the lives of those living and working in the locality of the school and to society more widely;*

- *enable students to acquire a broad general knowledge of and respect for public institutions and services in England;*

- *further tolerance and harmony between different cultural traditions by enabling students to acquire an appreciation of and respect for their own and other cultures;*

- *encourage respect for other people; and*

- *encourage respect for democracy and support for participation in the democratic processes, including respect for the basis on which the law is made and applied in England.*

(p5)

Time and again, when discussing the teaching of British values with teachers, there is a common issue with the use of the word tolerance. According to the *Cambridge Dictionary* (2016), tolerance is *The ability or willingness to tolerate the existence of opinions or behaviour that one dislikes or disagrees with* and many teachers feel uncomfortable with the connotations that holds. One option would be to discuss this value with the children and the definition of the term, then opt to use the word acceptance in its place. Dictionaries can be used to find how the meanings are different and even allow children to try to come up with a word to use in its place themselves. Even through such a simple discussion you can open the children's minds to how important words are and how language can be interpreted in many different ways. A discussion can also take place analysing the wording of the value and whether or not all opinions and behaviours should be accepted. What about racist, sexist and homophobic opinions? Should these be accepted without question? How can we respond to comments which may cause offence and be unacceptable in the classroom?

As mentioned earlier, the National Curriculum is brimming with objectives that our children have to be taught and time constraints are often problematic for teachers. However, SMSC and the teaching of British values are extremely easy to weave into many other areas of the curriculum, allowing highly creative and informed pieces of writing to take place. A very simple lesson, which encourages young children to express opinions and listen to and respect those of their peers, is described below

Case study

Year 1 class discussing what makes them feel happy

The children entered the classroom to the song *Happy* by Pharrel Williams. They all joined in with singing the chorus and some began dancing on the carpet. Annette, their teacher, asked the children to sit on the carpet once the song had finished.

(Continued)

(Continued)

She then asked her class what made them happy. She heard answers such as getting presents, playing with friends, spending time with family members and visiting places such as beaches or parks. Annette then showed the class six pictures of children doing six different things. The first was a child eating pizza, the second was a child talking to another child, the third was a child sitting in a dentist chair, the fourth was a child looking at an Ipad, the fifth was a child kicking a ball and the sixth was a child writing.

The children were asked which activity would make them the happiest. They took turns giving their opinions and then shared their thoughts in partners. Annette then gave the children the same six images photocopied and cut out into small squares. They were asked to go to their places and use blobs of Blu-Tak to stick the images in order of what would make them the most happy at the top of an A4 sheet of card and what would make them the least happy at the bottom of the sheet. Once completed, the children returned to the carpet to discuss and compare their own sheets to their friends.

The class discussed why some activities were more popular than others. Annette partnered children who had totally different results and asked them to discuss their choices. She then asked the children if any of them wanted to change where they had placed their images after talking to their friends. A lot of changes were made and Annette asked the children why they wanted to make changes. She then asked the class if what their friends thought meant a lot to them.

The children were finally asked to write next to their top and bottom images their reasons for placing them there. Annette wrote on the board 'This makes me happy because _____' and 'This makes me less happy because _____'.

Some children came up with their own sentences, whereas others used the framework offered by Annette. She supported the lower ability children.

Lessons such as the one in the case study above are a good way for children to practise expressing their opinions and justifying them to their peers. It also enables them to examine how other opinions and viewpoints can alter our own. This can also lend itself to opportunities that enable children to give their own opinions not just orally but also in the written form. Expressing your own opinion through spoken word is different from writing. The more children can practise this the better they will get at it.

- How could the case study above be adapted for your own class or other year groups?

- What subject area will you discuss?

- How will the children share their ideas?

- What writing will be the outcome?

- What music, video or other such media could you use to support the lesson?

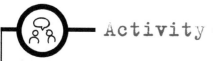

Activity

Writing a recipe for a family

Add a sprinkle of I love yous then put in the fridge to chill. After 1-2 hours your family is complete. Enjoy! Year 6 pupil from County Durham.

Writing a recipe is a good way to get children thinking, talking then writing about what a family actually is and more importantly what it needs. *The Great Big Book of Families* by Mary Hoffman is an excellent starting point to allow the children to realise that families come in many shapes and sizes. If the book is unavailable, then allowing the children to share who is in their family will open up a discussion that is sure to showcase a diverse range of families. In a modern-day society it can be assumed that every class will have children living with biological parents, some with step-parents and some who are looked after by people who aren't related to them directly. Having looked at what different families look like, pose the question: 'What does a family actually need?' Encourage the children to think creatively and suggest things like bedtime stories, kisses and cuddles and family dinners. At this point with older children, it is good to allow them to use *a consensus map* to brainstorm their own ideas, which they can then discuss as a group to allow them to reach a consensus on the key ingredients and this can be done through the use of consensus maps. With younger children, it is easier to brainstorm the ideas they suggest, then allow the children to vote on which ones they think are needed.

Once children have reached an agreement on what every family needs, model how to write a recipe using imperative and modal verbs, and creating a bank of 'quantities' for the children to use. Younger children may use a template to aid their writing, while older children may be able to write independently. This is an easily adaptable idea that lends itself to all age ranges and allows the children to write in a creative way.

A lesson plan complete with resources for the above activity can be downloaded free from www.educate andcelebrate.org/product/recipe-for-a-family

Research focus

Narrative style

Schools often focus on writing genres, with argument and persuasive writing styles being used when children are expected to put a point of view across. However, Riley and Reedy (2000, p159) assert that a narrative style also has a place:

> *if we aim to teach children how to use the language of persuasion, we delude ourselves and them if we do not give the message to children that narrative texts can also argue and persuade and that this may be one of the main reasons for their existence.*

There are many examples of literature that have conveyed powerful messages about societal problems and issues, including books by Dickens, Steinbeck, Orwell and Gaskell for adults, and Fine, Morpurgo, Hoffman and Binch, and Walliams for children.

Creating an LGBT+ inclusive curriculum

When teaching children about equality in SMSC, they will very often learn about discrimination of race, religion and gender through looking at important historical figures and events such as Rosa Parks, Martin Luther King, The Holocaust and women fighting for the right to vote. While these are extremely important issues that should indeed be discussed in schools, there seems to be a gap in the curriculum regarding the other diverse groups and their struggles for equality.

The Equality Act 2010 (c.1) states that the following are protected characteristics:

- age;

- disability;

- gender reassignment;

- marriage and civil partnership;

- pregnancy and maternity;

- race;

- religion or belief;

- sex;

- sexual orientation.

In a survey conducted by the charity Educate&Celebrate it was found that nearly 50 per cent of the children in our schools were not receiving any LGBT education in any area of the curriculum (2015) and this led to the question of why? Why aren't children in our schools being talked to about different types of relationships? Why are children not being educated on the correct use of the word gay to stop them using it as an insult? To help combat this, Educate&Celebrate deliver training that supports schools in implementing an LGBT+ inclusive curriculum to successfully eradicate homophobia, biphobia and transphobia from schools drawing on the findings from NatCen Social Research (HM Government, 2014) that a whole school integrated approach was *regarded as working better than only using stand-alone teaching on homophobic, biphobic and transphobic bullying specifically* (p6).

Educate&Celebrate actively seek to find new and innovating ways to teach about LGBT+ equality and the British value of having respect for others and their beliefs in a cross-curricular way. One County Durham school embarked on the Educate&Celebrate best practice programme in their school and followed the advice to take a whole school approach. The decision was made by the senior leadership team that LGBT+ would not be taught as an isolated issue in SMSC lessons, but rather be incorporated into the teaching of English lessons to enable the issues discussed to be 'usualised' – not singled out as something 'different' but an everyday part of the society we live in.

Each year group was bought a series of books that look at a range of issues surrounding LGBT+, such as stereotypes, celebrating being different from one another, families with same-sex parents, boys who want to play with dolls, and celebrating different types of relationships. These books were used to plan a week-long module of English once a term, leading up to a piece of writing. It was found that using the books as a starting point gave teachers much more confidence to discuss the underlying issues. As an example when discussing the concept of a child having two fathers, a Year 3 teacher read the children the story *And Tango Makes Three* by Justin Richardson and Peter Parnell, a book in which a zookeeper gives two male penguins an egg to hatch. When the baby penguin was born, the teacher was able to discuss with the children that it would grow up with two male parents, just like some children do. The children then worked on rewriting the story themselves and concentrated on English objectives, but the social content of the lesson was extremely valuable to promote the usualising of LBGT+ in the curriculum.

In a further example, a Year 6 teacher was teaching the children how to write biographies within a topic on 'The Olympics'. The children researched the life of Tom Daley, his early life, his road to Olympic success and also his personal life – how he 'came out' on YouTube and is now engaged to a man.

The English objectives were met successfully, but again the social side of the lesson allowed the children to use the word *gay* in the correct context. It allowed them to gain a greater understanding of terminology such as 'coming out' and it also allowed them to gain an insight into same-sex marriage and how that will be embedded as an important step forward to equality.

At the end of the best practice programme, the school was thrilled to witness the children in the school embracing and celebrating the differences found in society. Some outstanding pieces of writing had been produced as a result of the work surrounding the books, and teachers felt able to move on to create their own modules of work that weren't centred on the bought-in texts. One Year 5 teacher took the poem *Stop All the Clocks* by W.H. Auden and had the confidence to explain that this was written about his lover, the relationship with whom he had to keep secret because homosexuality was illegal in the past. Children were then encouraged to write poems in a similar style about someone who was very important to them.

If teachers are brave enough to look for the opportunities to discuss all areas of equality and the writing that can be produced from this, the possibilities are endless as to how we can socially educate our children and give them a greater understanding of the world we live in.

The *Star Wars* film franchise features the character Yoda. In *Episode One, The Phantom Menace* Yoda says *Fear is the path to the dark side … fear leads to anger … anger leads to hate … hate leads to suffering.*

It is often what we do not know or understand that leads to fear. The author, Andrew Smith, adds, *People fear what they don't understand and hate what they can't conquer* (www.goodreads.com/author/quotes/26810.Andrew_Smith).

By delivering LGBT+ lessons in our classrooms like the ones above, we are teaching children valuable empathic lessons for life. We can also look at, and write about, famous LGBT+ historical figures from the past such as Alexander the Great, Walt Whitman, Eleanor Roosevelt, Virginia Woolf or Leonardo da Vinci. Mark Pino states in his *Huffington Post* article 'The Necessity of LGBT-Inclusive Curriculum' (2016).

> *By seeing the great accomplishments of past LGBT people, students are able to associate a positive image of the LGBT community and would become more aware of the homophobic slurs that are ingrained in their vocabulary. The LGBT community has been dehumanized for far too long, and this is the way to rehumanize them. Being gay or lesbian or trans wouldn't be seen as something lesser, and bullying as a whole could be mollified. Schools would be safer for not just LGBT students, but for anyone who could be perceived as LGBT, and school would become a positive affirming environment that optimizes learning potential.*

Case study

Year 6 class discussing hate crimes

Claire, a Year 6 teacher, was teaching the topic 'Crime and Punishment'. During an English lesson, the children entered the classroom to a Northumbria Police 'Hate Crime' video being played. In the video a man can be seen, but not heard, as he shouts aggressively at people in the street. At various points of the video, Claire paused it and asked the children to discuss why they thought the man was shouting at the various people. The discussion was rich due to the video showcasing race, disability and sexual orientation as differences. Many children picked up on the fact that the man in the wheelchair was being targeted because of his disability, but only one girl expressed that she thought it was a racist attack due to the man's race.

At the point of the video where two women are seen to be holding hands, the children seemed reluctant to use the correct terminology to describe their sexual orientation. A very matter of fact discussion of the terms *lesbian, gay, bisexual* and *transgender* was able to take place here to extend the children's vocabulary and ensure that the terms were being used in the correct context. At the end of the video, Claire asked the children to think about the concept of a hate crime and what indeed *hate* is.

Children were encouraged to think literally and find the definition of the term in the dictionary and use a thesaurus to find synonyms. They were then asked to produce a mind map of metaphors, similes and personification of the word *hate*, which the children then transformed into poems entitled 'Hate is ... '

After the lesson, Claire used the school blog to showcase the children's writing and sent Northumbria Police a tweet to show them the work they had produced using their video. The police retweeted this and it spread quickly across Twitter, resulting in the children receiving a visit from Northumbria officers to discuss their work in the Hate Crime department and receiving several certificates of recognition from charities such as Stop Hate UK.

A downloadable lesson plan complete with resources for the above activity can be downloaded for free from www.educateandcelebrate.org/product/ks2-citizenship-what-is-a-hate-crime

---

Giving children the chance to discuss the terminology surrounding LGBT+ may be problematic at first unless teachers are confident about such matters. The lesson in the case study is a good place to start discussing the terms lesbian, gay, bisexual and transgender, as it is done within the context of looking at hate crimes and protected characteristics rather than an isolated discussion of the terms. This then encourages the children to understand the terms so they can use them correctly in further discussions.

Further questions that could be asked regarding terminology are as follows.

- When have you heard the word gay being used?

- Have you ever heard any of the terms being used incorrectly?

- Why do you think people use LGBT terms in a negative way?

- How can we combat the incorrect use of LGBT terms in school?

Using videos

Love is the moment your heart stops, the final piece of the puzzle. Year 6 pupil, County Durham.

Using videos in the classroom is becoming more and more common as this is a medium that the children are exposed to every day and one which they relate to very well. There are many good quality videos that can be used in SMSC teaching that will also lend themselves to encouraging children to write. The following videos can be found easily on YouTube and similar sites.

Love Has No Labels A good starting point is the *Love Has No Labels* video which sees skeletons behind a screen. Pause the video and ask the children who they think the skeletons belong to and why before the people behind the screen are revealed. The tag line 'Love Has No Labels' is a good topic to discuss: what do the children actually think that means? Love as a concept can be explored in the same way as hate was in the earlier case study. Children can think of their own definitions, metaphors and similes for love as a result of watching this video and create a 'love is' poem.

What Boy Does With Doll May Shock You

We think you grossly underestimate just how fierce a dolly can be. Mikki Willis, YouTube.

Another excellent video that can be used to challenge toys and gender stereotyping from a young age is *What Boy Does With Doll May Shock You* posted on YouTube by Mikki Willis. This video sees a father and son discussing how some people were negative towards the boy choosing a doll to play with, so they have decided to show these people that a dolly is not just for girls. After watching, engage the children in discussing toys and gender stereotypes, show them other adverts that target one gender specifically for certain toys and allow them to write letters to the manufacturers and toy stores challenging this concept and actually post them. If a school blog is available, publish work there and tweet it to various toy stores. The quality of the children's work will be of a higher level when you tell them that the whole world will be their audience and the letters that they are writing will actually be sent.

 **Activity**

Weddings

Key Stage 1

Weddings are a universally recognised celebration that can be explored from all faiths and cultures through use of stories, videos and photographs. Often this work takes place in RE, but it is easy to explore weddings through stories allowing the children to look at same-sex marriages

(Continued)

(Continued)

and create pieces of writing such as invitations, thank you letters and letters to the characters. The following texts can be used when looking at *who* can get married: *Prince Henry* by Olly Pike and *The Scarecrows' Wedding* by Julia Donaldson.

Start by reading *The Scarecrows' Wedding* to the children and discussing who is getting married (Harry (a man) and Betty (a woman)). Ask the children to think about why Harry and Betty are getting married and establish it is because they are in love. Then read *Prince Henry* with the children and again ask them who is getting married (this time two men, Henry and Thomas) and why they think they are getting married (again because they are in love). Discuss how the marriages are the same and how they are different, then allow the children to create wedding invitations for both weddings. Invitations are ideal for writing the different sentences found in the Key Stage 1 English curriculum: statements, questions, exclamations and commands can all be incorporated into an invitation. *Prince Henry* is also an ideal book for SMSC because it raises issues surrounding social class as well as gay marriage. The king in fact does not have an issue with his son wanting to marry another man: his issue is with the fact that Thomas is poor. This is an ideal opportunity for the children to discuss whether or not this is fair and to write letters to the king asking him to allow Henry and Thomas to marry each other.

 Research focus

Alternative versions

As highlighted earlier, stories can be an ideal stimulus to use with younger children and can often stimulate discussion among children higher up the school. Tales such as *Prince Henry* are based on the style of traditional tales, but have an interesting twist. However, Zipes sums up criticisms by feminists of the content of traditional tales.

> *Not only are the tales considered to be too sexist, racist and authoritarian, but the general contents are said to reflect the concerns of semi-feudal, patriarchal societies.*

(1983, p170)

Zipes, like Tatar (1992), approved of some of the alternative versions of such tales, which challenged stereotypes. Winston sums up their views.

> *They attack the oppressive moralizing of the literary fairy tale and the outmoded values they embody, advocating new, more radical tales to restore the original role of the fairy tale, one whose moral force lies in its drive towards social and cultural liberation.*

(Winston, 1998, p34)

Activity

Find examples of traditional tales retold to present characters in a different light and which challenge stereotypes. You will find examples at the end of the chapter, but might start with Roald Dahl's *Revolting Rhymes* and Eric Braun's *Trust Me, Jack's Beanstalk Stinks!: The Story of Jack and the Beanstalk as Told by the Giant (The Other Side of the Story)*. Such versions promote discussion and can stimulate children to write their own versions of tales.

Stories provide a wealth of writing opportunities alongside those for role play and discussion, particularly in those that have a moral as these promote empathy, something that is crucial in SMSC. The case study below provides an example.

Case study

Year 3 class finding out about stories from other cultures

Alan, a Year 3 teacher, was reading his class a traditional tale from Russia called *Baba Yaga Bony Legs*. Before the story he had shown the class a Russian doll and asked if any of the children knew what it was. Most did and he demonstrated how each doll got smaller by removing the first, largest doll from the others.

The story involved the main character, Masha, being sent by her parents to Baba Yaga's house. Baba Yaga tried to eat the girl, but Masha's kind acts toward a cat, dog and mouse save her in the end.

As Alan read the story, a lot of unfortunate events befall Masha. Each time something unpleasant or scary happened in the story, he made the Russian doll smaller and smaller until she became the last tiny doll. But then, as the story developed, Masha was helped to escape and better things began to happen to her. Alan built the doll back up to its larger size as each good thing occurred in the story. The ending sees Masha being reunited with her family and the witch is defeated. As the story closes, the Russian doll is back to its original size.

Alan asked the class what things made Masha smaller. He made a list on the board. He then asked what made her bigger again. Another list was made on the board. He then asked his class what made them feel smaller. The responses included name calling, shouting, breaking toys and bereavement.

The class were next asked what made them feel bigger. This time the responses were things like being complimented, telling jokes, birthdays and hugs. Alan explained to the class that we all sometimes feel small and that the things that make us feel bigger are what we should remember

(Continued)

(Continued)

when we do have those negative feelings. He gave the class a sheet with an image of a Russian doll in the middle. The class were asked to write in sentences around the doll all of the things that made them feel bigger. He told them that this writing would be going home. He explained to the class that they should ask their parents if they could put their writing on the wall of their bedrooms. If they ever felt sad or small they should look at this writing to remind them of the things that made them feel good or bigger.

 Research focus

There are many books on the importance and meaning of the traditional tale, for example, Bettelheim's *The Uses of Enchantment*, Campbell's *The Hero With a Thousand Faces* and Estes's *Women Who Run With the Wolves*. These are all well researched and thorough studies. Angela Carter's reimagining of the fairy tale from a feminist perspective in her book *The Bloody Chamber* is an insightful study and a highly recommended read but certainly not suitable to read in primary schools as it is a very dark, adult-themed book. It redefines the traditional tale and makes us look at something very familiar in an unfamiliar way. This is exactly what we can do with traditional tales with children. We can rewrite them to challenge fixed mindsets and alter perspectives. For example, *Sleeping Beauty* could be *Sleeping Handsome*.

Fairy stories and traditional tales can be a means to discuss any topic. They can be a stimulus to compare the written word to the world around us. Maria Tatar (2002, p16) from Harvard University maintains,

> Through the medium of (fairy) stories, adults can talk with children about what matters in their lives, about issues ranging from fear of abandonment and death to fantasies of revenge and triumphs that lead to happily-everafter endings ... and offer guidance for thinking about similar matters in the real world.

Conclusion

SMSC and the teaching of British values is an important part of the curriculum, which is often only found in the assembly hall. With an ever-changing and increasingly diverse society, it has never been more important to teach children about the country and the world they live in. By incorporating SMSC into other areas of the curriculum, teachers can allow children to look at the world in a respectful manner, stand up for what they think is right, and discuss the many different choices, beliefs and lifestyles that they will encounter as they move through life. Listen to the discussion that happens in the classroom during SMSC; take in the values and opinions that the children hold, then allow them to write with a passion and empathy that they will hopefully keep throughout their lives.

Further reading

For alternative versions of fairy stories try:

Bettelheim, B. (1977) *The Uses of Enchantment: The Meaning and Importance of Fairy Tales.* New York: Vintage/Random House.

Braun, E (2012) *Trust Me, Jack's Beanstalk Stinks!: The Story of Jack and the Beanstalk as Told by the Giant (The Other Side of the Story).* North Mankato, MN: Picture Window Books.

Braun, E., Speed Shaskan, T. and Loewen, N. (2015) *The Other Side of the Story: Fairy Tales with a Twist.* North Mankato, MN: Picture Window Books.

Campbell, J. (1993) *The Hero With a Thousand Faces.* London: Fontana Press.

Estes, C.P. (2008) *Women Who Run With Wolves.* London: Random Press.

References

Cambridge Dictionary (2016). Cambridge: Cambridge University Press, available from: www.dictionary.cambridge.org/dictionary/English/tolerance

Carter, A. (2007) *The Bloody Chamber.* London: Vintage.

DfE (2014) *Promoting Fundamental British Values as Part of SMSC in Schools.* London: Department for Education.

HM Government (2010) The Equality Act 2010. Available from: www.legislation.gov.uk/ukpga/2010/15/part/2/chapter/1

HM Government (2014) Tackling homophobic, biphobic and transphobic bullying among school-age children and young people. NatCen Social Research. Available from: www.natcen.ac.uk/media/563016/natcen-social-research-hbt-bullying-findings.pdf

Pino, M. (2016) The necessity of LGVBT-inclusive curriculum, *The Huffington Post*, 2 February. Available from: www.huffingtonpost.com/mark-pino/the-necessity-of-lgbt-inclusive-curriculum_b_6928438.html

Riley, J. and Reedy, D. (2000) *Developing Writing for Different Purposes.* London: Sage.

Tatar, M. (1992) *Off with Their Heads! Fairy Tales and the Culture of Childhood.* Princeton, NJ: Princeton University Press.

Tatar, M. (2002) *Classic Fairy Tales.* London: Norton.

Winston, J. (1998) *Drama, Narrative and Moral Education.* London: Falmer Press.

Zipes, J. (1983) *Fairy Tales and the Art of Subversion.* London: Heinemann.

Conclusion

We hope that reading this book has helped you to reflect on the wide range of possibilities for inviting children to write across the curriculum. We hope, too, that you draw upon the suggestions for wider reading and links to useful websites to develop your thinking and to enable you to justify your approaches to writing.

This book was created by people who are passionate about primary education, who have made use of their wide experience to offer practical guidance on writing, underpinned by theoretical understanding. If the authors have shown that writing is an essential and integral feature of all curricular subjects, their work will have been worthwhile.

Adam Bushnell
David Waugh
March 2017

Index